Advances in Experimental Philosophy of Language

Advances in Experimental Philosophy

Series Editor:
James Beebe, Associate Professor of Philosophy, University at Buffalo, USA

Editorial Board:
Joshua Knobe, Yale University, USA
Edouard Machery, University of Pittsburgh, USA
Thomas Nadelhoffer, College of Charleston, UK
Eddy Nahmias, Neuroscience Institute at Georgia State University, USA
Jennifer Cole Wright, Psychology, College of Charleston, USA
Joshua Alexander, Siena College, USA

Empirical and experimental philosophy is generating tremendous excitement, producing unexpected results that are challenging traditional philosophical methods. *Advances in Experimental Philosophy* responds to this trend, bringing together some of the most exciting voices in the field to understand the approach and measure its impact in contemporary philosophy. The result is a series that captures past and present developments and anticipates future research directions.

To provide in-depth examinations, each volume links experimental philosophy to a key philosophical area. They provide historical overviews alongside case studies, reviews of current problems and discussions of new directions. For upper-level undergraduates, postgraduates and professionals actively pursuing research in experimental philosophy these are essential resources.

Titles in the series include:
Advances in Experimental Epistemology, edited by James R. Beebe
Advances in Experimental Moral Psychology, edited by Hagop Sarkissian and Jennifer Cole Wright
Advances in Experimental Philosophy and Philosophical Methodology, edited by Jennifer Nado
Advances in Experimental Philosophy of Mind, edited by Justin Sytsma
Advances in Religion, Cognitive Science, and Experimental Philosophy, edited by Helen De Cruz and Ryan Nichols

Advances in Experimental Philosophy of Language

Edited by
Jussi Haukioja

Advances in Experimental Philosophy

Bloomsbury Academic
An imprint of Bloomsbury Publishing Plc

B L O O M S B U R Y
LONDON · OXFORD · NEW YORK · NEW DELHI · SYDNEY

Bloomsbury Academic
An imprint of Bloomsbury Publishing Plc

50 Bedford Square	1385 Broadway
London	New York
WC1B 3DP	NY 10018
UK	USA

www.bloomsbury.com

BLOOMSBURY and the Diana logo are trademarks of Bloomsbury Publishing Plc

First published 2015
This paperback edition first published 2016

© Jussi Haukioja and Contributors, 2015

Jussi Haukioja has asserted his right under the Copyright, Designs and Patents Act, 1988, to be identified as Author of this work.

All rights reserved. No part of this publication may be reproduced or transmitted in any form or by any means, electronic or mechanical, including photocopying, recording, or any information storage or retrieval system, without prior permission in writing from the publishers.

No responsibility for loss caused to any individual or organization acting on or refraining from action as a result of the material in this publication can be accepted by Bloomsbury or the author.

British Library Cataloguing-in-Publication Data
A catalogue record for this book is available from the British Library.

ISBN: HB: 978-1-4725-7073-4
PB: 978-1-3500-1441-1
ePDF: 978-1-4725-7075-8
ePub: 978-1-4725-7074-1

Library of Congress Cataloging-in-Publication Data
Advances in experimental philosophy of language / edited by Jussi Haukioja.
pages cm. – (Advances in experimental philosophy)
Includes bibliographical references and index.
ISBN 978-1-4725-7073-4 (hardback) – ISBN 978-1-4725-7074-1 (epub) – ISBN 978-1-4725-7075-8 (epdf) 1. Language and languages–Philosophy.
I. Haukioja, Jussi, editor.
P107.A39 2015
401–dc23
2014045776

Typeset by Newgen Knowledge Works (P) Ltd., Chennai, India

Contents

List of Figures	vi
List of Contributors	vii

1	Introduction *Jussi Haukioja*	1
2	Kripke's Gödel Case *Max Deutsch*	7
3	Testing Theories of Reference *Michael Devitt*	31
4	A Rylean Argument against Reference *Edouard Machery*	65
5	The Metaphilosophy of Language *Daniel Cohnitz*	85
6	Experimental Semantics: The Case of Natural Kind Terms *Sören Häggqvist and Åsa Wikforss*	109
7	Ambiguity and Referential Machinery *Ángel Pinillos*	139
8	General Terms, Hybrid Theories and Ambiguity: A Discussion of Some Experimental Results *Genoveva Martí*	157
9	Testing Transparent Ascriptions: A Plea for an Experimental Approach *Mark Phelan*	173
Index		203

List of Figures

4.1	Results from Machery et al. (2004)	70
4.2	Results of Machery et al. (2009) and of Machery and Olivola (unpublished)	72
4.3	Results of Machery et al.'s (forthcoming) Study 5	73
9.1	Mean saying scores	187
9.2	Percentage of transparency assessments per vignette	188
9.3	Mean saying/conveying scores across first- and third-person vignettes	191
9.4	Mean overall agreement with meaning equivalence statements	194
9.5	Mean agreement with meaning equivalency statements for those who judged the hedged claim was conveyed	195

List of Contributors

Daniel Cohnitz: Department of Philosophy, University of Tartu.

Max Deutsch: Department of Philosophy, The University of Hong Kong.

Michael Devitt: Philosophy Program, Graduate Center, City University of New York.

Jussi Haukioja: Department of Philosophy and Religious Studies, Norwegian University of Science and Technology.

Sören Häggqvist and Åsa Wikforss: Department of Philosophy, Stockholm University.

Edouard Machery: Department of History and Philosophy of Science, University of Pittsburgh.

Genoveva Martí: Department of Philosophy, Western University and ICREA, University of Barcelona.

Mark Phelan: Department of Philosophy, Lawrence University.

Ángel Pinillos: School of Historical, Philosophical & Religious Studies, Arizona State University.

1

Introduction

Jussi Haukioja

Experimental philosophy has, in the last ten years or so, caused a wide variety of reactions, ranging from excitement and elation to irritation and exasperation. More and more experimental work is being done on intuition and judgement concerning values, free will, consciousness, and so on – and last but not least, language. Whatever view one takes on the relevance of experimental data, it is undeniable that experimental philosophy has contributed enormously to the recent interest in metaphilosophy and philosophical methodology, and thereby to increased self-reflection in analytic philosophy.

One should resist the urge to make sweeping generalizations about philosophical methodology, whether one is defending the armchair or throwing it away. As Daniel Cohnitz stresses in his contribution to this volume, it is by no means obvious – or even likely – that the same kind of reaction to the use of experimental methods is justified *across all subfields* of philosophy (even of analytic philosophy). Different subfields are concerned with different questions, and may even have different explanatory goals. In philosophy of language, many questions are concerned with how *our* language functions, rather than with how *all* languages *must* function. As a consequence, empirical considerations and also experimental methods may well be more directly relevant here than in other areas of philosophy. Thus, philosophers who are otherwise sceptical of experimental philosophy may well think that in the case of the philosophy of language, experimental results do have a role to play. Given the difficulty of drawing a clear line between philosophy of language and linguistics, this should not be surprising.

Indeed, many philosophers of language – most likely the majority – do acknowledge that experimental data *can* be relevant to questions that are typically thought to belong to philosophy of language, but they disagree on *which* questions should be studied experimentally, and in particular, as *what kind of data* is relevant. Many theorists appear to feel that the kinds of survey studies currently available, while perhaps interesting in many ways, do not really tell us anything interesting about *semantics* but acknowledge that future studies, perhaps using different methodologies, might be able to do so.

The methodological battles continue, then, as new experimental data keeps coming in. Unlike in (many areas of) linguistics, there is no consensus on what kind of data is relevant, and for which questions. Experimental philosophy of language is, in many ways, still in its early stages. This volume reflects this. All of the papers engage, more or less directly, in the methodological debates surrounding experimental philosophy of language. At the same time, two of the papers present new data, two others discuss results that are as of yet unpublished, and the remaining four discuss the conclusions (if any) that can be drawn from existing studies, and suggest ways of improving on current experimental methods.

1. How it started: MMNS 2004 and the challenge to traditional armchair methodology

Much of the current interest in experimental philosophy of language is due to Machery, Mallon, Nichols and Stich's (MMNS) provocative 2004 paper "Semantics, Cross-Cultural Style". MMNS presented an experimentally based challenge to what they take to be the standard methodology in philosophy of language in general (and in much of analytical philosophy outside philosophy of language) and theories of reference in particular. As they see it, theories of reference have been formulated by appealing to philosophers' own *intuitions* about reference: such intuitions have been taken to be the primary *evidence* that a theory of reference should adequately capture in order to be successful. MMNS went on to present experimental data gathered on vignettes closely modelled after Kripke's Gödel/Schmidt example and claimed their results show that the kinds of intuitions that have been taken to be evidence in theorizing about reference are culture-relative and, thus, far from as universal as philosophers of language have been assuming.

MMNS's paper created a voluminous discussion that is still ongoing. Various aspects of the original study have been criticized, but Machery and other experimental philosophers have been remarkably quick in coming up with new experiments to improve on the earlier ones. (For helpful summaries of the state of the research, see Genone 2012; Hansen forthcoming.)

Yet doubts remain about the assumption underlying the experimental project, as described by MMNS. In his contribution to this volume, Max Deutsch argues that MMNS, as well as many of their critics, are simply *wrong* in assuming that Kripke and other philosophers of language have been centrally relying on intuitions in theorizing about reference. Deutsch argues that the sections of Kripke (1980) that are often taken to signal an evidential appeal to intuitions have been misinterpreted and that the primary evidence for causal-historical theories is to be found in our ordinary, empirical knowledge about language and the world (cf. also Deutsch 2009; Cappelen 2012). Consequently, if it is intuitions that experimental philosophers such as MMNS are probing in their studies, their results are simply not directly relevant to theories of reference.

Michael Devitt, however, accepts that intuitions have played a central role in theorizing about reference, also in Kripke's groundbreaking work. Having said that, Devitt urges that philosophy of language should mature in its methodology and adopt experimental methods to study, not intuitions, but *linguistic usage*. In his "Testing Theories of Reference", Devitt summarizes his argument for this view, presented earlier (e.g. Devitt 1996, 2011). He then goes on to discuss in more detail exactly how theories of reference *should* be empirically tested, suggesting the use of corpus studies and/or elicited production. He also reports on a study he carried out with Wesley Buckwalter and Kate Devitt (unpublished), where they attempted to use the method of elicited production to study the reference of proper names. This study was unsuccessful but informative, in uncovering some pitfalls that should be avoided by future work.

In "A Rylean Argument against Reference", Edouard Machery develops further a particular strand in his earlier argumentation. Machery's attention here is on the notion of *type* reference rather than *token* reference – on the relation between a *type* of proper name and a particular. After reviewing experimental data (some of it new and as of yet unpublished) that appears to indicate substantial demographic variation in speakers' judgements about reference, he focuses on a particular kind of response that has seemed promising to many philosophers: claiming that the data does not need to be taken seriously because the folk have at best confused concepts of reference and extension. Machery argues that this move comes at a significant cost: theories of reference and extension could no longer be seen as dealing with a subject matter that is pre-theoretically grasped. The burden of proof, Machery claims, is now on the theorist of reference, to show that the relations of (type) reference and extension are real and that theorizing about them serves some explanatory purpose.

Daniel Cohnitz argues in his contribution that experimental work may have more promise of giving directly informative results in philosophy of language, and philosophical semantics in particular, than in other subfields of philosophy. Drawing on the meta-internalist perspective on reference developed in earlier work (Cohnitz and Haukioja 2013 and forthcoming), he claims that the intuitive application and interpretation of language should be seen as *constituting* the relevant semantic facts rather than *tracking* an independently existing realm of facts. Empirical data about our semantic dispositions will then be immediately relevant to theorizing about reference, at least to the extent that we expect theories of reference to play a role in explaining successful linguistic communication between speakers. Cohnitz goes on to suggest that experimental philosophers should adopt methods from psycholinguistics to get more informative data. For example, eye-tracking studies have been used with success to study the reference of anaphoric pronouns. This methodology could also be used by philosophers to study the intuitive application and interpretation of referring expressions, as well as to study related issues such as the discrimination between speaker's reference and semantic reference.

2. Beyond proper names

The focus on proper names in recent experimental philosophy of language is understandable, given the origin of the recent debates. But reference (though central) is just one among many philosophically interesting linguistic phenomena, and proper names (though important) are just one class of referring expressions. Both Kripke (1980) and Putnam (1975) took the central ideas in the new causal-historical theory of reference also to apply to natural kind terms – indeed, Putnam's Twin Earth thought experiment has been just as central and influential in recent philosophy of language as Kripke's Gödel/Schmidt experiment is (if not more so).

In their "Experimental Semantics: The Case of Natural Kind Terms", Sören Häggqvist and Åsa Wikforss distinguish between various different things that might be meant by "semantic theory", and discuss the role of both empirical evidence and theoretical expertise in the construction of theories according to each way of construing the central questions. Informed by this, they then go on to review the existing evidence concerning the semantics of natural kind terms, presented from the armchair *and* from experimental studies, as well as from the history of science. Häggqvist and Wikforss argue that, contrary to widespread impressions, this evidence lends some support to *cluster* theories of natural kind terms, but more evidence, and more carefully designed experiments, are sorely needed.

Ángel Pinillos suggests in his contribution that perhaps *both* main contenders, descriptivist theories *and* causal-historical theories, are (partly) correct when it comes to the reference of natural kind terms and proper names. He reviews the data from a recent study on natural kind terms (Nichols et al. forthcoming) and concludes that the view that natural kind terms are *ambiguous* between descriptivist and causal-historical readings at least deserves to be taken seriously. Pinillos then goes on to present new experimental data, where he explores a similar theory for proper names, and argues that his data lends support to the view that names are, indeed, ambiguous in the same way.

In her "General Terms, Hybrid Theories and Ambiguity: A Discussion of Some Experimental Results", Genoveva Martí also discusses theories of this kind, as well as the theory (also experimentally motivated) presented by Genone and Lombrozo (2012) for a *hybrid* semantics for natural kind terms. Martí finds the motivation for such theoretical moves wanting. Even if the data turns out to support a hybrid theory, or an ambiguity theory, this does not represent a radical departure from the causal-historical theories that have been formulated during the last decades. Traditional descriptivist theories were driven by the assumption that all reference has to be *mediated* by descriptions, and any causal-historical theorist will agree that *some* terms, or some uses of terms, have their reference determined by descriptions. A hybrid theory, or an ambiguity theory, will then *agree* that not all reference has to be mediated, and only represent a minor adjustment to the causal-historical picture rather than a wholesale rejection of it.

3. Beyond reference and extension

Appeals to 'what we would say' in philosophy of language are not limited to theories of reference and extension. It is therefore to be expected that empirical data can be highly relevant for a number of other projects in philosophy of language. However, the precise relevance of experimental results of a given kind to a given problem will have to be resolved on a case-by-case basis.

The final paper in this book, Mark Phelan's "Testing Transparent Ascriptions: A Plea for an Experimental Approach" tackles the problem of first-person belief attributions. Do utterances of the form "I believe that p" always directly express the mental state of the speaker, and only *imply* information about the non-psychological world (as Grice 1989 would have it)? Or do they on some occasions express the speaker's belief states, and on others hedged information about the world (the 'direct expression' view)? Phelan clarifies the two competing theories and presents the data from a series of experiments he conducted, finding *prima facie* support for the direct expression view.

References

Cappelen, H. (2012), *Philosophy without Intuitions*. Oxford: Oxford University Press.

Cohnitz, D. and Haukioja, J. (2013), 'Meta-externalism vs meta-internalism in the study of reference'. *Australasian Journal of Philosophy*, 91, 475–500.

Cohnitz, D. and Haukioja, J. (forthcoming), 'Intuitions in philosophical semantics'. *Erkenntnis*.

Deutsch, M. (2009), 'Experimental philosophy and the theory of reference'. *Mind and Language*, 24 (4), 445–466.

Devitt, M. (1996), *Coming to Our Senses: A Naturalistic Program for Semantic Localism*. Cambridge: Cambridge University Press.

Devitt, M. (2011), 'Experimental semantics'. *Philosophy and Phenomenological Research*, LXXXII, 418–435.

Genone, J. (2012), 'Theories of reference and experimental philosophy'. *Philosophy Compass*, 7, 152–163.

Genone, J. and Lombrozo, T. (2012), 'Concept possession, experimental semantics, and hybrid theories of reference'. *Philosophical Psychology*, 25, 717–742.

Grice, P. (1989), *Studies in the Way of Words*. Cambridge, MA: Harvard University Press.

Hansen, N. (forthcoming), 'Experimental philosophy of language'. *Oxford Handbooks Online*.

Kripke, S. A. (1980), *Naming and Necessity*. Cambridge, MA: Harvard University Press.

Machery, E., Mallon, R., Nichols, S. and Stich, S. P. (2004), 'Semantics, cross-cultural style'. *Cognition*, 92, B1-B12.

Nichols, S., Pinillos, A. and Mallon, R. (forthcoming), 'Ambiguous reference'. *Mind*.

Putnam, H. (1975), 'The meaning of "meaning"', *Philosophical Papers Vol. 2: Mind, Language, and Reality*. Cambridge: Cambridge University Press.

2

Kripke's Gödel Case

Max Deutsch

1. Introduction

In earlier work (Deutsch 2009), I argued that Saul Kripke does not, in *Naming and Necessity* (henceforth, "*NN*"), treat intuitions about his famous *Gödel Case* as evidence for what he takes to be true in the case. I claim that this shows that empirical data collected by experimental philosophers of language, to the effect that speakers from different cultural backgrounds have conflicting intuitions about the case[1], does not in any way affect Kripke's argument for his conclusion about the case. One thing I emphasized in my earlier work is that there really is an *argument* in Kripke's book, as opposed to a simple appeal to intuition, for what he takes to be true in the Gödel Case.

I have two aims in the present chapter. First, I aim to bolster the argument I've made for the view that there are no evidential appeals to intuition in Kripke's argument for his conclusion about the Gödel Case. The argument needs bolstering, apparently; despite my earlier efforts, there are still many philosophers (and not just experimental ones) who insist that Kripke makes such appeals in arguing for that conclusion. Second, I aim to discuss a passage in *NN* that has been interpreted by many commentators as indicating an explicit endorsement, by Kripke, of the metaphilosophical view that intuitions are evidence for philosophical claims. I will argue that this is misinterpretation; reading the passage in context reveals that it is very likely not intended as such an endorsement.

2. The case

The thesis that Kripke means to establish in the passages in which the Gödel Case appears is the anti-descriptivist thesis that the reference of an ordinary proper name is not determined by definite descriptions that users of the name associate with it. The Gödel Case is intended to reveal a counterexample to descriptivism; it involves an ordinary proper name, "Gödel", which, relative to the circumstances Kripke hypothesizes in the case, does not, Kripke claims, refer to the object to which it *would* refer if its reference were determined by associated definite descriptions. Here is the case as Kripke presents it:

The Gödel Case

Let's take a simple case. In the case of Gödel that's practically the only thing many people have heard about him – that he discovered the incompleteness of arithmetic. Does it follow that whoever discovered the incompleteness of arithmetic is the referent of "Gödel"?

Imagine the following blatantly fictional situation. (I hope Professor Gödel is not present.) Suppose that Gödel was not in fact the author of this theorem. A man named "Schmidt", whose body was found in Vienna under mysterious circumstances many years ago, actually did the work in question. His friend Gödel somehow got hold of the manuscript and it was thereafter attributed to Gödel. On the view in question, then, when our ordinary man uses the name "Gödel", he really means to refer to Schmidt, because Schmidt is the unique person satisfying the description, "the man who discovered the incompleteness of arithmetic". Of course you might try changing it to "the man who *published* the discovery of the incompleteness of arithmetic". By changing the story a little further one can make even this formulation false. Anyway, most people might not even know whether the thing was published or got around by word of mouth. Let's stick to "the man who discovered the incompleteness of arithmetic". So, since the man who discovered the incompleteness of arithmetic is in fact Schmidt, we, when we talk about "Gödel", are in fact always referring to Schmidt. But it seems to me that we are not. We simply are not. (Kripke 1980, pp. 83–84)

Kripke's conclusion about his example is that, in the hypothesized "blatantly fictional" circumstances, "Gödel" refers to the man who stole the incompleteness proof, namely Gödel, not to the man who discovered the proof, Schmidt. If this conclusion is correct, then the Gödel Case is a counterexample to those varieties of descriptivism that imply the opposite. Henceforth, I will refer to Kripke's conclusion about the Gödel Case as the *Gödel Judgement*.

3. Evidential appeals to intuitions

The question I turn to in the next section is *how* Kripke means to establish the truth of the Gödel Judgement. A very common view is that he means to do so at least in part by making an evidential appeal to his own and his readers' *intuition* that the Gödel Judgement is true. I will argue that that this common view is mistaken, but before turning to that argument it will be helpful to get clearer about what, exactly, constitutes an evidential appeal to an intuition.

Fortunately, despite many disagreements over details, there has emerged something of a consensus about the nature of intuitions. For example, there is widespread agreement that "intuition" names a kind of *propositional attitude*; one intuits *that p*, where "p" names the propositional content that individuates the intuition. Another point of (more or less) agreement is that intuition is a species of *non-inferential* propositional attitude; that is, when one intuits that *p*, this is not in virtue of inferring *p* from other attitudes one holds. A last point of agreement is that intuitions are not perceptions, memories, or introspections; they have their own source, perhaps 'rational insight' (though how to positively characterize this other source is more controversial).

As I understand it in this paper, to make an *evidential appeal* to an intuition thus characterized is to treat the *having*, or *instantiation*, of the intuition that *p* as evidence for *p* itself. So, on this understanding, Kripke makes an evidential appeal to an intuition in defence of the Gödel Judgement just in case he treats the instantiation (in him and perhaps his readers) of a propositional attitude – whose content matches that of the Gödel Judgement's – as evidence for the truth of that very content.[2]

But what is it to treat the instantiation of such a propositional attitude as *evidence* for the content of that very attitude? There are several possibilities here. For example, it might be to treat the instantiation of the attitude as *increasing the likelihood of its content's truth*. Alternatively, it might be to treat the instantiation of the attitude as *justifying a corresponding belief in, or judgement of, the truth of its content*. I will remain neutral among these and other possibilities and will content myself with saying what I mean to be compatible with all of them, namely that to treat the having of an intuition that *p* as evidence for *p* itself is to treat it as bestowing some kind of *positive epistemic* status on belief in p (should one form that belief on the basis of having the intuition).[3]

4. The argument

I have said that it is common to hear Kripke's method in presenting the Gödel Case described as making an evidential appeal to the intuition that the Gödel Judgement is true. A first point to make about this common view is that *if* there is such an appeal, it is not explicit in the passages that constitute the presentation of the Gödel Case. Neither "intuition" nor a cognate appears in the passages, and there is no other language in them that suggests that Kripke intends to be citing evidence for the truth of the Gödel Judgement via an appeal to the fact that he or his readers instantiate a propositional attitude with the Gödel Judgement's content.

Some will say: "But what of Kripke's use of 'seems' in the penultimate sentence of the presentation of the Gödel Case – 'But it seems that we are not'? Isn't that 'intuition talk', suggestive of an evidential appeal to an intuition? Indeed, doesn't Kripke fairly clearly intend, in the transition from this sentence to the last – 'We simply are not' – to be moving from the fact that it is *intuitive* that the Gödel Judgement is true to the fact that it *is* true?"

I have heard this complaint many times in informal conversations with other philosophers, and, in John Bengson's (2014) recent commentary on Herman Cappelen's (2012) *Philosophy without Intuitions*, the complaint has now made it into print. The problem with the complaint is that there is a better interpretation: Kripke's use of "seems" at the end of the presentation of the Gödel Case is a *hedging or understating* use; it expresses less than full commitment to the Gödel Judgement, a commitment that is then strengthened in the final, "seems"-free sentence of the presentation. Kripke, on this better interpretation, is doing something very different, in the last two sentences of the presentation of the Gödel Case, from providing evidence for the Gödel Judgement. Instead, he is simply asserting its truth, less committedly at first, and then more firmly a sentence later.

Support for this interpretation comes from Kripke himself, in a precursor to *Naming and Necessity*, his paper, "Identity and Essence". There, Kripke comments on his own use of "seems", writing, "I, like other philosophers, have *a habit of understatement* in which 'it seems plainly false' means 'it is plainly false'" (Kripke 1971, p. 6; my emphasis). I don't claim that this constitutes proof that Kripke is using "seems" in the presentation of the Gödel Case in this hedging or understating way. But I do think the quotation from "Identity and Necessity" shows that this is far more likely than an interpretation that takes Kripke to be making an explicit evidential appeal to intuition in support of the Gödel Judgement.

Such an appeal could be implicit, however, and evidence for an implicit evidential appeal to intuition would be lack of genuinely argumentative support for the Gödel Judgement. However, Kripke offers a complex (and, to my mind, highly compelling) argument for the Gödel Judgement. The argument does not appear in the presentation of the Gödel Case itself. Instead it appears in the surrounding passages, some of which are not explicitly linked to the Gödel Case or the Gödel Judgement but which are nevertheless clearly meant by Kripke to have a bearing on their assessment. I turn now to laying this argument out as perspicuously as possible.

4.1 Comparison to actual cases

Part of Kripke's argument for the Gödel Judgement occurs in the passages immediately following his presentation of the Gödel Case (pp. 84–87). One theme of these passages is a comparison between the Gödel Case and three actual (not hypothetical) cases involving actual speakers and actual uses of the names "Peano", "Einstein", and "Columbus". The point of the comparison, Kripke says, is to discourage the impression that the circumstances imagined in the Gödel Case are unusual in some way:

> But it may seem to many of you that this [The Gödel Case] is a very odd example, or that such a situation occurs rarely. This also is a tribute to the education of philosophers. Very often we use a name on the basis of considerable misinformation. (Kripke 1980, p. 84)

Consider first the *Peano Case*: Many of *us* – that is, many people in Kripke's audience at the time of the lectures from which *NN* derives, and many later readers of the text as well – use "Peano" believing it to name the discoverer of the so-called Peano axioms. However, as Kripke reminds us, *Dedekind* discovered those axioms, not Peano. Supposing that the Gödel Judgement is true, the Gödel Case is then a fictional example of the real-life phenomenon exhibited by the Peano Case: In each case, a group of speakers uses a name to refer to a certain man even though that man is *not* picked out by the 'identifying descriptions' associated by those speakers with the name. The other two actual cases, the *Einstein Case* and the *Columbus Case*, exhibit the same phenomenon. Einstein is not the inventor of the atomic bomb, though some actual speakers believe him to be. Despite this, their uses of "Einstein" refer to Einstein, not the inventor of the atomic bomb. Likewise for "Columbus": Some misinformed speakers think that "Columbus" names the man who first realized that the earth is round. However, this misconception does not affect the referential facts; "Columbus", even out of the mouths of these misinformed speakers, does not refer to the man who first realized that the earth is round.

I take Kripke's comparison between the Gödel Case and the actual cases to constitute a reason for accepting the Gödel Judgement, and hence as part of the argument for its truth. Indeed, as I said above, Kripke explicitly says that the presentation of the Peano, Einstein, and Columbus cases is meant to counter a potential objection to his view of the Gödel Case, namely the objection that the circumstances described in the presentation of the Gödel Case are unusual in some way that would blunt its anti-descriptivist force. In my view, Kripke's point is that the similarities between the hypothetical case and the actual ones are so strong that, whatever the correct characterization of the referential facts in the actual cases happens to be, an analogous characterization should apply to the hypothetical case. There is also an assertion of – *not* an intuition about – the correct characterization of the actual cases: In the actual cases, speakers who are misinformed in various ways about the bearers of the names they use, nevertheless refer to those bearers with their uses. This is strong evidence that the misinformed users of "Gödel"' in the hypothetical Gödel Case, refer to Gödel, not Schmidt, and hence that the Gödel Judgement is true.

However, it would be wrong to describe this evidence as *intuitive* evidence; Kripke's strategy, in presenting the actual cases, is *not* to elicit further anti-descriptivist intuitions about them. I will return to this important point in the next (main) section, for there are some (e.g. Devitt 2011a, 2011b, 2012) who describe Kripke's strategy in just this mistaken way.

Does Kripke beg the question against descriptivism by asserting (things that imply) that descriptivism is false of actual uses of "Peano", "Einstein", and "Columbus"? Only in the way that anyone who objects to a generalization by citing a counterexample counts as begging the question. No one thinks that Gareth Evans's famous *Madagascar Case* counterexample to certain (anti-descriptivist) causal theories of reference begs the question against those theories. Dialectically, Kripke's appeal to the Peano, Einstein and Columbus cases is no more suspect than Evans's appeal to the Madagascar Case. Just as we know that Madagascar is not part of the African mainland, so too we know that Peano did not discover the Peano axioms, that Einstein did not invent the atomic bomb, and that Columbus was not the first person to realize that the earth is round. This knowledge, all of it knowledge of straightforwardly *empirical* (i.e. not intuitive) truths, when combined with knowledge of how to express these truths in English, has implications for the correct theory of reference for (English) proper names.[4] To put the underlying idea in general terms: A theory of reference is tested against the referential facts, many of which we already know (e.g. that "Einstein" does not refer to the inventor of the atomic bomb). No questions are begged by saying, as in effect Kripke does, that descriptivism is to be tested against known facts about reference; indeed, it is difficult to imagine how else a theory of reference *could* be tested.

Testing theses related to descriptivism in this way, by comparing their implications to antecedently known truths about reference, occurs earlier in *NN* as well. Jonathan Ichikawa, Ishani Maitra and Brian Weatherson (2012) remind us in a recent paper that Kripke presents the Gödel Case, and the actual cases to which he compares it, *after* he has presented other, related (and also actual) cases, ones in which speakers use a name but cannot themselves cite any uniquely identifying properties of the names' bearers – the *Cicero* and *Feynman* cases (Kripke 1980, pp. 81–82). Some speakers, Kripke says, use the name "Feynman", thinking of its bearer only as 'a famous physicist or something'; similarly, some speakers use "Cicero" knowing no more than that it names *a* famous roman orator (Kripke 1980, p. 82). However, such speakers make definite reference to Feynman and Cicero with their uses – this we know already, in advance of theory – despite being unable to uniquely identify the bearers of these names in descriptive terms. The lesson would seem to be that the descriptive material that speakers associate with the names they use does not in general determine the reference of those names.

Strictly speaking, that lesson leaves it open whether there are other cases in which associated descriptive material does determine reference, and so leaves it open whether descriptivism, as I characterized it above – that is, as a thesis about the role of associated *definite* descriptions in the determination of a name's reference – is true. However, Kripke's assessment of the Feynman and Cicero cases clearly has a bearing on what he says about the later cases (viz. the Gödel, Peano, Einstein and Columbus cases) that more directly challenge descriptivism: we learn from the earlier cases that associated descriptive material is sometimes irrelevant to the referential facts and hence that, if it is sometimes relevant, this is not because there is some necessary connection between associated descriptive material and the determination of reference.

It is in this context, after discussing the Feynman and Cicero cases, that Kripke presents the Gödel Case, where the question becomes whether associated *definite* descriptions determine a name's reference. In fact, I think (and here my view differs from that taken in Ichikawa et al. 2012) that the question is somewhat subtler even than this. The question that the Gödel Case is meant to test is whether, in those cases in which *we know already* that a certain description commonly associated with a name *does* in fact denote the bearer of that name (this, Kripke points out, is true of "Gödel" and "the discoverer of incompleteness" as we actually, in real life, use the terms – the Gödel Case, remember, is 'blatantly fictional'), the name refers to its bearer *because* the description denotes that person.[5] If that were true, then, in the blatantly fictional circumstances imagined in the Gödel Case, it should be true that 'Gödel' refers to Schmidt, not Gödel. That this is not so – that, in those imagined circumstances, 'Gödel' refers, still, to Gödel – is then argued for by appeal to the actual Peano, Einstein and Columbus cases, in which we know already that certain definite descriptions associated by some speakers with the relevant names do *not* denote the bearers of those names.

4.2 Immunity from error

Kripke's argument for the Gödel Judgement does not end with the comparison to the actual cases, however. In a footnote to his discussion of the Gödel Case (Kripke 1980, p. 85, n. 36), Kripke observes that if descriptivism were true, then certain sentences that express misconceptions – his example is "Peano discovered the axioms of number theory" – would express trivial truths instead.[6] The point, cast as it is in terms of the nature of the content of certain name-containing sentences, counts against descriptivism about the *meanings* of names, but Kripke does not always carefully separate the varieties of descriptivism, and it is clear, given that the note's context is a discussion focused on descriptivism about reference, that his intention is to say something against that variety as well.

To bring out its force as a point against descriptivism about reference, it can be put in terms, not of triviality, but of immunity from error. According to descriptivism about reference, the reference of "Peano", for speakers who associate "the discoverer of the axioms of number theory" with the name, will be whoever is uniquely identified by that description. That implies that such speakers are immune from error when they utter Kripke's example sentence. Such speakers cannot *but* refer to the discoverer of the axioms of number theory when using "Peano", so they can only speak the truth if they utter, "Peano was the discoverer of the axioms of number theory."[7] The argument against this implication is straightforward: *No* speaker who utters that sentence speaks truly; Dedekind, not Peano, discovered the relevant axioms.

The application of the point to the Gödel Case is also straightforward: If one is inclined, on descriptivist grounds, to say that the speakers in Kripke's imagined circumstances refer to Schmidt with their uses of "Gödel", then one will be forced to say that those speakers are not, and cannot be, wrong when they say, for example, "Gödel discovered the incompleteness of arithmetic." But when they utter that sentence, they say something false, not something they could not but be correct in saying.

This lack of immunity from error figures in an indirect argument for the truth of the Gödel Judgement: the only reason for making the opposite judgement, namely the reason given by the descriptivist theory of reference for names, has false consequences concerning a certain kind of immunity from error. That provides a reason for *not* making the opposite judgement, and for concluding, with Kripke, that the Gödel Judgement is true.

4.3 Speaker's reference

There is a further argument for the Gödel Judgement in note 36 of *NN*. Indeed, the bulk of the relatively long note is given over to this other argument, in which Kripke describes the connection (or rather lack thereof) between the notion of *speaker's reference* and the truth of the Gödel Judgement.

The issue in this part of the note is not whether descriptivism is true in general, but whether, instead, there are certain *uses* of a name, such that the name, relative to these uses, has its reference determined by associated definite descriptions. Here is Kripke's description of the sorts of uses he has in mind:

> Some who have conceded such cases to me have argued that there are other uses of the same proper names satisfying the cluster theory. For example, it is argued, if we say, "Gödel proved the incompleteness of arithmetic," we are, of course, referring to Gödel, not to Schmidt. But, if we say, "Gödel relied on a diagonal argument in this step of the proof," don't we here, perhaps, refer to whoever proved the theorem? Similarly, if someone asks, "What did Aristotle (or Shakespeare) have in mind here?", isn't he talking about the author of the passage in question, whoever he is? (Kripke 1980, p. 85, n. 36)

Kripke makes two replies to the claim that descriptivism might be true of at least uses of this variety. First, he says that, even if the claim is correct, there are many uses of names, including many uses of "Gödel" in the hypothesized circumstances of the Gödel Case, for which descriptivism is not true. Second, and more importantly, he denies that the claim is correct; that is, Kripke denies that descriptivism is true of uses of the relevant sort. Sketching a view mentioned in an earlier note in *NN* (p. 25, n. 3) and elaborated in other work (especially in Kripke 1977), Kripke admits that, relative to such uses, it might be correct to say that the *speaker* refers to whomever is picked out by an associated definite description, but this does not imply that the name *itself* refers to, or that its *semantic* reference is, that person – not even on those very occasions of use. Descriptivism is a theory of semantic reference; facts about what a *speaker* refers to in using a name do not, therefore, have a clear bearing on its truth, since what a speaker refers to in using a name need not coincide with what the name itself refers to. In fact, Kripke's evidence for the view that the relevant uses are cases in which a speaker makes merely speaker's reference to the objects picked out by associated descriptions is that the speaker in such a case is inclined to *withdraw* the claim he or she makes with the use when he or she learns that the semantic reference of the name lacks the associated uniquely identifying property. And the same is true for misidentifications involving two names, as opposed to a name and a definite description, as in the Smith/Jones case to which Kripke compares the uses in question:

> If I mistake Jones for Smith, I may refer (in an appropriate sense) to Jones when I say that Smith is raking the leaves; nevertheless I do not use "Smith" ambiguously, as a name sometimes of Smith and sometimes of Jones, but univocally as a name of Smith. Similarly, if I erroneously think that Aristotle wrote such-and-such passage, I may perhaps sometimes use "Aristotle" to refer to the actual author of the passage, even though there is no ambiguity in my use of the name. In both cases, I will withdraw my original statement, and my original use of the name, if apprised of the facts. (Kripke 1980, p. 86, n. 36)

Likewise, a speaker who says, "Gödel relied on a diagonal argument in this step of the proof", will withdraw the statement on learning that Schmidt was responsible for the discovery of the proof. As in the Smith/Jones and Aristotle cases, the hypothetical speakers in the Gödel Case do not use "Gödel" ambiguously, sometimes as a name for Gödel and other times for Schmidt. At most, such speakers sometimes make speaker's reference to Schmidt, using a name, "Gödel", whose semantic reference, across every use, is Gödel.

How does this point about speaker's reference add up to a further argument for the truth of the Gödel Judgement? If correct, it shows that there is a reason to reject the claim that there are special uses of "Gödel", relative to the circumstances hypothesized in the Gödel Case (as in "Gödel relied on a diagonal argument in this step of the proof") for which descriptivism gives the correct account of the determination of these uses' semantic reference. In other words, the invocation of the speaker's/semantic reference distinction defuses what is perhaps the best reason for thinking that descriptivism applies to at least some uses of names, namely the fact that there really *is* a sense, on some occasions of use, in which *speakers* refer to the objects denoted by associated definite descriptions. That, Kripke argues, is perfectly consistent with the name, even on the uses in question, not having its semantic reference determined by those associated definite descriptions.

4.4 The causal picture

As is well known, *NN* is highly critical of descriptivism, and a great many of its points and arguments are negative. However, it is also well known that an alternative 'picture' of reference for names is sketched in *NN*, the so-called *Causal Picture* of reference. Without entering into the details of Kripke's positive arguments for the Causal Picture, let me make this fairly obvious point about them: They are, one and all, arguments also for the Gödel Judgement. Arguing for an account of reference determination for names that has, as a consequence, the truth of the Gödel Judgement, is of course to argue for the truth of the Gödel Judgement. Suffice it to say, then, that Kripke's general remarks about 'initial baptisms' and names being passed from 'link to link', along with his discussion of referential intentions and what might or might not be necessary or sufficient for definite reference, all of this counts – indirectly, but nonetheless – as a further raft of considerations that favour the Gödel Judgement.

5. Insistence on intuitions

Here is a striking fact about Kripke's argument for the Gödel Judgement as I have reconstructed it in Section 4 but which derives directly from the original text of *NN*: *There is nowhere, in any of it, any hint that Kripke is, or intends to be, making evidential appeals to intuitions, as I described such appeals in Section 3, in support of the Gödel Judgement.* In fact, the presence of the rather long and multifaceted argument that I described in Section 4 makes the claim that Kripke means us to accept the Gödel Judgement on the basis of it being intuitively true downright laughable.

Despite this, many philosophers continue to insist that it is the intuitiveness of the Gödel Judgement that Kripke intends as the main ground for our belief in its truth, or at least that intuitions of some kind do or might play a significant role in justifying that belief. Experimental philosophers insist on this. Of course, this insistence is a main component of Edouard Machery, Ron Mallon, Shaun Nichols and Stephen Stich's original (2004) experimental paper on the topic. But, despite my best efforts at correcting their mistake, they still insist on it. For example, here is Machery (2011) writing in a recent paper about what counts as evidence for the Gödel Judgement:

> Thus, the Gödel case elicits the judgement that in the circumstances described by the case "Gödel" refers to the man originally called "Gödel." This judgement

is evidence that in these circumstances "Gödel" does refer to the man originally called "Gödel". (Machery 2011, p. 192)

In their most recent paper on the subject, Machery et al. (2013) insist again and again that an evidential appeal to intuition is what Kripke intends as justification for the Gödel Judgement. In fact, their main line of response to the critics they address (Devitt 2011a; Ichikawa et al. 2012) is that a primary goal in their work on topic has been not to reject Kripke's argument against descriptivism, but instead to challenge the use of intuitions as evidence for theories of reference – Kripke's use of intuition in justifying the Gödel Judgement being *the* case in point, according to them.[8] The problem is that they have said next to nothing about why we should believe that Kripke makes an evidential appeal to intuition in support of the Gödel Judgement.[9]

At one point in Machery et al. (2013), the authors mention the fact that they have never replied to my objection that Kripke does not make an evidential appeal to intuition in support of the Gödel Judgement. About this they write:

> but it [my objection] strikes us as clearly mistaken. The evidence that 'Gödel' refers to Gödel rather than Schmidt in the counterfactual situation that Kripke describes (or that our vignette characterizes) is an intuition (or 'spontaneous judgement' if you prefer) that it does. (Machery et al. 2013, p. 630)

This is table pounding. It's insensitive to the textual evidence too. Anyone who has actually read the relevant passages of *NN* can see that Kripke says a great deal in defence of the Gödel Judgement that has nothing to do with its intuitiveness. Indeed, appeals to intuition, let alone 'spontaneous judgements', appear to be entirely absent, as I have tried to show in Section 4.

But an insistence that there are evidential appeals to intuition in philosophy is to be expected from experimental philosophers; unfortunately, they have a vested interest in finding such appeals, even when there are none to be found. What's worse is that even philosophers who have objected to Machery et al.'s (2004) criticism of Kripke's argument for the Gödel Judgement continue to insist that evidential appeals to intuitions might play a role in that argument. Ichikawa et al. (2012), which is an otherwise intelligent and detailed rebuttal of Machery et al.'s position, says things such as:

> Now perhaps we'll get new experimental evidence that even in these cases [Here Ichikawa et al. are discussing the Cicero and Feynman cases, which they take, as I do too, to be relevant to the justification of the Gödel Judgement.], some experimental subjects have descriptivist intuitions. Some people might intuit

that if a speaker does not know of any property that distinguishes Feynman from Gell-Mann, their name "Feynman" is indeterminate in reference between Feynman from Gell-Mann. We're not sure what such an experiment would tell us about the metaphysics of reference, but maybe someone could try undermining Kripke's argument this way. (Ichikawa et al. 2012, p. 5)

At least Ichikawa et al. are 'not sure' what their imagined experiment would show; still, the suggestion is that experiments on intuitions might have some bearing on Kripke's argument for the Gödel Judgement and this it could not do if that argument were, as I claim it is, completely free of evidential appeals to intuitions.

The worst offender in this regard, however, is Michael Devitt, who, though not terribly impressed by the use to which Machery et al. put their original (2004) results, has insisted that Kripke's argument for the Gödel Judgement does rely on an evidential appeal to intuition. In fact, Devitt goes so far as to describe "the consulting of intuitions" as the "*modus operandi* of the philosophy of language" (Devitt 2011b, p. 5), and says that I am "strangely critical of this account of the philosophical methodology" (Devitt 2011b, p. 5, n. 1).[10]

A main objection that Devitt raises against Machery et al. is that they focus on the wrong *kind* of referential intuition. According to Devitt, Kripke's case against descriptivism leans far more heavily on intuitions about the 'humdrum' actual cases (Peano, Einstein, etc.) rather than on intuitions about 'fanciful' hypothetical cases, such as the Gödel Case.[11]

There are many problems with Devitt's objection. Logically speaking, the actual and hypothetical cases are on a par. That is, descriptivism has entailments with respect to hypothetical cases just as much as with respect to actual ones. The truth of the Gödel Judgement falsifies descriptivism just as much as the truth of (what might as well be called) the Peano Judgement. Given this, it seems odd, to claim that intuitions about the entailments of descriptivism relative to hypothetical cases somehow matter less, given that one thinks, as Devitt does, that intuitions matter in the first place.[12]

Devitt will say that it is the *fancifulness* of the Gödel Case that makes intuiting about it trickier business than intuiting about the humdrum actual cases. But, as a matter of fact, fanciful hypotheticals are often easier to reason about than actual cases, precisely because they, in their fanciful way, can eliminate distracting real-world detail.[13] Besides, there's nothing *that* fanciful about the Gödel Case anyway.[14]

Another problem with Devitt's objection is that it simply concedes one of Machery et al.'s main points, which is that the *method* by which Kripke means to justify the Gödel Judgement is via an evidential appeal to intuition. Now, Devitt is upfront about this concession, but the rhetoric of his papers on the topic make it seem as though the concession matters very little to Machery et al.'s overall aims, and *that* – the claim that Machery et al. are right about the method but that it doesn't matter overall – is definitely strange. One of Machery et al.'s main points is, and has always been, that Kripke makes an evidential appeal to intuition in justifying the Gödel Judgement, but, given cross-cultural variability in that judgement, we ought to be highly suspicious of the method. One can't concede this and proceed to suggest that it doesn't matter to the overall debate; it's one of the central conclusions that Machery et al. aimed to establish!

Furthermore, Devitt's view of the relationship between the Gödel Case and the actual cases is mistaken and is denied by Kripke himself. On Devitt's view, the hypothetical cases and the actual cases function independently of each other, each a separate intuitive counterexample to descriptivism. But recall, as I explained in Section 4.1, that Kripke introduces the actual cases in order to respond to a potential objection to his claims about the Gödel Case. Also, as I claimed in Section 4.1, the Gödel Case functions as a rejection of the claim that, in those cases in which we know already that a certain definite description, associated with a certain name, picks out the bearer of that name, the name refers to that bearer *because* he, she, or it is the referent of the description. That is, the Gödel Case plays a special role in a rather intricate argument against several subtly different varieties of descriptivism about reference, a role that Devitt's view can't accommodate.

The most significant problem with Devitt's objection, however, is that he is wrong to claim that *intuitions* about the actual cases provide evidence against descriptivism, and wrong too that this is how Kripke intends the actual cases. Consider, for example, Kripke's presentation of the Einstein and Columbus cases:

> Even worse misconceptions, of course, occur to the layman. In a previous example I supposed people to identify Einstein by reference to his work on relativity. Actually, I often used to hear that Einstein's most famous achievement was the invention of the atomic bomb. So when we refer to Einstein, we refer to the inventor of the atomic bomb. But this is not so. Columbus was the first man to realize that the earth was round. He was also the first European to land in the western hemisphere. Probably none of these things are true, and therefore, when people use the term "Columbus" they really refer to some Greek if they use the roundness of the earth, or to some Norseman, perhaps, if they use the "discovery of America". But they don't. (Kripke 1980, p. 85)

This is not the sound of someone who thinks evidence of any kind, let alone intuitive evidence, must be adduced for the claims that "Einstein" does not refer to the inventor of the atomic bomb or that "Columbus" does not refer to the first man to realize that the earth was round. The questions are not treated as open; Kripke simply takes it for granted – as surely he may – that the claims are true. In any case, one needn't and shouldn't 'consult intuitions' in order to know that Einstein did not invent the atomic bomb and, hence, that "Einstein" does not refer to the inventor of the atomic bomb. And no one came to know that Columbus was not the first man to realize the earth was round, and hence that "Columbus" does not refer to that man, in the non-inferential way allegedly characteristic of intuiting that something is so. This knowledge about Einstein and Columbus (and "Einstein" and "Columbus") is ordinary, empirical, inferential knowledge, and knowledge that Kripke just takes for granted. The idea that Kripke is, or intends to be, making evidential appeals to intuitions to justify judgements about the actual cases is simply a mistake.

6. The heavy evidence passage

Judging by the number of times it has been cited by philosophers who insist that there are evidential appeals to intuitions in *NN* in general, and in Kripke's argument for the Gödel Judgement in particular, there is a single passage in *NN* that strikes many philosophers as sufficient grounds for this insistence. I will call it the *Heavy Evidence* passage:

> **Heavy Evidence**
>
> Of course, some philosophers think that something's having intuitive content is very inconclusive evidence in favor of it. I think it is very heavy evidence in favor of anything, myself. I really don't know, in a way, what more conclusive evidence one can have about anything, ultimately speaking. (Kripke 1980, p. 42)

All of Boghossian (2014), Bengson (2014), Machery et al. (2013), Pust (2000) and Devitt (2012b) have interpreted the Heavy Evidence passage as an endorsement, by Kripke, of the view that intuitions are evidence for philosophical claims.[15] However, none of these papers or books situates the Heavy Evidence passage in its textual context in *NN*. I will argue that, read in context, the Heavy Evidence passage appears to be making a very different point.

Though one would never know it from reading it in isolation (which is, of course, one main problem with citing it in isolation), the Heavy Evidence passage's textual context is a discussion of *de re* modality that runs from page 39 to at least page 49 of *NN*. One of Kripke's claims in these pages is that *de re* modal notions possess "intuitive content", and hence that arguments for scepticism about *de re* modality premised on these notions' alleged lack of intuitive content are unsound. The phrase, "intuitive content", appears three times, once in the Heavy Evidence passage, but twice before it too. When it makes its first appearance, Kripke says explicitly what he means by it:

> It is even suggested in the literature, that though a notion of necessity may have some sort of intuition behind it (we do think some things could have been otherwise; other things we don't think could have been otherwise), this notion [of a distinction between necessary and contingent properties] is just a doctrine made up by some bad philosopher, who (I guess) didn't realize that there are several ways of referring to the same thing. I don't know if some philosophers have not realized this; but at any rate it is very far from being true that this idea [that a property can meaningfully be held to be essential or accidental to an object independently of its description] is a notion which has no intuitive content, *which means nothing to the ordinary man*. (Kripke 1980, p. 41; my emphasis)

Then, in the sentence immediately preceding the Heavy Evidence passage, the phrase occurs again:

> If someone thinks that the notion of a necessary or contingent property (forget whether there are any nontrivial necessary properties [and consider] just the *meaningfulness* of the notion) is a philosopher's notion with no intuitive content, he is wrong. (Kripke 1980, p. 42; Kripke's emphasis)

Just this much more textual context is already enough, I think, to make the usual interpretation of the Heavy Evidence passage very doubtful. One thing that leaps out from the other passages in which "intuitive content" appears is that Kripke does not seem to mean the phrase as the usual interpretation of the Heavy Evidence passage takes him to mean it. For Kripke, it is *notions* and *distinctions*, not propositions or claims, which possess intuitive content, and their possession of it is evidence only of their 'meaningfulness', not of the truth of some or another proposition.

Also, consider Kripke's explicit definition: A notion has intuitive content when it *means something to the ordinary man*. I take it that that – meaning something to the ordinary man – comes to something along the lines of *being present in the thought and talk of ordinary people*. According to Kripke, the 'usual argument'[16] for scepticism about *de re* modality hinges on the idea that *de re* modal notions are philosophical fictions, 'made up by some bad philosopher'. Against this, Kripke, argues that, no, ordinary people speak and think in *de re* modal terms:

> Suppose that someone said, pointing to Nixon, "That's the guy who might have lost". Someone else says "Oh no, if you describe him as 'Nixon', then he might have lost; but, of course, describing him as the winner, then it is not true that he might have lost". (Kripke 1980, p. 41)

Kripke goes on to characterize the second person, who Kripke takes to be representative of someone who holds that there are only *de dicto* possibilities and necessities (and thus that whether it is possible that Nixon lost depends on how he is described) as the "unintuitive man", in the sway of "a philosophical theory" (p. 41). The first person, by contrast, is answering the "intuitive question" of "whether in some counterfactual situation, *this man* would in fact have lost the election" (p. 41; Kripke's emphasis).

So, not just "intuitive content", but also "unintuitive man" and "intuitive question", are to be understood in terms of a notion's presence in the thought and talk of ordinary people. The second person is the unintuitive man because he professes to find some flaw in thinking that Nixon, independently of how he is described, might be such that he is possibly the loser of the election. In so doing, the second person reveals that he is not operating with ordinary modal notions, notions of *de re* modality that are constitutive of ordinary peoples' understanding of questions such as, "Might Nixon have lost the election?" According to Kripke, the first man understands that question just as anyone not in the grip of bad philosophical theory would, namely as a question about Nixon's *de re* modal properties.

However, what is most striking about the explicit definition of "intuitive content", and the implied definitions of "unintuitive man" and "intuitive question", is that the concept of the intuitive thus defined is very different from that operative in the usual understanding of the Heavy Evidence passage. Kripke's argument against scepticism about *de re* modality is not an argument that proceeds from the fact that he or his readers instantiate a propositional attitude of a certain special kind, the instantiation of which provides evidence for the content of that very attitude.[17] And he is indicating in neither the Heavy Evidence passage, nor in the surrounding context, that he approves of such a method, generally speaking. Instead, he appeals to what strikes me as a straightforwardly empirical premise about the presence of a certain notion in the thought and talk of ordinary people and then wields this premise against the view that the notion is a philosophical fiction.

The Heavy Evidence passage does make a somewhat more general point, namely that presence in the thought and talk of ordinary people (i.e. intuitive content) is evidence, very heavy evidence even, for the meaningfulness of *any* notion, not just the notion of *de re* modality. That is, the "somethings" to which Kripke refers, when saying in the Heavy Evidence passage that 'something's having intuitive content is (. . .) very heavy evidence in favor of anything', are *notions*. The claim is that, in general, a notion's presence in the thought and talk of ordinary people – its possession of intuitive content – is very heavy evidence for its meaningfulness. The claim is *not* that intuiting *p* is heavy evidence for the truth of *p*, and so is not the claim that 'intuitions are evidence', given the way that claim has been understood in recent metaphilosophical discussions.

7. Conclusion

One of Devitt's recent papers begins like so:

> How should we go about finding the truth about language? The received view is that we should proceed by consulting our intuitive judgements about language, our 'intuitions'. Indeed, it would be hard to exaggerate both the apparently dominant role of such intuitions in the philosophy of language and the agreement among philosophers that these intuitions should have this role. (Devitt 2012, p. 554)

Devitt might be right about the received view. But I think, *pace* Devitt, that it is *very* easy to exaggerate the role of intuitions in first-order philosophy of language. If, as Devitt claims, there is agreement among philosophers that intuitions *should* have this role, I hope this chapter will at least make them pause to reconsider.

Kripke and *NN* are often held up as examples of how the received view came to be the received view. Devitt holds them up for this purpose, writing:

> Saul Kripke's *Naming and Necessity*, one of the most influential works in the philosophy of language, is often, and rightly, cited as an example of heavy reliance on intuitions. (Devitt 2012, p. 554)

He then cites the Heavy Evidence passage as proof.

I have argued that, given Kripke's intuition-free presentation of an argument for the Gödel Judgement, and given the fact that the standard interpretation of the Heavy Evidence passage is a misinterpretation, the reasons usually given for taking NN to be an example of 'heavy reliance on intuitions' do not justify that view.

That will strike readers as a quite modest conclusion, I hope. I haven't established that there are no evidential appeals to intuitions anywhere in NN, let alone in the philosophy of language as a whole. I haven't established that there are not places elsewhere in NN in which Kripke commits himself, either explicitly or implicitly, to a method of philosophizing about language that involves regular evidential appeals to intuition. However, I do think that my modest conclusion is suggestive: Perhaps NN and other work in the philosophy of language is not as rife with such appeals as some philosophers have come to believe.

The question of whether the philosophy of language contains regular evidential appeals to intuition is an empirical one, to be answered at least in part by empirical methods. Not by social scientific studies of peoples' intuitions, since many such studies *presuppose* a "yes" answer. Rather, we must review those books and papers that strike us as important contributions to the philosophy of language to *see* whether there are evidential appeals to intuitions in them. My view is that Kripke and NN are innocent, but I cannot yet say so definitively – that is work in progress. However, I would recommend this method to other philosophers of language interested in their discipline's metaphilosophy: Look and see whether intuitions play some fundamental role.

This looking and seeing must be carried out before we can properly assess contributions to *experimental* philosophy of language. I think it is safe to say, right now, that experimental work on intuitions about the Gödel Case is irrelevant. And I also think that, to the extent that experimental philosophy of language has been motivated by the Heavy Evidence passage, it is poorly motivated. But that is not to say that there is no conceivable experimental work that might shed light on issues in first-order philosophy of language. In fact, some extant experimental work already qualifies, in my opinion.[18]

However, if one's study involves surveying intuitions, or claims that this or that philosopher of language makes evidential appeals to intuition in his or her work, these methods and claims must be justified. For too long experimental philosophy has simply proceeded from the assumption that intuitions play a major role in the methods of philosophy, but that's all that it is at this point – an assumption. Overturning it or justifying it will take time, and a careful examination of the actual practices and methods of the philosophy of language.

Notes

1 To date, the main data is that reported in Machery, Mallon, Nichols and Stich (2004). Recently, the same authors have claimed that the main cross-cultural finding of their 2004, namely that Chinese English speakers' intuitions appear to favour a descriptivist theory of reference for names, while Western English speakers' intuitions do not, has been replicated in unpublished work by Jonathan Livengood, Justin Sytsma, Ryoji Sato and Oguchi Mineki. However, the finding in this case is with respect to a difference between Japanese and Western subjects, the Japanese subjects, like the earlier Chinese ones, tending toward intuitions consistent with descriptivism.

2 This slightly awkward formulation is meant to be neutral between those views inclined to simply identify intuitions with judgements or beliefs of a certain sort and those (such as 'intellectual seemings' accounts) that deny that intuitions are a species of judgement or belief.

3 I take this formulation, in terms of 'positive epistemic status' from Bengson (2014).

4 Jussi Haukioja has suggested to me that it might be this latter sort of knowledge, knowledge about how to express a given truth in a given language – for example, knowledge about how to express, in English, the truth that Einstein did not invent the atomic bomb, that might be what philosophers of language are getting at when they claim that intuitions have a role to play in arriving at the correct theory of reference. I think there is something to this interesting idea but it is a good distance away from the idea that yours or my intuitions about which object is referred to by "Einstein" has a significant evidential bearing on the question of which object is referred to by "Einstein", and it is this latter idea (in its general form) that I am mainly concerned with criticizing. See Cohnitz and Haukioja (forthcoming) on ambiguities in "intuition" as it is used in the philosophy of language.

5 In a footnote (Ichikawa et al. 2012, p. 6, n. 5), Ichikawa et al. note this 'distinctive feature' of the Gödel Case and even suggest that Kripke might take the feature to be significant in just the way I claim it is, but then go on to say that, no, the point made by the Gödel Case is the same as that made by the actual cases to which Kripke compares it. In my view, the feature is quite significant and Kripke clearly realizes this; he needs an argument against that variety of descriptivism that says that, *when a certain associated definite description does, in fact, uniquely identify the bearer of a name*, then the name's referent is determined by that description.

6 Kripke notes this in the first sentence of footnote 36. The rest of the note contains a somewhat different strand of his argument for the Gödel Judgement. I discuss this different strand of the argument in Section 4.3.

7   Strictly speaking, speakers *can* go wrong in uttering "Peano discovered the axioms of number theory", even if descriptivism about reference is true. It could turn out that *no one* discovered the axioms of number theory. That possibility also shows that Kripke's example sentence does not express a trivial truth, even if descriptivism about meaning is true. This means only that the wrong example sentences have been chosen; the underlying point still holds. Consider: "Peano, *if he exists*, discovered the axioms of number theory." On meaning descriptivism, this sentence is trivially true, while, in fact, it is false. Similarly, the sentence, given reference descriptivism, cannot be uttered falsely, when, in fact, any actual utterance of it is false.

8   This is how Machery et al. describe their strategy in their 2013, though given that Machery et al. think that Kripke argues against descriptivism *by* appealing to intuitions as evidence, it is unclear how they think they can object to the latter without rejecting the former.

9   Machery et al. (2013) do mention the now notorious passage from *NN* in which Kripke claims that something having 'intuitive content' is 'heavy evidence' for it. I discuss this passage, which I call the *Heavy Evidence* passage, in detail, in Section 6 of the main text. For now, suffice it to say that I think that Machery et al. badly misinterpret this passage; it certainly does nothing to support the view that Kripke makes an evidential appeal to intuition to justify the Gödel Judgement.

10 Devitt means that it is strange that I don't share his view that 'the consulting of intuitions' is the m.o. in the philosophy of language. His view is that this *is* the m.o. but that it shouldn't be. Instead, it should be supplemented, he thinks, with other methods. My view is that it isn't the m.o. in the first place. Devitt never says why my view is strange. My view is empirically based; when I study papers and books in the philosophy of language, I don't find that the consulting of intuitions is the m.o. Sometimes philosophers of language *say* things that suggest that they, like Devitt, *think* this is the m.o. But there's a significant 'disconnect' between what some philosophers say is the m.o. and how the actual practice of the philosophy of language proceeds. For example, Devitt quotes from a paper by Stephen Neale in which Neale says, 'Our intuitive judgements about what *A* meant, said, and implied, and judgements about whether what *A* said was true or false in specified situations constitute the primary data for a theory of interpretation, the data it is the theory's business to explain' (Neale 2004, p. 79; quoted in Devitt 2012, p. 554). But Neale is mistaken, independently of the correct view of the role of intuition. The primary data for a theory of interpretation are facts about what *A* meant, said and implied, not 'our' intuitive judgements about these facts. Devitt's other evidence that the consulting of intuitions is the m.o. in the philosophy of language is Kripke and the method he adopts in *NN*. It should be clear from the rest of what I say in this paper that I take Devitt to be mistaken about Kripke and *NN*, but one point worth

mentioning here is that Devitt is looking in the wrong place for insight about the m.o. of the philosophy of language. That insight is to be found by taking the case-study approach, adopted, for example, in Herman Cappellen's excellent 2012. It is by carefully examining 'first-order' philosophizing about language that we will be able to discern the methods employed therein. Metaphilosophical pronouncements, such as Neale's, are not, in my opinion, very reliable (unless of course they come from philosophers such as myself and Cappelen who have bothered to adopt the case-study approach!). Furthermore, like Machery et al., Devitt misinterprets the metaphilosophical passage he cites from Kripke (this is the Heavy Evidence passage I mentioned in note 8), which I discuss in detail in Section 6. One last point: There is no *single* method employed by philosophers of language; they adopt a dizzying array of techniques and methods. It should be obvious that nothing as pat and anaemic as 'the consulting of intuitions' could count as the correct description of the m.o.

11 The *humdrum and actual* versus *fanciful and hypothetical* distinction is first drawn at page 421 of Devitt (2011a).
12 In fact, there is a reason to think they matter more: Suppose that no speaker ever made the kinds of errors with names and descriptions illustrated by the Peano, Einstein and Columbus cases. That is, imagine that every speaker associates definite descriptions with names they use that do, in fact, pick out the bearers of those names. Even so, we could come to see the falsity of descriptivism by reflecting on cases such as the hypothetical Gödel Case.
13 Think, for example, of Judith Jarvis Thomson's (1971) case of the violinist and the conclusions we're meant to draw from the example about the morality of abortion. Presumably, Thomson presented the fanciful case because she thought matters were clearer in that case than they would be just thinking about actual cases of the kinds of killings that she wanted to discuss.
14 This is a point made in Ichikawa et al. (2013) as well, on page 63.
15 The metaphilosophical view attributed to Kripke by the papers that cite the Heavy Evidence passage – the view that intuitions are evidence for philosophical claims – is equivalent, I take it, to the view that intuiting that *p* bestows positive epistemic status on one's belief in *p*, should one believe *p*. That is, I read the relevant papers as claiming that, in the Heavy Evidence passage, Kripke endorses the view that *having* or *instantiating* an intuition increases the likelihood of its content, or justifies belief in that content's truth, or something along such lines.
16 Kripke describes it as such on page 42, note 12. This has always struck me as a bit unfair to Quine (1943), if that's who Kripke has in mind in these passages. Quine is mentioned earlier, on page 40, but not specifically in connection with the view that the notion of *de re* modality lacks intuitive content.
17 What propositional content would this be, anyway? That there *are de re* modal properties of objects? No, because Kripke says explicitly that he is interested only

in the *meaningfulness* of *de re* modal notions and does not treat the considerations he advances in the relevant pages as adding up to a case for the existence of *de re* modal properties. That there is a *notion* of *de re* modality? No, because he and his opponents agree that there is such a notion; their dispute is over whether its source is bad philosophy or ordinary thought and talk. That *de re* modal notions can be used to meaningfully characterize properties of objects? No, because this is the *conclusion* that the premise that the notion of *de re* modality has intuitive content is meant to justify (and is not, itself, characterized as intuitive).

18 For example, I am a fan of Mark Phelan's (2010) experimental work on the philosophy of metaphor.

References

Bengson, J. (2014), 'How philosophers use intuition and "intuition"', in D. Sosa (ed.), Symposium on Herman Cappelen's *Philosophy without Intuitions* (2012), *Analytic Philosophy*. In Press.

Boghossian, P. (2014), 'Cappelen on intuitions', in David Sosa (ed.), Symposium on Herman Cappelen's *Philosophy without Intuitions* (2012), *Analytic Philosophy*. In Press.

Cappelen, H. (2012), *Philosophy without Intuitions*. Oxford: Oxford University Press.

Cohnitz, D. and Haukioja, J. (forthcoming), 'Intuitions in philosophical semantics'. *Erkenntnis*.

Deutsch, M. (2009), 'Experimental philosophy and the theory of reference', *Mind and Language*, 24 (4), 445–466.

Devitt, M. (2011a), 'Experimental semantics'. *Philosophy and Phenomenological Research*, 82 (2), 418–435.

Devitt, M. (2011b), 'Whither experimental semantics?', *Theoria*, 27, 5–36.

Devitt, M. (2012b), 'The role of intuitions', in G. Russell and D. Graff Fara (eds.), *A Companion to the Philosophy of Language*. New York: Routledge, pp. 554–566.

Ichikawa, J., Maitra, I. and Weatherson, B. (2012), 'In defense of a Kripkean dogma'. *Philosophy and Phenomenological Research*, 85 (1), 56–68.

Kripke, S. (1971), 'Identity and necessity', in M. K. Munitz (ed.), *Identity and Individuation*. New York: New York University Press, pp. 135–164.

Kripke, S. (1977), 'Speaker's reference and semantic reference', *Midwest Studies in Philosophy*, 2, 255–276.

Kripke, S. (1980), *Naming and Necessity*. Cambridge, MA: Harvard University Press.

Machery, E. (2011), 'Thought experiments and philosophical knowledge', *Metaphilosophy*, 42 (3), 191–214.

Machery, E., Mallon, R., Nichols, S. and Stich, S. P. (2004), 'Semantics, Cross-cultural Style', *Cognition*, 92 (3), B1–B12.

Machery, E., Mallon, R., Nichols, S. and Stich, S. P. (2013), 'If folk intuitions vary, then what?' *Philosophy and Phenomenological Research*, 86, 618–635.

Neale, S. (2004), 'This, that, and the other', in A. Bezuidenhout and M. Reimer (eds), *Descriptions and Beyond*. Oxford: Oxford University Press, pp. 68–82.

Phelan, M. (2010), 'The Inadequacy of paraphrase is the dogma of metaphor', *Pacific Philosophical Quarterly*, 91 (4), 481–506.

Pust, J. (2000), *Intuitions as Evidence*. New York: Garland.

Quine, W. V. (1943), 'Notes on existence and necessity', *The Journal of Philosophy*, 40 (5), 113–127.

Thomson, J. J. (1971), 'A defense of abortion', *Philosophy and Public Affairs*, 1 (1), 47–66.

3

Testing Theories of Reference

Michael Devitt

"Semantics, cross-cultural style", an important piece of "experimental philosophy" by Edouard Machery, Ron Mallon, Shaun Nichols and Steve Stich (2004), tested theories of reference against the referential intuitions of undergraduates. Whatever we make of the significance of its results – and there has been lots of discussion of this[1] – the paper is important because it raises a very serious methodological question: *How should we test theories of reference?* I have been much occupied with this question in recent years (2011b, c; 2012a, b). In this chapter, I bring together some earlier conclusions (particularly in Sections 3 and 4) and offer some further thoughts (particularly in Sections 5 and 6).

I have argued that Machery et al. are right to criticize the standard methodology in the philosophy of language, a methodology that simply tests theories of reference against philosophers' referential intuitions. But Machery et al. are wrong to propose that we should instead test the theories against the folk's referential intuitions. The primary goal for experimental semantics should not be testing theories against anyone's referential intuitions but rather testing them against the reality that these intuitions are about: theories should be tested against *linguistic usage*. The challenge then is to figure out how to do that.

1. "Reference"

What do we mean by "reference"? The word "reference" and its cognates are ordinary English words with a range of common meanings. When used in philosophy, however, they are technical terms. Many philosophers use "reference" in a quite restricted sense that picks out a relation that holds only between a *singular* term of a certain type – for example, proper names and demonstratives – and one semantically significant object. This restricted use is illustrated in *The Reference Book* (Hawthorne and Manley 2012) and in the large literature that the book discusses.[2] But experimental semanticists favour a generic use of "refer". We need some word in semantics to cover the many different semantically significant relations that expressions bear to the world. "Refer" seems as good choice as any for this role. So, on this usage, not only proper names and demonstratives but count nouns, mass nouns, verbs, adjectives and so on, all refer.

I talk here of "reference" picking out "semantically significant relations" between expressions and the world. Which relations are those? They are, or at least should be, ones identified by the explanatory work the term "reference" does in a theory of language.

This raises the very important question: What are languages and why are they theoretically interesting? Languages are representational systems that are parts of the natural spatio-temporal world and are of theoretical interest because of their causal roles in that world, particularly their roles in communicative behaviours. Thus, Karl von Frisch won a Nobel Prize for discovering that the bees' "waggle dance" is a language communicating messages about food sources. Another scientist, C. N. Slobodchikoff (2002), discovered that the "barks" of Gunnison's prairie dogs form a language that communicates messages about predators. And it is a truism that humans have languages that communicate messages that are the contents of thoughts: "language expresses thought". So, just as the bees and the prairie dogs have representational systems used for communicating messages to each other, so do we.[3] In light of this, the properties of languages that we need to explain – let's call them *meanings* – are those that enable languages to play their causally significant roles in the lives of the organisms that have them, in particular their roles in communication.

A popular idea, and one that I subscribe to, is that reference, along with syntactic properties, are the central notions in an explanation of meanings: they are the core notions in the theory of language. Thus, consider "Jack thinks that Fred loves himself". The idea is that its meaning is largely explained by its syntactic structure and the reference of its expressions ("Jack", "loves", etc.). So the semantically significant relations of expressions to the world that we should pick out as "reference" are the ones that contribute to explaining meanings. It is partly in virtue of standing in those relations that expressions play their important causal roles. I have argued for this naturalistic view of semantics elsewhere (1981, 1996, 2013b).

So we identify referential relations by their causal roles. Then we need to explain those relations: we need theories of reference.

2. Theories of reference

Three general types of theory seem possible. (1) According to "description" theories, the reference of *E* is fixed by certain descriptions that competent speakers associate with *E*; *E* refers to whatever those descriptions, or a weighted most of them, uniquely describe. The received view for decades was that the reference of proper names was to be explained by a description theory. But then came the revolution, led by Saul Kripke (1980).[4] Description theories of names were seen to have serious problems, particularly the problem of "ignorance and error": speakers who seem perfectly competent with a name are too ignorant to provide the descriptions of its referent demanded by description theories; worse, speakers are often so wrong about the referent that the descriptions they would provide apply not to the referent but to another entity or to nothing at all. There were similar problems for description theories of some other terms. (2) These problems with description theories stimulated interest in theories that took the reference of *E* to be explained not indirectly via associated descriptions but rather by some direct relation between *E* and the world, presumably some sort of causal relation, historical, reliablist, or teleological. (3) Finally, there is the possibility of theories that explain reference partly in terms of the associated descriptions of (1) and partly in terms of the direct relations of (2).

I have often emphasized a crucial point about theories of reference: *description theories are essentially incomplete* (e.g. Devitt 1996, p. 159). A theory of type (1) explains the reference of *E* by appealing to the referential properties of descriptions associated with *E*: *E* refers to whatever those other expressions jointly refer to; thus, perhaps, "vixen" refers to whatever its associated descriptions, "female" and "fox", jointly refer to. How then are the references of those other expressions to be explained? What explains the reference of "female" and "fox"? Perhaps we can use description theories to explain those other references too. This process cannot, however, go on forever: there must be some expressions whose referential properties are not parasitic on those of others, else language as a whole is cut loose from the world. Description theories pass the referential buck, but the buck must stop somewhere. It stops with theories of type (2) that explain reference in terms of direct relations to reality.[5] Those theories offer, we might say, *ultimate* explanations of reference.

If any expressions refer then some expressions must be amenable to ultimate explanations. So theorists of reference should always be on the lookout for likely candidates for ultimate explanations (and theorists should not have needed problems with description theories to stimulate interest in other theories).

We turn now to our main question: How should we test what theory of reference is right for an expression?

3. The received view[6]

3.1 The role of intuitions

The received view is that we should test theories of reference, indeed any semantic theory, by consulting our intuitive judgements about language, our metalinguistic "intuitions". It would be hard to exaggerate both the apparently dominant evidential role of such intuitions in the philosophy of language and the agreement among philosophers that these intuitions should have this role.[7] This emphasis on intuitions reflects, of course, a widely held view about the methodology of "armchair philosophy" in general.[8]

Why is this reliance on intuitions appropriate? Machery et al. (2004) have noted that the intuitions that play this evidential role are usually those of the philosophers themselves and have questioned the appropriateness of this: Why should theories of reference rest on the intuitions of philosophers rather than those of the folk, for example, on those of the undergraduates in Rutgers and Hong Kong that they tested? I think our objection to the standard philosophical practice should be more radical: the problem is not that of relying on philosophers' intuitions rather than the folk's, the problem is that of relying on intuitions at all (2011b, c). The right response to armchair philosophy is not to move in more armchairs for the folk.[9]

I am not alone in being concerned about the role of intuitions. Thus, Jaakko Hintikka remarks: "One searches the literature in vain for a serious attempt to provide" a justification for the appeal to intuitions (1999, p. 130). In a similar vein, Timothy Williamson remarks: "[T]here is no agreed or even popular account of how intuition works, no accepted explanation of the hoped-for correlation between our having an intuition that P and its being true that P." He describes this as "a methodological scandal" (2007, p. 215).

3.2 "Cartesianism"

So why do philosophers think that the use of intuitions is appropriate? It clearly would be appropriate if we could be confident that the intuitions reflected *knowledge*. And the received view is that a competent speaker of a language does indeed have knowledge about her language, *propositional* knowledge, "tacitly" at least, *simply by virtue of being competent* in the language:

> It is an undeniable feature of the notion of meaning... that meaning is *transparent* in the sense that, if someone attaches a meaning to each of two words, he must know whether these meanings are the same. (Dummett 1978, p. 131)

> The natural view is that one has *some kind of* privileged semantic self-knowledge. (Loar 1987, p. 97)

The idea of this sort of privileged access – that we are in a special position to know about our own competence – is an instance of general "Cartesianism":

> Since Descartes, it has seemed undeniable to most philosophers that each of us has a privileged way of knowing about his or her own mental states... whenever we have a thought, belief, intention, or desire, we can in principle come to know *what* we think, believe, intend, or desire just by internal examination, without engaging in an empirical investigation of the external world. (McKinsey 1994, p. 308)

The idea that we have a Cartesian access to semantic facts seems to be an almost unquestioned part of the semantic traditions of Frege and Russell.

3.3 A priori knowledge?

Why should we suppose that ordinary competent speakers have this knowledge of semantic facts? Many seem to think that the knowledge is a priori. Thus Jerrold Katz claims: "We know sense properties and relations of expressions on the basis [of] the speaker's a priori linguistic intuitions in clear cases" (1997, p. 21). And Michael McKinsey thinks that it is "fairly clear" that "the principle that the meanings of words are knowable a priori... is taken for granted by most philosophers of language and by many linguists" (1987, p. 1).

Now, of course, the idea that some knowledge is a priori is widespread in philosophy. Nonetheless, Quine has raised serious doubts about it. The main problem with the idea, in my view, is that we do not have even the beginnings of an account of what a priori knowledge *is*. We are simply told what it *isn't*, namely empirical knowledge. Still, suppose we set such general doubts aside and accept that at least our knowledge of mathematics and logic is a priori, what could be the basis for supposing that our knowledge of *meanings* is too? The meaning of a word is presumably constituted by relational properties of some sort: "internal" ones of the sort described by description theories of type (1); or "external" ones of the sort described by causal theories of type (2); or a combination of internal and external relations of the sort described by theories of type (3) (Section 2). I have argued that we have no reason to suppose that we have some non-empirical way of forming a justified belief about which of these relations constitute the meaning of a word (Devitt 1994, 1996, 1998, 2011a, 2014a).

3.4 Embodied theory?

If the view that competent speakers have a priori knowledge of semantic facts does not hold up, what else could justify the ubiquitous reliance on intuitions in the philosophy of language? Perhaps philosophers can take a leaf out of the book of linguists.

The common linguistic view of intuitive judgements is expressed in passages like the following:

> it seems reasonably clear, both in principle and in many specific cases, how unconscious knowledge issues in conscious knowledge . . . it follows by computations similar to straight deduction. (Chomsky 1986, p. 270)

I have described the common view as follows: linguistic competence, all on its own,

> provides information about the linguistic facts . . . So these judgements are not arrived at by the sort of empirical investigation that judgements about the world usually require. Rather, a speaker has a privileged access to facts about the language, facts captured by the intuitions, simply in virtue of being competent. (Devitt 2006a, p. 96)

On this view, intuitive syntactic judgements are, "noise" aside, "the voice of competence" and so provide good evidence about the language. Let's call this thesis "VoC."

The evidence that VoC is the orthodox Chomskian view of linguistic intuitions strikes me as overwhelming (Devitt 2006a, b, 2010b, 2013a).[10] Indeed, if Chomskians did not hold VoC, they would have no view of the source of linguistic intuitions.

Stich has suggested that philosophers of language may be implicitly embracing VoC as a justification for the authoritative role given to referential intuitions (1996, p. 40; see also Hintikka 1999 and Williamson 2007). Philosophers may think that speakers derive their referential intuitions from embodied referential principles. So, just as the true grammar is already embodied in the mind of every speaker, so too, according to this suggestion, are true semantic theories of reference. Referential intuitions, like syntactic ones, are the result of something like a deduction from a represented theory.[11]

Although VoC is much more promising than the view that we have a priori knowledge of meaning, I have argued that it is wrong (2006a, b, 2010b, 2013a). The main problems with it are, first, that, to my knowledge, it has never been stated in the sort of detail that could make it a real theory of the source of intuitions. Just *how* do the allegedly embodied principles yield the intuitions? We need more than a hand wave in answer. Second, again to my knowledge, no argument has ever been given for VoC until Georges Rey's recent attempt (2013), which, I argue (Devitt 2013a), fails. Third, given what else we know about the mind, it is unlikely that VoC could be developed into a theory that we would have good reason to believe.

I have pointed out some other implausibilities of VoC. These are briefly as follows. (i) If competence really spoke to us, why would it not use the language of the embodied theory and why would it say so little? (ii) There would be a disanalogy between the intuitions provided by the language faculty and by perceptual modules. (iii) Developmental evidence suggests that the ability to speak a language and the ability to have intuitions about the language are quite distinct, the former being acquired in early childhood, the latter, in middle childhood as part of a *general* cognitive development.

Perhaps the best reason for rejecting VoC is that there is a better explanation of intuitions and their evidential role.

4. The modest explanation of intuitions

If VoC is not the right theory of intuitions, what is? I argue that intuitive judgements about language, *like intuitive judgements in general*, "are empirical theory-laden central-processor responses to phenomena, differing from many other such responses only in being fairly immediate and unreflective, based on little if any conscious reasoning" (Devitt 2006a, p. 103).[12] Although a speaker's competence in a language obviously gives her ready access to the *data* of that language, the data that the intuitions *are about*, it does not give her ready access to the *truth* about the data; the competence does not provide the *informational content* of the intuition. In this respect my view is sharply different from VoC. And it is sharply different in another respect: it is *modest*, making do with cognitive states and processes we were already committed to. So, following Mark Textor (2009), I now call it "the Modest Explanation".

According to the Modest Explanation, intuitions about language, like other intuitions, are 'theory-laden'. This could do with some explanation. First, the view is *not* that these intuitions are theoretical judgements or the result of theorizing. Rather, the intuitions are mostly *the product of experiences* of the linguistic world. They are like 'observation' judgements; indeed, some of them *are* observation judgements (2006a, p. 103) As such, they are 'theory-laden' in just the way that we commonly think observation judgements are. The anti-positivist revolution in the philosophy of science, led by Thomas Kuhn and Paul Feyerabend, drew our attention to the way in which even the most straightforward judgements arising from observational experiences may depend on background expertise. We would not make the judgements if we did not hold certain beliefs or theories, some involving the concepts deployed in the judgements. We would not make the judgements if we did not have certain predispositions, some innate but many acquired in training, to respond selectively to experiences.[13] There is need for some cautionary words about this theory ladenness.

- The power of background expertise to influence judgements should not be exaggerated. Thus a person observing the Müller-Lyer arrows will judge that one "looks longer" than the other even though she knows perfectly well that they are the same length.
- The view is not that we consciously bring the background into play in a way that amounts to *theorizing* about the experience. Surely, we mostly don't. Nonetheless, the background plays a causal role in the judgement.
- The view is not that we need to have done a great deal of thinking about language before having linguistic intuitions: a thoroughly ignorant person may *learn* to have intuitions in an experimental situation (Devitt 2006a, p. 114).[14]
- Finally, the theory ladenness we are discussing is *epistemic*. It should not be confused with *semantic* theory-ladenness, the view that the meaning of an observation term is determined by the theory containing it. This "semantic holism", also part of the revolution, has little to be said for it in my view (Devitt 1996, pp. 87–135).

It is not a methodological consequence of the Modest Explanation of intuitions that they should have no evidential role in theorizing about the nature of some area of reality. However, it is a consequence that they should have that role only to the extent that they are likely to be reliable about that area of reality, only to the extent that they are *reliable indicators*. And this reliability needs to be assessed using independent evidence about the reality. But we need that independent evidence anyway:

> Although we may often be right to trust an intuition in the short run, it is crucial to see that nothing rests on it in the long run. We can look for more direct evidence

in scientific tests. In such a scientific test we examine the reality the intuition is *about*. These scientific examinations of reality, not intuitions about reality, are the primary source of evidence. The examinations may lead us to revise some of our initial intuitions. They will surely show us that the intuitions are far from a complete account of the relevant bit of reality. (Devitt 2011b, p. 425)

The intuitions in question here are ones identifying objects as having properties *of the sort adverted to in the very theory being tested*; for example, intuitions about fish when testing a biological theory of fish, about money when testing an economic theory of money and about reference when testing a semantic theory of reference. Such intuitions from people who are reliable about the reality in question, are of course good evidence about the nature of that reality. But I make two points about the intuitions. First, they are only indirect evidence. Second, their reliability needs to be established. Both these points show the need for more direct evidence: *the primary evidence for a theory about a certain reality comes not from aforementioned intuitions about the reality but from more direct examinations of that reality*. We don't rest biology on intuitions about fish and the like, or economics on intuitions about money and the like. No more should we rest semantic theories on intuitions about reference and the like. We should examine linguistic reality more directly. That reality is to be found in linguistic usage.

I shall consider the task of gathering this evidence in Section 6.

But first we need to clarify this contrast between indirect and direct evidence by distinguishing different sorts of intuitions. And we need to say something about the *likelihood* that intuitions, particularly referential intuitions, are reliable. All this requires distinguishing among intuitions according to the degree to which they are theory laden and according to the expertise of those who have them.

5. Varieties of intuitions

5.1 Perceptual judgements as intuitions

After introducing the Modest Explanation of intuitions in *Ignorance of Language*, I immediately make a clarification:

> It may be that there are many unreflective empirical responses that we would not ordinarily call intuitions: one thinks immediately of perceptual judgements like "That grass is brown" made on observing some scorched grass, or "That person is angry" made on observing someone exhibiting many signs of rage. Perhaps we count something as an intuitive judgement only if it is *not really obvious*. I shall

> not be concerned with this. My claim is that intuitions are empirical unreflective judgements, *at least*. Should more be required to be an intuition, so be it. (Devitt 2006a, p. 103)

Some perceptual judgements that are "not really obvious" are among my later examples of intuitions. The following one is in the text:

> Consider, for example, a paleontologist in the field searching for fossils. She sees a bit of white stone sticking through grey rock, and thinks "a pig's jawbone". This intuitive judgement is quick and unreflective. She may be quite sure but unable to explain just how she knows. (p. 104)

The next ones are in a note:

> other nice examples: of art experts correctly judging an allegedly sixth-century Greek marble statue to be a fake; of the tennis coach, Vic Braden, correctly judging a serve to be a fault before the ball hits the ground. (p. 104, n. 12)

However, I also treat some "really obvious" perceptual judgements as intuitions in a discussion of the visual module (pp. 112–113). And I did also in an earlier work (1996).

So I have a generous view of what counts as an "intuition", including even such "really obvious" judgements as that the grass is brown and the person angry. Given my view that all of these perceptual judgements, whether really obvious or not, are immediate, empirical, and theory-laden, it is an uninteresting verbal issue whether I am "right" to be so generous. These perceptual judgements are certainly all intui*tive*. There seems to be no theoretically interesting reason for grouping some but not all together under the term "intuition". This having been said, the difference in the obviousness of these intuitions is interesting. The less obvious an intuition of a certain sort, the more expertise, the more 'theory', is required to have reliable ones of that sort. So whereas judging brown grass requires little expertise, judging a pig's jawbone requires a lot.

I have used (Devitt 2006a, pp. 104–105) the following quote from the cognitive psychologist, Edward Wisniewski, to demonstrate the importance of expertise:

> researchers who study behavior and thought within an experimental framework develop *better* intuitions about these phenomena than those of the intuition researchers or lay people who do not study these phenomena within such a framework. The intuitions are better in the sense that they are more likely to be correct when subjected to experimental testing. (1998, p. 45)

The role of expertise has obvious methodological consequences. Although the intuitions of the inexpert may often be reliable enough about some matter, we should in general prefer the intuitions of the expert: "the more expert a person is in an area, the better the person's theory, the wider her range of reliable intuitions in the area" (Devitt 2010b, p. 860).

On the generous view, all immediate perceptual judgements count as intuitions. So there obviously cannot be any blanket dismissal of intuitions as evidence. For, at bottom, all theories rest on immediate judgements about what is perceived and hence on intuitions, generously conceived. The most direct contact we can have with reality is via the experiences of it that yield perceptual judgements. These judgements at the periphery of our 'web of belief' provide the empirical justification for our theories (Devitt 2011c, p. 30). And the evidential question that concerns us should be not *whether* to use intuitions as evidence but *what* intuitions to use as evidence.

In light of this, return to our contrast between resting on certain intuitions and seeking more direct evidence. The intuitions in question were, as noted, ones that identify objects as having properties *of the sort adverted to in the very theory being tested*. We note now that, on the generous view, the more direct evidence is also to be found in intuitions, albeit different ones that are more basic and less theory-laden; for example, perceptual judgements about animal behaviour when doing biology, about human behaviour when doing economics, about colours and smells when doing chemistry, about instrument readings when doing physics. I shall bring out this contrast by considering the evidence for a theory of reference.

Suppose that Jill witnesses an utterance by Jack in condition C. Here is a series of immediate perceptual judgements that Jill makes in response to this event, judgements roughly ordered for theory ladenness:

Jack emitted a noise

Jack uttered something

Jack said something in English

Jack said, "Einstein was a physicist"

Jack said that Einstein was a physicist

Jack referred to Einstein

All of Jill's judgements are 'intuitive' and, on the generous view, all count as 'intuitions'. But only the last is a *referential* intuition. The other judgements, perhaps obtained in scientific tests, are examples of 'more direct evidence' of linguistic usage on which a theory of reference should ultimately be based. Thus, suppose that a theory of reference for names predicted that, in condition C, Jack would not say 'Einstein was a physicist'.[15] Then, Jill's judgement that Jack did say this is likely clear evidence against the theory. And it is *primary* evidence in a way that Jill's judgement about what, if anything, Jack referred to is not, however reliable Jill is in such referential judgements.

It is an empirical question just how reliable a person's intuitive judgements are and hence how good they are as evidence. However, supposing that Jill is an ordinarily educated English speaker, we can surely count on her being very reliable in her perceptual judgements of most of the sorts illustrated above; they are at the really obvious end of the scale. Thus, when Jill judges that someone utters a certain English sentence like "Einstein was a physicist", it is very likely that she is right. What about her perceptual judgements *about reference*, like that Jack referred to Einstein? This is the most theory-laden of Jill's judgements. How likely is a judgement of that sort to be true? Provided that Jill's judgements are about reference in ordinary humdrum situations, I predict that they would be quite reliable. In order for the folk to make reliable judgements about reference, they will doubtless have to have reflected on language a bit, aided by some minimal education. But that is what we can expect from normal members of our society. So I predict that if we tested folk referential intuitions about humdrum situations against evidence from usage, we would find the intuitions fairly reliable. Nonetheless, we should prefer the judgements of the experts here for the same reason we should prefer them anywhere: we can expect them to have a wider range of reliable intuitions. So we should prefer the intuitions of philosophers.

So far as I know, perceptual judgements about reference by the folk have not played a significant evidential role with theories of reference. But judgements of this sort by philosophers surely have. I have given this example: my intuitions about names, formed when I first heard Kripke in 1967, "have been confirmed, day in and day out for forty years, by observations of people using a name to refer successfully to an object that they are ignorant or wrong about" (2011c, pp. 21–22). This sort of approach to referential intuitions is surely common in philosophy. Philosophers who favor truth-referential theories of meaning – and there are many of them – surely find support for their theories in their observations of paradigm instances of reference. Indeed, if they did not make such observations, they would surely not suppose that reference could play a key explanatory role in a theory of meaning.

5.2 Memory judgements as intuitions

Suppose that Mary is another witness to Jack's utterance in condition C. She arrives at just the same judgements from this experience as does Jill but she does so the next day, based on her *memory* of John's utterance. All of Mary's judgements, like Jill's, are 'intuitive' and, continuing my generous policy, I count them all as "intuitions". Once again, the epistemic status of each judgement depends on the details of Mary's reliability. And there is no basis for a blanket dismissal of them.

Arguably, many of the intuitions of philosophers, led by Kripke, about the reference of names like "Cicero", "Catiline", "Feynman", "Einstein", and "Columbus" out of the mouths of the ignorant, intuitions central to the most powerful argument against description theories of names, are memory judgements of this sort (as Genoveva Marti [2014] also points out).[16] Kripke and others likely make many of these judgements in response to *remembered observations of the actual uses of these names, or analogous ones, by the ignorant*.

So, I am suggesting, it is likely that many of the referential intuitions that play a role in testing theories of reference are about *actual* cases, perceived or remembered. It seems to be easy for philosophers to overlook this likelihood, slipping into the view that all the evidence for these theories comes from *thought experiments* about *hypothetical* cases. Machery et al. are an example, as I noted (2011b): they talk of the theories of reference being "assessed by consulting one's intuitions about the reference of terms in *hypothetical* situations" (2004, B1; emphasis added).[17]

5.3 Intuitions in thought experiments

Now consider the intuitive judgements expressed by Frank in the following situation. Frank did not witness Jack saying anything but is presented with a *description* of an utterance by Jack in condition C and asked what he would say about it. So Frank is engaged in a thought experiment about a hypothetical case. Frank immediately forms just the same judgements as Jill and Mary, including the judgement that Jack referred to Einstein. Referential judgements of this sort are what philosophers seem mostly to have in mind as the intuitions that provide evidence for or against a theory of reference. I agree that such intuitions do, of course. So, although, I have just claimed, a philosopher's referential intuition about a humdrum use of a name by the ignorant will sometimes be a perceptual or memory judgement, it will sometimes not be: it will be based not on the experience of an actual use of the name but on a thought experiment. Think, for example, of the judgement I made about a nice case invented by Donnellan:

> A child is gotten up from sleep at a party and introduced to a person called "Tom". "Later the child says to his parents, "Tom is a nice man" . . . nothing the child possesses in the way of descriptions, dispositions to recognize, serves to pick out in the standard way anybody uniquely" ([Donnellan]1972: 364). Yet the child is talking about that very person he was introduced to. (Devitt 2011b, p. 421, n. 3)

My judgement here is made in a thought experiment and is not based on perception. Still, judgements arising from thought experiments like this about *humdrum* hypothetical situations should be distinguished from those arising from thought experiments about *fanciful* hypothetical situations, cases like Kripke's one of "Gödel". What makes the humdrum situations humdrum is they are of just the sort that we all, folk and philosophers alike, are perceiving day in and day out, situations of ignorant people using familiar names. So, although the judgements we make in thought experiments like Donnellan's are not perceptual, they are closely related to perceptual ones, for they are about situations *just like many that we remember in our experience*. So, if we were to seek judgements of this type from the folk, it seems to me *quite likely* that they would be about as reliable as the perceptual judgements that they are related to. They don't require much expertise. Still, once again, we should prefer the judgements of philosophers.

When we move to intuitions about hypothetical fanciful cases like "Gödel", I have argued that we should forget about the folk (as indeed we had until Machery et al.): these intuitions require too much expertise (Devitt 2011b, pp. 420–423). As Stich aptly remarked, with cases like Twin Earth in mind (and long before he was seized by experimental philosophy), "nonphilosophers often find such cases so outlandish that they have no clear intuitions about them" (1983, p. 62, n.*). For cases like this, the only intuitions worth worrying about are those of philosophers and similar experts.[18]

So, we have made some distinctions among the immediate and unreflective empirical judgements that I generously count as intuitions. There are the perceptual ones, memory ones and ones formed in thought experiments. Among the latter there are ones about humdrum hypothetical cases and ones about fanciful hypothetical cases. And among them all there are differences in the degree to which their reliability depends on expertise. I conjecture that referential intuitions about humdrum cases, whether perceptual or not, are likely to be fairly reliable without much expertise about language. In contrast, referential intuitions about fanciful hypothetical cases probably require a good deal of expertise.

5.4 Consequences for Machery et al.

The Modest Explanation of intuitions that I have presented has consequences for the methodology of Machery et al.

First, they tested the wrong referential intuitions. If we are going to test referential intuitions, we should prefer to test ones about humdrum cases like Kripke's "Einstein" and "Columbus", or even Donnellan's sleeping child, rather than ones about fanciful cases like Kripke's "Gödel". For, we should expect intuitions about humdrum cases to be more reliable.

Second, they tested the wrong people. If we are going to test referential intuitions, we should prefer to test those of philosophers, particularly if the intuitions are about fanciful cases like "Gödel", because philosophers are more expert (2011b, pp. 425–426).[19] This line of thought yielded an example of what has become known as "the Expertise Defense" against the findings of Machery et al. The Expertise Defense has led to a lively exchange of opinion: Weinberg et al., 2010; Devitt 2011c, 2012b; Machery 2011, 2012; Machery and Stich 2012; Machery et al. 2013.[20]

One objection that Machery et al. have to preferring the referential intuitions of philosophers to those of the folk is that the philosophers' intuitions may be theoretically biased (2013). Indeed, they may be, but that is the sort of epistemic risk that we *always* run in science, since all judgements are theory-laden. And there are two points to make about it. First, we can try to control for bias, just as we do elsewhere in science. Second, the risk should not be exaggerated. The intuitive judgements that scientists make about their domains tend to be in agreement. For evidence of this among linguists, see Sprouse and Almeida (2013). For evidence among reference theorists, one has to look no further than the response to Kripke's intuitions about names. These intuitions were devastating for the sorts of description theories of names that were the received theories at that time. Yet philosophers who wanted to save description theories did not reject the intuitions, whether about humdrum cases or fanciful Gödel cases but rather tried to construct novel description theories that were compatible with those intuitions (see Devitt and Sterelny 1999, sec. 3.5 for discussion). And it is not surprising that, despite theory ladenness, experts tend to share intuitions because those intuitions are not determined simply by theoretical background:

they are determined largely, we hope, by experiences of the reality of that domain.

Third, my main disagreement with Machery et al. is with their focusing experimental semantics on testing anyone's intuitions about reference. I have argued that the focus should be on testing linguistic usage. So I disagree with the following:

> that philosophers of language should emulate linguists, who are increasingly replacing the traditional informal reliance on their own and their colleagues' intuitions with systematic experimental surveys of ordinary speakers' intuitions. (Machery and Stich 2012, p. 495)

The syntactic intuitions elicited by linguists are at best indirect evidence of the nature of the syntactic reality that they are about. Linguists need more direct evidence and that is to be found by examining linguistic usage. The story for philosophers is much the same. Referential intuitions are at best indirect evidence of the nature of referential reality. Philosophers need the more direct evidence that can be found by examining linguistic usage. The focus of experimental semantics should be on that. And that is what I now turn to.

6. Testing usage

How are we to test theories of reference against usage? I think that we should get inspiration from linguistics. Even though the received methodology in linguistics, like in philosophy, is dominated by attention to the role of intuitions – far too much so, in my view (2006a, pp. 98–100) – linguistics is importantly different from philosophy in that linguistics often acknowledges the role of usage as a source of evidence. Thus evidence for grammars is found in the corpus and in elicited production.[21] I shall consider these in turn.

6.1 The corpus

I have elsewhere emphasized that a major source in linguistics of evidence about syntax comes from the corpus, the vast mass of linguistic sounds and inscriptions that competent speakers produce as they go about their business without prompting from linguists. Linguists observe these performances and seek answers to questions like: "Do people ever say *x*?"; "How do they respond to *y*?"; "In what circumstances do they say *z*?" (Devitt 2006a, p. 98). Philosophers can also look to the corpus for evidence about reference. I have illustrated what a rich source this could be, in principle, with a bit of the corpus provided, ironically enough, by Machery et al. In going about their business, which is testing folk referential intuitions, Machery et al. use the name 'Gödel' many times. These uses are in vignettes presented to their experimental subjects. Machery et al. are surely as competent as anyone with "Gödel" and yet, I point out, their use of the name in the following passage is inconsistent with what (standard)[22] description theories would predict: "Now suppose that Gödel was not the author of this theorem. A man called 'Schmidt', whose body was found in Vienna under mysterious circumstances many years ago, actually did the work in question" (2004, p. B6). If the description theory were true this utterance would be anomalous. (So Machery et al.'s experiment is biased against description theories.)

> For, if [Machery et al.]'s use of "Gödel" refers to that eminent logician in virtue of their associating with it the description, "the prover of the incompleteness of arithmetic", this passage is not something that [they] would be disposed to say. They would not, in one and the same breath, both refer to Gödel and suppose away the basis of that reference. (Devitt 2011c, p. 28)

I shall now give a similar illustration using a vignette from another, more recent, experiment. This experiment, by James Genone and Tania Lombrozo (2012), was designed to test descriptive and causal theories of reference for natural and nominal kind terms.

A stimulus that they provided to some subjects included the following:

> There is a small island in the Indian Ocean called "Alpha". Natives of Alpha, called "Alphians", sometimes catch diseases not found anywhere else in the human population. When this happens, they consult Alphian doctors. One of the diseases on Alpha is called "tyleritis".

> *Facts about the Alphian disease called "tyleritis":*
>
> - Tyleritis affects the muscles and causes muscle pain.
> - Tyleritis is only caused by exposure to a rare mineral.
> - Tyleritis can be diagnosed with a blood test.
> - Tyleritis can be cured by an injection.
>
> Alex is a native Alphian. Alex first heard of tyleritis when his uncle contracted it and he overheard other family members discussing it. Alex knows that tyleritis* is a disease, and that it can cause pain. Alex also has a number of other beliefs about tyleritis*.
>
> *Alex's beliefs about the Alphian disease tyleritis*:*

- Tyleritis* affects only the joints and causes joint pain.
- Tyleritis* is caused by a virus.
- Tyleritis* can only be diagnosed with a tissue biopsy.
- Tyleritis* is incurable. (asterisks added)

All of Genone and Lombrozo's uses of the invented term "tyleritis" that I have marked with asterisks are inconsistent with what description theories of "tyleritis" would predict.[23] (So this experiment is also biased against description theories.)[24]

(A) Suppose that a description theory was true of "tyleritis". Then its reference would be determined by descriptions drawn from the ones used above to state the "facts" about tyleritis. Furthermore, competent users of the term must associate those reference-determining descriptions with it. It follows, then, that Alex is not competent with the term. For, rather than associating those descriptions, he associates descriptions nearly all of which are false of tyleritis. So his uses of "tyleritis" do not refer to tyleritis but to something else or nothing at all.

(B) Next, consider Genone and Lombrozo's uses of "tyleritis" that I have marked. What do those uses refer to? Given the story, they must refer to the Alphian disease described in the list of "facts"; that is, the uses refer to tyleritis. For, when the term is properly used, that's what it refers to and we may assume that Genone and Lombrozo are using it properly: after all, they invented it!

(C) Finally, Genone and Lombrozo have some interesting things to say with the marked uses of "tyleritis". These remarks concern Alex's beliefs. I start with a presumption: Genone and Lombrozo are inviting us to suppose that they base their views of those beliefs largely, if not entirely, on *what Alex says* using "tyleritis". With this in mind, consider their remarks about Alex's beliefs. (i) One of these is that "Alex . . . has a number of . . . beliefs about tyleritis". We should see this as reflecting Genone and Lombrozo's referential intuition about Alex's use of "tyleritis". Since they are expert enough, we expect their intuition to be right (Sec. 5). Yet if "tyleritis" was covered by a description theory, this intuition would be wrong: Alex's use of "tyleritis", hence the beliefs he expresses with the term, would not be about tyleritis – see (A). So Genone and Lombrozo's remark is contrary to what the description theory predicts. (ii) Still, I am looking to the corpus for a test *against usage* not against referential intuitions. For this test we must consider Genone and Lombrozo's other remarks. These ascribe beliefs to Alex; for example, they ascribe the belief that Tyleritis is caused by a virus. But, if a description theory was true of "tyleritis", these are not beliefs that Genone and Lombrozo would be disposed to ascribe. For, their uses of "tyleritis", hence the beliefs they ascribe to Alex, are about tyleritis – see (B) – and yet Alex's beliefs would not be about tyleritis – see (A). And, Genone and Lombrozo, as competent users of "tyleritis", are disposed to ascribe beliefs about tyleritis on the basis of uses of "tyleritis" only to people whose uses refer to tyleritis. That is part of what their competence with "tyleritis" amounts to.

The sort of thinking that lies behind the final step could do with elaboration. I shall provide this in the discussion of elicited production to follow. I shall also point to a worrying flaw in the thinking: "the implicit-scare-quote problem".

These are two examples of how we can gather evidence about reference from usage in the corpus. But there are well-known difficulties in using the corpus as evidence. First, in this case, one has to note something in the linguistic phenomena that *is* evidence for/against some theory of reference. Then one has to have a record of it, which is problematic if it is spoken rather than written. And one may need to document quite a lot of information about the speaker and circumstances. Still, the examples illustrate what a mass of evidence the corpus provides that *could* be mined scientifically. And it indicates the important role that the corpus plays as informal evidence about reference.[25]

6.2 Elicited production

Fortunately, we don't have to rely on the corpus for direct evidence in usage: we can *induce* usage from competent speakers in experimental situations. Consider this description of "the technique of *elicited production*" in linguistics:

> This technique involves children in a game, typically one in which children pose questions to a puppet. The game orchestrates experimental situations that are designed to be uniquely felicitous for production of the target structure. In this way, children are called on to produce structures that might otherwise not appear in their spontaneous speech. (Thornton 1995, p. 140)

Clearly much direct evidence could be gathered in this way. However, contriving appropriate situations in an experiment is likely to be a laborious business.

I proposed an easier technique of elicited production for linguistics. Instead of *constructing* situations to see what people say and understand in those situations, "we can *describe* situations and ask people what they would say or understand in those situations" (Devitt 2006a, p. 99). Note that this method is not the common one of prompting *metalinguistic intuitions* about described situations, yielding indirect evidence about language. Rather it is prompting *linguistic usage* in described situations, yielding direct evidence about language.[26] I have suggested recently that this method could provide a rich source of evidence about reference. I think that this is the way forward in experimental semantics (Devitt 2011c, pp. 29–30).

The challenge then was, of course, to design elicited production experiments that would do the job. My earlier discussion of naturalized semantics in *Coming to Our Senses* (Devitt 1996, chapter 2; also, 1994) prompted an idea (Devitt 2011b, pp. 430–432). Wesley Buckwalter, Kate Devitt and I have conducted experiments along the lines of this idea. We started by testing theories of reference for proper names, using the name "Beyoncé" as an example. Here is a summary of the idea for the experiment:

1. Find participants who are 'experts' on pop stars in general and Beyoncé in particular.
2. Present two vignettes about a character, Dr. Marcus, in which he uses the name "Beyoncé". In one he associates with that name descriptions that do identify Beyoncé, in the other, he does not, including associating *mis*descriptions. Ask the participants to explain a certain behaviour of the character, Dr. Marcus.
3. Assumption. The participants, being 'experts', are competent users of the name "Beyoncé". So if a participant uses "Beyoncé", she will refer to the pop star. And if she uses it (or a pronoun anaphoric on it) in ascribing a thought that Beyoncé is . . . to Marcus in order to explain his behaviour she has understood Marcus as having referred to Beyoncé with the name. So, probably, Marcus did refer to Beyoncé.
4. Descriptivist prediction: the differences in the associated descriptions in the two vignettes will make a difference in the participants' readiness to use "Beyoncé" to ascribe thoughts to Dr Marcus: they will be much less likely to ascribe such thoughts in the vignette where the descriptions do not identify Beyoncé. Anti-descriptivist prediction: the differences in associated descriptions will make no difference in usage.

More needs to be said about why the description theory predicts that participants would not use "Beyoncé" to ascribe beliefs to Dr. Marcus. First, note that the prediction does not rest on any assumptions about the evidential status of referential intuitions, intuitions deploying the theoretical concept of *reference* (2011c, p. 30). So what does it rest on? The thinking is that it rests simply on *the assumption that participants are competent with the name "Beyoncé"*. What does this competence amount to? (a) On a fairly theory-neutral view of thoughts, this competence is the ability to use the inscription

"Beyoncé"[27] to express a part of a thought that refers to the famous singer and the ability to assign to an inscription "Beyoncé" that refers to the singer in the context of utterance a part of a thought that refers to the singer. (b) Adding more theory by assuming the Representational Theory of the Mind (RTM), we can simplify: the competence is the ability to translate back and forth between mental representations of the singer Beyoncé and "Beyoncé". (c) Adding even more theory by assuming the Language of Thought Hypothesis (LOTH): the competence is the ability to translate back and forth between the mental word <Beyoncé> referring to the singer and "Beyoncé". As a result of this competence, assuming LOTH for convenience, a participant tends, in understanding a "Beyoncé" utterance, to form a <Beyoncé> thought iff the utterance refers to the singer. And, as a result of this competence, her production of a "Beyoncé" utterance will refer to the singer iff it is produced by a <Beyoncé> thought. *This is simply how her competence with "Beyoncé" is manifested.* So, on the basis of this assumption of her competence, we theorists can then conclude that she will tend to use the name "Beyoncé" in her description of the mental states that explain Dr. Marcus' behaviour iff Dr. Marcus' use of the name refers to the singer. Our conclusion does not rest on any assumption that the participant thinks any thoughts about the reference of "Beyoncé"; she simply thinks whatever thoughts are expressed in the "Beyoncé" utterances she is understanding and producing.

6.3 The implicit-scare-quote problem

I had a worry about this line of thought from the beginning. How would an 'expert' participant *indicate* that she thinks that a character who associates 'incorrect' descriptions with an expression "E" does *not*, on those grounds, believe/hope/wonder whether/etc . . . E . . .? That is, suppose the description theory for "E" was *right*, what would be the predicted response? The prediction is that, because the character does not associate the descriptions that determine the meaning and reference of "E" the participants should treat the character as not using "E" in the conventional way and not referring to E. But the difficult question is: *How would participants indicate this?* Here are some of the ideas we came up with for Dr Marcus – "Beyoncé":

(a). "Dr. Marcus doesn't know who he is talking about with 'Beyoncé'"
(b). "Dr. Marcus is not talking about Beyoncé"
(c). "Dr. Marcus is thinking about someone else"

(d). "Dr. Marcus thinks that the invitation is for someone he wrongly calls 'Beyoncé'"
(e). Any explanation where the name "Beyoncé" is in scare quotes.

One concern about these possible responses is that at least two of them, (b) and (c), are expressions of referential intuitions and yet the idea was to test theories against usage not against referential intuitions. (e) raises a more worrying concern. Even where the character's associated descriptions are false of E and a participant responds that the character, say, "believes that . . . E . . .", this may be consistent with a description theory of "E" *because the participant may, without drawing attention to this, be distancing herself from the usage*: there may be *implicit* scare quotes.

Stories like the following give a feel for the implicit-scare-quote problem. Suppose that the word "vixen" really is covered by a description theory, as it likely is. Now imagine Harry is in a house where there is talk of a vixen in the garden. It quickly becomes apparent from Harry's near hysterical remarks using the word "vixen" that he has a belief that he would express "Vixens are tigers". Harry then rushes violently from the house just as Sam is entering. Might we not explain Harry's behaviour to Sam by saying, "Harry thinks that there is a ferocious vixen in the garden"? In so doing, there are implicit scare quotes around "vixen", indicating, as Wikipedia puts it, that the expression "may not signify its apparent meaning or that it is not necessarily the way the quoting person would express its concept"; we are describing Harry's belief the way *he* would even though critical of his usage; we are distancing ourselves from the usage. So our mere use of the term "vixen" does *not* show that we have understood Frank as having referred to vixens, hence does *not* count against the description theory of "vixen". Indeed, if our use does have scare quotes that is evidence *for* the description theory. This goes right against the assumption 3 in the above summary.

Though we were well aware of the implicit-scare-quote problem, our preliminary Beyoncé experiment did not address it. This cast doubt on the apparently decisive support it gave to Kripkean anti-descriptivism.[28] To get some idea just how serious this problem was, we decided to complicate our next set of experiments. We would not only test usage by eliciting an explanation of behaviour, as in the preliminary Beyoncé experiment, but we would also test usage by offering a choice of explanations, selected with the aim of showing whether there were indeed implicit scare quotes in the elicited usage.

These experiments covered not only proper names but also artefactual kind terms, which strike me as much more interesting than proper names. Philosophers have strong Kripkean intuitions about the reference of proper names, intuitions that favour anti-descriptivist theories. In contrast, we have little in the way of firm intuitions about the reference of artefactual kind terms. We really don't have much idea what sort of theory is right for these terms (Devitt and Sterelny 1999, pp. 93–100).

The results of these experiments were baffling, and we certainly could not draw any interesting conclusions about reference from them. But we did learn one thing: the implicit-scare-quote problem is very real. The results did seem to confirm that we were right to be worried about participants distancing themselves from usage. So this way of testing usage by elicited production is problematic.

These experiments support the idea that whenever a person x ascribes thoughts to another person y, there is a real risk of implicit scare quotes, a risk of x describing y's thought the way y would do so while distancing herself from this usage. This risk can be present not only in getting evidence from elicited production but also in getting it from the corpus. So there is a flaw in the earlier thinking about Genone and Lombrozo's uses of "tyleritis" in ascriptions of belief to Alex (Section 6.1). These uses are inconsistent with what description theories would predict only on the assumption that the uses are not implicitly accompanied by scare quotes. That assumption may be false.

Our other example of evidence from the corpus against a description theory was provided by the uses of "Gödel" by Machery et al. Should we be worried about implicit scare quotes here too? I suspect not. These uses are not in ascriptions of thoughts to others. There does not seem to be any reason why Machery et al. would want to distance themselves from their own usage.

6.4 The future

Where do we go from here? Most important of all, we must resist the reactionary response of simply resting our theories of reference on referential intuitions. One problem with that response is that, as the case of artefactual kind terms illustrates, we simply do not have intuitions that could do the job for many terms. But the deeper problem is that resting on referential intuitions is not scientifically respectable. Theories of reference, like any scientific theories, need to be tested directly against the reality that they concern. That reality for theories of reference is to be found in linguistic usage.

So we have to come up with ways to test theories of reference against linguistic usage. Experiments along the lines of our preliminary Beyoncé experiment have not been a success. Can we come up with a modification of this that solves the implicit-scare-quote problem? To do so we need to come up with a reliable way of detecting when people are distancing themselves from the language used in ascribing thoughts. Perhaps we can discover this by testing description theories that, intuitively, seem likely to be true; for example, a description theory of "vixen". Alternatively, perhaps we should abandon the idea of testing usage in ascriptions of thoughts altogether, given the implicit-scare-quote worry that the idea generates. Then we will need to find some other sort of test of usage that is relatively free of this worry. Can we get inspiration here from the corpus example provided by Machery et al.?

7. Conclusion

We need theories of reference because, it is widely thought, reference relations are explanatorily important relations in theories of language. This gives rise to the question that has concerned this paper: How should we test theories of reference?

The received view is that we should test them against referential intuitions. And the intuitions used have been those of philosophers. Machery et al. (2004) wonder why it is appropriate to rely on the intuitions of philosophers rather than those of the folk. I wonder why it is appropriate to rely on referential intuitions at all.

It is common for philosophers to think that their practice of relying on referential intuitions is appropriate because they are a priori. I have argued against this view. Stich has suggested another justification for the practice: philosophers might follow linguists in thinking that linguistic intuitions are 'the voice' of our linguistic competence. I have argued against this view too and instead urged 'the Modest Explanation' of intuitions.

According to the Modest Explanation, referential intuitions are empirical theory-laden central-processor responses to linguistic phenomena, differing from many other such responses only in being fairly immediate and unreflective. So we should rely on the intuitions only to the extent that they are reliable indicators of the nature of linguistic reality. And, at best, they are only indirect evidence. We should be seeking more direct evidence by examining the linguistic reality that these intuitions are about: we need to examine linguistic usage. The results of this direct examination can then also be used to assess the reliability of referential intuitions.

I generously include all immediate perceptual judgements among intuitions with the result that all of our theories rest ultimately on intuitions of some sort. So the contrast between indirect and direct evidence for a theory of reference becomes a distinction among intuitions. The indirect evidence comes from *referential* intuitions, whereas the direct comes from immediate perceptual judgements, particularly ones about usage, that deploy no concept of reference; for example, from the judgement that Jack said "Einstein was a physicist".

Referential intuitions differ among themselves in several significant ways. There are the perceptual ones, memory ones and ones formed in thought experiments. Among the latter there are ones about humdrum hypothetical cases and ones about fanciful hypothetical cases. And among them all there are differences in the degree to which their reliability depends on expertise. I conjecture that referential intuitions about humdrum cases, whether perceptual or not, are likely to be fairly reliable without much expertise about language. In contrast, referential intuitions about fanciful hypothetical cases, like the "Gödel" cases tested by Machery et al., probably require a good deal of expertise.

Finally, I have addressed the problem of testing theories of reference more directly against the evidence of linguistic usage. One source of this evidence is the corpus. I illustrate this with some material used by Genone and Lombrozo in their experiment testing theories of reference. Many of their uses of the invented term "tyleritis" seem to be inconsistent with what description theories of "tyleritis" would predict. But there are notorious difficulties in using the corpus as evidence. So, I have proposed, philosophers should follow linguistics in using the method of elicited production to test their theories of language. But it has so far proved difficult to come up with a satisfactory experimental test because of the "implicit-scare-quote" problem. The problem is that elicited production, indeed the corpus, provides the evidence we need only if speakers are not implicitly distancing themselves from their usage. We need experiments that control for this worry. The experiments conducted so far have not managed this.[29]

Notes

1   Including: Ludwig (2007); Deutsch (2009); Jackman (2009); Marti (2009); Devitt (2011b, c), (2012b); Ichikawa et al. (2011); Sytsma and Livengood (2011); Genone and Lombrozo (2012); Ostertag (2013).
2   I have taken a critical look at the theoretical role of "reference" in this literature in a review article on this book (2014b).

3 Strangely, this view of human language is rejected by Chomskians; see, for example, Chomsky (1986) and (1996); Dwyer and Pietroski (1996); Laurence (2003); Collins, (2008a, b); and Antony, (2008). They see a human language as an internal state not as a system of external symbols that represent the world. I have argued against this view: Devitt 2003, 2006a, c, 2008a, b, c and 2009.

4 Devitt and Sterelny (1999), chapters 3–5, is an account of the revolution.

5 Could the buck stop with theories of type (3)? I doubt it, but we would need to see the details of such a theory to be confident in rejecting it. A danger with any such theory is that it will lead to a totally unacceptable semantic holism; see Devitt (1996, pp. 127–132).

6 The brief accounts of the received view in this section, and of the Modest Explanation in the next, are based on earlier works: Devitt (1994), (1996), (2006d) and (2012a). There is a related discussion of intuitions in linguistics in Devitt (2006a, b). This discussion was criticized in Collins (2006), Matthews (2006), Miščević (2006), Rattan (2006), Rey (2006) and Smith (2006). Devitt (2006c) is a response. There have been some later critics: Pietroski (2008), responded to in Devitt (2008a); Textor (2009), responded to in Devitt (2010a); Culbertson and Gross (2009), which led to the exchange, Devitt (2010b), Gross and Culbertson (2011); Miščević (2009), responded to in Devitt (2014c); Fitzgerald (2010), responded to in Devitt (2010b); Ludlow (2011) and Rey (2013), responded to in Devitt (2013a).

7 For evidence of this, see Devitt (2012a, pp. 554–555).

8 This widely held view has recently been challenged by Herman Cappelen in a splendidly iconoclastic book (2012). (An earlier article by Max Deutsch [2009] also challenges the view.) Cappelen mounts an impressively detailed argument against what he calls "Centrality", the thesis that "contemporary analytic philosophers rely extensively on intuitions as evidence" (p. 1). Cappelen's challenge deserves an argument in response. I have offered one elsewhere (forthcoming). Here is a brief summary of my response: (1) Cappelen first argues against the support that Centrality seems to get from the fact that philosophers often "characterize key premises in their arguments as 'intuitive'" (p. 4). He finds this intuition talk very hard to interpret and claims that under none of the interpretations that he proposes does the talk support Centrality. I present two objections. (i) The talk is in fact easy to interpret: for the most part, "intuitive" and "intuition" are not technical terms and so mean here just what they ordinarily mean. In thinking about this, it is important to note that differing theories of intuitions do not entail differing meanings of "intuition". (ii) Cappelen does not produce convincing reasons for not taking these philosophers at their word in their characterization of their premises. So this characterization does support Centrality (in which "intuition" also has its ordinary meaning). (2) Cappelen argues next that Centrality gets no support from

philosophical practice. He proposes three "diagnostics" to detect the presence of intuitions: intuitions 'seem true or have a special phenomenology; they are default justified, or can justify other propositions without themselves requiring justification; and they are based solely on conceptual competence' (p. 111). He then examines many well-known cases in the philosophical literature and finds no evidence of philosophers relying on items satisfying these diagnostics and hence concludes that Centrality is false (chapter 8). I present four objections. (I) The diagnostics are based on philosophers' *theories* of intuitions (chapter 6), theories that, I have argued (see items cited in note 6), are largely false. So the diagnostics based on them are inappropriate. (II) The thesis of Centrality no more needs to be supported by a theory-based diagnostic for intuitions than, say, the thesis that lonely people tend to have dogs needs to be supported by a theory-based diagnostic for dogs. Testing these theses simply requires *abilities to recognize* intuitions and dogs, abilities that almost everyone, including proponents of Centrality, surely have. (III) If we *must* have a diagnostic for intuitions, the place to look for one is in not in philosophical theories but in dictionaries. Based on a quick look at a few dictionaries, I propose a diagnostic along the following lines: "an immediate judgement without much conscious reasoning or inference". Indeed, Cappelen himself notes something like this 'interpretation' in his struggle with intuition talk (pp. 33, 62). (IV) Using our ordinary ability to recognize intuitions, aided by this minimal diagnostic if necessary, Centrality gets ample support from the cases that Cappelen examines. (3) Finally, I think that Cappelen is insufficiently struck by the need to answer the following question: If philosophers are not really relying on intuitions as evidence in the cases he examines, what are they relying on? He rightly insists that these cases are full of arguments; that is the way of philosophy, as he emphasizes. But arguments need premises and it is hard to see what the premises could be in *these* cases – though I certainly do not say in *all* philosophical cases – other than intuitions. Claiming that philosophers rely on propositions that are "pre-theoretic" (p. 61) or "common ground" (p. 119) is only the beginning of an answer. Why are these propositions thought to be evidence if not because they are intuitively true?

9   I owe this nice remark to Genoveva Martí who thinks she heard or read it somewhere but can't recall the circumstances.
10 So I was surprised to find three knowledgeable philosophers rejecting the attribution: John Collins (2008a, pp. 17-19), Gareth Fitzgerald (2010) and Peter Ludlow (2011, pp. 69-71). I have responded to Fitzgerald (Devitt 2010b, pp. 845-847) and to Ludlow (Devitt 2013, pp. 274-278). Ludlow's discussion is notable for its egregious misrepresentation of the evidence. I have also provided more evidence (2013, p. 273) in the works of Barry Smith (2006), Mark Textor (2009) and Georges Rey (2013). I still think that the evidence is overwhelming. But see Jeffrey Maynes and Steven Gross (2013) for a nice discussion of the matter.

11 Interestingly, Chomsky, who holds VoC for grammatical intuitions seems to reject it for semantic ones (1995, p. 24). For discussion, see Devitt (2012a, pp. 558–559).
12 This theory of intuitions could be seen as starting from the minimal dictionary-based diagnostic I proposed in response to Cappelen; see note 8 above. Should Cappelen, indeed anyone, object that the theory is not true, my positive proposals for testing theories of reference would lose nothing, so far as I can see, from replacing "intuition" by "intuition*" in the following discussion and turning my theory of intuitions into a definition of "intuition*".
13 So "theory" in "theory-laden" has to be construed *very* broadly to cover not just theories proper but also these dispositions that are part of background expertise.
14 I claim that this is the way to view intuitions of the ignorant in the ingenious 'minimal pair' experiments (2006a, p. 110).
15 It is sadly difficult to come up with such predictions; see Section 6.
16 In support of Centrality, the thesis rejected by Cappellan (note 8 above), it is *obvious* that Kripke uses referential intuitions as evidence in this argument; for example, in judging that "the man in the street . . . uses the name 'Feynman' as a name for Feynman" (1980, p. 81). So does just about every theorist of reference.
17 They have since modified their position to include intuitions about actual cases (2013).
18 I have pointed out that Gödel experiments have put us well on the way to showing that philosophers are indeed more reliable than the folk in their referential intuitions about fanciful cases (Devitt 2011c, p. 24).
19 James Genone and Tania Lombrozo may have misunderstood the similar criticism I made (Devitt 2010d) in commenting on a draft of their paper (Genone and Lombrozo 2012). For, they respond by doubting that "expert intuitions are superior to folk intuitions when it comes to ordinary referential practices, or that there could be specialists in the practice of using names and concepts in general" (2012, p. 734). But my criticism does not rest on the view that philosophers are more expert than the folk at "using names and concepts in general" but that they are more expert at making intuitive judgements about the reference of those names and concepts. Genone and Lombrozo's experiment elicits the latter referential intuitions not "ordinary referential practices". (I am all for eliciting the practices; see Section 6.)
20 See also the following exchange arising out of my analogous claim (Devitt 2006a, pp. 108–109) that we should prefer the grammatical intuitions of linguists over those of the folk: Culbertson and Gross (2009); Devitt (2010b); Gross and Culbertson (2011).
21 Also in reaction time studies, eye tracking and electromagnetic brain potentials. Perhaps philosophers can get inspiration from these experiments too, but I have no idea how.
22 This qualification is necessary to exclude theories that are not along the lines of those offered by Frege, Russell and Searle. So we are excluding what I call "circular

descriptivism" and "causal descriptivism" (Devitt and Sterelny 1999, pp. 60–61). The qualification should be taken as read in what follows.

23 Interestingly, in another passage, Genone and Lombrozo's usage is inconsistent with what a *causal* theory would predict: "Bob's beliefs were always identical to Alex's" (2012, p. 725). Bob is on another island, Brom, and has a number of beliefs about a disease found only on Brom and also called "tyleritis". But this disease "affects only the joints and causes joint pain" and so is a different disease from the one called "tyleritis" on Alpha. So, even though Bob and Alex express their beliefs in identical words, their beliefs are *not* identical according to a causal theory, because they have different origins. (Similarly, if Putnam is right, when Oscar and Twin-Oscar say "Water is refreshing", they do not express the same beliefs because one is about H_2O, the other about XYZ.)

24 I pointed this out before (Devitt 2010d); for a response, see Genone and Lombrozo (2012, pp. 740, n. 24).

25 I made a similar point about the evidential role of the corpus in linguistics as part of a response to the tendency in linguistics to exaggerate the role of speakers' intuitive judgements (Devitt 2006a, pp. 98–99).

26 I sum up my discussion of linguistic evidence: "The main evidence for grammars is not found in the intuitions of ordinary speakers but rather in a combination of the corpus, the evidence of what we would say and understand, and the intuitions of linguists" (Devitt 2006a, p. 100).

27 Similarly, of course, the sound /Beyoncé/ and so on. Take this addition as read in what follows. I focus on inscriptions because they are what we are dealing with in the experiment.

28 Nat Hansen pressed this concern in comments on the experiment.

29 The first version of this chapter was delivered as the Presidential Address at the Society for Philosophy and Psychology 39th Meeting at Brown University in June 2013. I acknowledge the support of the Spanish Ministerio de Economía y Competitividad. ("Reference, selfreference and empirical data" FFI2011–25626). Finally, many thanks to Mark Phelan for helpful comments on the penultimate version.

References

Antony, L. (2008), 'Meta-linguistics: Methodology and ontology in Devitt's *Ignorance of Language*'. *Australasian Journal of Philosophy*, 86, 643–656.

Cappelen, Herman. (2012), *Philosophy without Intuitions*. Oxford: Oxford University Press.

Chomsky, N. (1986), *Knowledge of Language: Its Nature, Origin, and Use*. New York: Praeger Publishers.

Chomsky, N. (1995), 'Language and nature'. *Mind*, 104, 1–61.
Chomsky, N. (1996), *Powers and Prospects: Reflections on Human Nature and the Social Order*. Boston, MA: South End Press.
Collins, J. (2006), 'Between a rock and a hard place: a dialogue on the philosophy and methodology of generative linguistics'. *Croatian Journal of Philosophy*, VI, 469–503.
Collins, J. (2008a), 'Knowledge of language redux'. *Croatian Journal of Philosophy*, VIII, 3–43.
Collins, J. (2008b), 'a note on conventions and unvoiced syntax'. *Croatian Journal of Philosophy*, VIII, 241–247.
Culbertson, J. and Gross, S. (2009), 'Are linguists better subjects?' *British Journal for the Philosophy of Science*, 60, 721–736.
Deutsch, M. (2009), 'Experimental philosophy and the theory of reference'. *Mind and Language*, 24, 445–466.
Devitt, M. (1981), *Designation*. New York: Columbia University Press.
Devitt, M. (1994), 'The methodology of naturalistic semantics,' *Journal of Philosophy*, 91, 545–572.
Devitt, M. (1996), *Coming to Our Senses: A Naturalistic Program for Semantic Localism*. Cambridge: Cambridge University Press.
Devitt, M. (1998), 'Naturalism and the a priori'. *Philosophical Studies* 92, 45–65 (reprinted in Devitt, 2010c).
Devitt, M. (2003), 'Linguistics is not psychology', in A. Barber (ed.), *Epistemology of Language*. Oxford: Oxford University Press, pp. 107–139.
Devitt, M. (2006a), *Ignorance of Language*. Oxford: Clarendon Press.
Devitt, M. (2006b), 'Intuitions in linguistics'. *British Journal for the Philosophy of Science*, 57, 481–513.
Devitt, M. (2006c), 'Defending *Ignorance of Language*: Responses to the Dubrovnik papers'. *Croatian Journal of Philosophy*, VI, 571–606.
Devitt, M. (2006d), 'Intuitions', in V. G. Pin, J. I. Galparaso and G. Arrizabalaga (eds), *Ontology Studies Cuadernos de Ontologia: Proceedings of VI International Ontology Congress (San Sebastian, 2004)*. San Sebastian: Universidad del Pais Vasco, pp. 169–176 (reprinted in Devitt 2010c).
Devitt, M. (2008a), 'Explanation and reality in linguistics'. *Croatian Journal of Philosophy*, VIII, 203–231.
Devitt, M. (2008b), 'a response to Collins' note on conventions and unvoiced syntax'. *Croatian Journal of Philosophy*, VIII, 249–255.
Devitt, M. (2008c), 'Methodology in the philosophy of linguistics'. *Australasian Journal of Philosophy*, 86, 671–684.
Devitt, M. (2009), 'Psychological conception, psychological reality: a response to Longworth and Slezak'. *Croatian Journal of Philosophy*, IX, 35–44.
Devitt, M. (2010a), 'What 'intuitions' are linguistic evidence?' *Erkenntnis*, 73, 251–264.
Devitt, M. (2010b), 'Linguistic intuitions revisited,' *British Journal for the Philosophy of Science*, 61, 833–865.

Devitt, M. (2010c), *Putting Metaphysics First: Essays on Metaphysics and Epistemology*. Oxford: Oxford University Press.
Devitt, M. (2010d), 'Comments on Genone and Lombrozo'. Delivered at the Society for Philosophy and Psychology Conference, Portland (OR), June 2010.
Devitt, M. (2011a), 'No place for the a priori', in M. J. Shaffer and M. L. Veber (eds), *What Place for the A Priori?* Chicago and La Salle: Open Court Publishing Company, pp. 9–32 (reprinted in Devitt 2010c).
Devitt, M. (2011b), 'Experimental semantics'. *Philosophy and Phenomenological Research*, LXXXII, 418–435.
Devitt, M. (2011c), 'Whither experimental semantics?' *Theoria*, 27, 5–36.
Devitt, M. (2012a), 'The role of intuitions', in G. Russell and D. G. Fara (eds), *Routledge Companion to the Philosophy of Language*. New York: Routledge, pp. 554–565.
Devitt, M. (2012b), 'Semantic epistemology: Response to Machery'. *Theoria*, 74, 229–233.
Devitt, M. (2013a), 'Linguistic intuitions are not "the voice of competence"', in M. Haug (ed.), *Philosophical Methodology: The Armchair or the Laboratory?* London: Routledge, pp. 268–293.
Devitt, M. (2013b), 'What makes a property "semantic"?', in A. Capone, F. L. Piparo and M. Carapezza (eds), *Perspectives on Pragmatics and Philosophy*. Cham: Springer, pp. 87–112.
Devitt, M. (2014a), 'We don't learn about the world by examining concepts: a response to Carrie Jenkins', in R. Neta (ed.), *Current Controversies in Epistemology*. New York: Routledge, pp. 23–34.
Devitt, M. (2014b), 'Lest auld acquaintance be forgot'. *Mind and Language,* 29, 475-484.
Devitt, M. (2014c), 'Linguistic intuitions: In defense of "ordinarism"'. *European Journal of Analytic Philosophy.*
Devitt, M. (forthcoming), 'Relying on intuitions: Where Herman Cappelen goes wrong'. *Inquiry.*
Devitt, M. and Sterelny, K. (1999), *Language and Reality: An Introduction to the Philosophy of Language*, 2nd edn (1st edn 1987). Oxford: Blackwell Publishers.
Donnellan, K. S. (1972), 'Proper names and identifying descriptions', in D. Davidson and G. Harman (eds), *Semantics of Natural Language*. Dordrecht: D. Reidel, pp. 356–379.
Dummett, M. (1978), *Truth and Other Enigmas*, Cambridge, MA: Harvard University Press.
Dwyer, S. and Pietroski, P. (1996), 'Believing in language'. *Philosophy of Science*, 63, 338–373.
Fitzgerald, G. (2010), 'Linguistic intuitions'. *British Journal for the Philosophy of Science*, 61, 123–160.
Genone, J. and Lombrozo, T. (2012), 'Concept possession, experimental semantics, and hybrid theories of reference'. *Philosophical Psychology*, 25, 717–742.
Gross, S. and Culbertson, J. (2011), 'Revisited linguistic intuitions'. *British Journal for the Philosophy of Science*, 62, 639–656.

Hawthorne, J. and Manley, D. (2012), *The Reference Book*. Oxford: Oxford University Press.
Hintikka, J. (1999), 'The emperor's new intuitions'. *Journal of Philosophy*, 96, 127–147.
Ichikawa, J., Maitra, I. and Weatherson, B. (2011), 'In defense of a Kripkean dogma'. *Philosophy and Phenomenological Research*, 82, 418–435.
Jackman, H. (2009), 'Semantic intuitions, conceptual analysis, and cross-cultural variation'. *Philosophical Studies*, 146, 159–177.
Katz, J. (1997), 'Analyticity, necessity, and the epistemology of semantics'. *Philosophy and Phenomenological Research*, 57, 1–28.
Kripke, S. A. (1980), *Naming and Necessity*. Cambridge, MA: Harvard University Press.
Laurence, S. (2003), 'Is linguistics a branch of psychology?' in A. Barber (ed.), *Epistemology of Language*. Oxford: Oxford University Press, pp. 69–106.
Loar, B. (1987), 'Subjective intentionality'. *Philosophical Topics*, 15, 89–124.
Ludlow, P. (2011), *The Philosophy of Generative Linguistics*. Oxford: Oxford University Press.
Ludwig, K. (2007), 'The epistemology of thought experiments: First-person approach vs. Third-person approach'. *Midwest Studies in Philosophy*, 31, 128–159.
McKinsey, M. (1987), 'Apriorism in the philosophy of language'. *Philosophical Studies*, 52, 1–32.
McKinsey, M. (1994), 'Individuating belief', in J. Tomberlin (ed.), *Philosophical Perspectives, 8: Logic and Language*. Atascadero, CA: Ridgeview Publishing Company.
Machery, E. (2011), 'Expertise and intuitions about reference'. *Theoria*, 27, 37–54.
Machery, E. (2012), 'Semantic epistemology: a brief response to Devitt'. *Theoria*, 74, 223–227.
Machery, E., Mallon, R., Nichols, S. and Stich, S. P. (2004), 'Semantics, cross-cultural style'. *Cognition*, 92, B1–B12.
Machery, E., Mallon, R., Nichols, S. and Stich, S. P. (2013), 'If folk intuitions vary, then what?' *Philosophy and Phenomenological Research*, 86, 618–635.
Machery, E. and Stich, S. P. (2012), 'The role of experiments in the philosophy of language', in G. Russell and D. G. Fara (eds), *Routledge Companion to the Philosophy of Language*. New York: Routledge, pp. 495–512.
Martí, G. (2009), 'Against semantic multi-culturalism'. *Analysis*, 69, 42–48.
Martí, G. (2014), 'Empirical data and the theory of reference', in M. O'Rourke (ed.), *Topics in Contemporary Philosophy, Volume 10: Reference and Referring*. Cambridge, MA: MIT Press.
Matthews, R. J. (2006), 'Could competent speakers really be ignorant of their language?' *Croatian Journal of Philosophy*, VI, 457–467.
Maynes, J. and Gross, S. (2013), 'Linguistic intuitions'. *Philosophy Compass*, 8 (8), 714–730.
Miščević. N. (2006). 'Intuitions: The discrete voice of competence'. *Croatian Journal of Philosophy*, VI, 523–548.

Miščević. N. (2009). 'Competent voices: a theory of intuitions'. http://oddelki.ff.uni-mb.si/filozofija/en/festschrift
Ostertag, G. (2013), 'The 'Gödel' effect'. *Philosophical Studies*, 166, 65–82.
Pietroski, P. (2008), 'Think of the children'. *Australasian Journal of Philosophy*, 86, 657–669.
Rattan, G. (2006), 'The knowledge in language'. *Croatian Journal of Philosophy*, VI, 505–521.
Rey, G. (2006), 'Conventions, intuitions and linguistic inexistents: a reply to Devitt'. *Croatian Journal of Philosophy*, VI, 549–569.
Rey, G. (2013), 'The possibility of a naturalistic Cartesianism regarding intuitions and introspection', in M. Haug (ed.), *Philosophical Methodology: The Armchair or the Laboratory?* London: Routledge, pp. 243–267.
Slobodchikoff, C. N. (2002), 'Cognition and communication in prairie dogs', in C. Allen and G. M. Burchardt (eds), *The Cognitive Animal: Empirical and Theoretical Perspectives on Animal Cognition.* Cambridge MA: MIT Press, pp. 257–264.
Smith, B. C. (2006), 'Why we still need knowledge of language'. *Croatian Journal of Philosophy*, VI, 431–456.
Sprouse, J. and Almeida, D. (2013), 'The role of experimental syntax in an integrated cognitive science of language', in K. Grohmann and C. Boeckx (eds), *The Cambridge Handbook of Biolinguistics.* Cambridge: Cambridge University Press, pp. 181–202.
Stich, S. P. (1983), *From Folk Psychology to Cognitive Science: The Case against Belief.* Cambridge, MA: Bradford/MIT Press.
Stich, S. P. (1996), *Deconstructing the Mind.* New York: Oxford University Press.
Sytsma, J. and Livengood, J. (2011), 'a new perspective concerning experiments on semantic intuitions'. *Australasian Journal of Philosophy*, 89, 315–332.
Textor, M. (2009), 'Devitt on the epistemic authority of linguistic intuitions'. *Erkenntnis*, 71, 395–405.
Thornton, R. (1995), 'Referentiality and *wh*-movement in child English: Juvenile d-linkuency'. *Language Acquisition*, 4, 139–175.
Weinberg, J. M., Gonnerman, C., Buckner, C. and Alexander, J. (2010), 'Are philosophers expert intuiters?' *Philosophical Psychology*, 23, 331–355.
Williamson, T. (2007), *The Philosophy of Philosophy.* Oxford: Blackwell Publishing.
Wisniewski, E. J. (1998), 'The psychology of intuitions', in M. R. DePaul and W. Ramsey (eds), *Rethinking Intuition: The Psychology of Intuition and Its Role in Philosophical Inquiry.* London: Rowan and Littlefield Publishers, pp. 45–58.

4

A Rylean Argument against Reference*

Edouard Machery

Rylean arguments, narrowly conceived, conclude that philosophers' claims about topic x (e.g. free will) are nonsensical on the grounds that, when they formulate these claims, philosophers' use of the relevant concepts (e.g. the concept of voluntariness; see Ryle 1949) contravenes to their proper use, as manifested (at least typically) by laypeople's use of the predicates expressing them in, for example, English. Broad Rylean arguments, which are particularly congenial to experimental philosophy, question whether philosophers' concept of x refers in part on the grounds that it differs from laypeople's (see Sytsma and Machery [2010] on philosophers' concept of phenomenal consciousness) or question whether philosophers' judgements (sometimes called 'intuitions') about philosophical cases (e.g. the fake-barn case) are justified in part on the grounds that their judgements differ from laypeople's. Clearly, broad and narrow Rylean arguments differ in various ways: Among other things, broad Rylean arguments merely lead to sceptical conclusions – they call into question the justification for accepting some proposition (expressed by a judgement about some case) or for assuming that some concept is not empty – and they do not go as far as arguing that the relevant proposition is false or that the relevant concept does not refer, but, just like narrow Rylean arguments, they crucially appeal to differences between laypeople's and philosophers' concepts or concept uses.

The goal of this chapter is to put forward a broad Rylean argument about reference on the basis of the empirical work about the demographic variation in judgements about the reference of proper names (Machery et al. 2004; Machery, Olivola and de Blanc 2009; Lam 2010; Machery et al. 2010; Beebe and Undercoffer 2013a; Machery, Sytsma and Deutsch forthcoming; Sytsma et al. forthcoming) and about the extension of natural kind terms (Machery et al. ms; Olivola and Machery 2014).[1] In substance, I argue that, if one responds to this diversity by claiming that laypeople's judgements about reference and extension can be ignored because laypeople have at best confused concepts of reference and extension, then it becomes unclear whether philosophers' concepts of reference and extension are about anything at all – that is, whether there is any such thing as reference and extension.

Here is how I will proceed. In Section 1, I clarify the notions of reference and extension at play in this chapter. In Section 2, I review the empirical research on judgements about the reference of proper names. In Section 3, I review the more recent empirical research on judgements about the extension of natural kind terms. In Section 4, I put forward the broad Rylean argument against reference and extension.

1. Clarifications

Proper names are used to refer: When I say, "Barack Obama is the forty-fourth president of the United States", I use the proper name "Barack Obama" to refer to, or talk about, the man who has been president of the United States since 2009, and the sentence "Barack Obama is the forty-fourth president of the United States" is used to assert something of, or attribute something to, that man. This much is uncontroversial.

Let's look more closely at this phenomenon. It is common, and natural, to apply the distinction between a type and its tokens to proper names, predicates, sentences, and other phrases, although how to typify linguistic expressions is a difficult question that I will bracket (Kaplan 1990). When I use "Obama" to complain about the killing of innocents by drones and when some pundit rages on Fox that Obama's socialist policies are destroying the US economy, the occurrences of "Obama" are two tokens of the same type, which are used to refer to the same individual. When a proper name is used to refer, it occurs in a particular context, which includes, but does not reduce to, the communicative intention of the speaker (whom or what the speaker intends to be talking about).

In addition to being used to refer, proper names are also said to refer qua types. Proper names qua types do not have any context, and they are not tied to any communicative intention. For instance, "Barack Obama" qua type is often assumed to refer to the man who happens to be the forty-fourth president of the United States, independently of any context and communicative intention; similarly, "Paris" qua type is assumed to refer to the capital of France.

So, we need at least the following distinction: the reference of a proper name, as it is used in a context, and the reference of a proper name qua type. The former is a relation between a token proper name, a context of use (including a speaker and her communicative intention), and a particular, the second a relation between a type of proper names (an abstract object) and a particular. Theories of reference, such as descriptivist theories (Searle 1958; Jackson 1998) and causal-historical theories (Kripke 1980; Devitt 1981), are about the latter relation.[2]

This distinction may not exhaust the distinctions needed to theorize about names. In particular, the reference of a proper name, as it is used in a given context, is not to be identified unreflectively with Kripke's (1977) speaker's reference – roughly, what the speaker intends to refer to with a proper name in a given occasion – since, in contrast to speaker's reference, what determines the reference of a proper name as it is used in a given context may not be determined (fully or at all) by the speaker's communicative intention. Be it as it may, while other notions such as the notion of speaker's reference may be needed to theorize about names, this chapter will focus on the distinction between the use of a proper name to refer to an individual and the reference of a proper name qua type.

While the distinction between being used to refer and referring qua type has typically been drawn for referring phrases (proper names, demonstratives and indexicals, definite descriptions), it is possible to draw a similar distinction for the extension of predicates. It is uncontroversial that predicates are used to pick out sets of objects; in addition to this three-place relation (a token predicate, a context of use, and a set), predicates are also often thought to have an extension qua types (a two-place relation).[3]

As noted above, there is no doubt that proper names are used to refer, although what aspect of the context of use determines the reference of a proper name, as it is used in a given context, is not clear. By contrast, reference, as a property of proper names qua types, is a controversial notion (mutatis mutandis for extension). When discussing 'theories of reference' or when expressing doubts about reference in this chapter, I will be concerned with the two-place relation allegedly picked out by this latter, controversial notion.

Famously, Strawson rejected the idea that proper names refer qua types (1950, p. 326): "'Mentioning,' or 'referring,' is not something an expression does; it is something that someone can use an expression to do." Names don't refer, people do. Davidson (1977, 1979, reproduced in Davidson 1984) rejected the notion of a unique relation between proper names and particulars (reference) or predicates and sets of individuals (extension) (see also Quine

1960): "Reference drops out. It plays no essential role in explaining the relation between language and reality" (1984, p. 225). Davidson's argument proceeded in two steps. He first noted that reference cannot be explained in non-linguistic terms and concluded that reference and satisfaction (hence, extension) are to be thought of as theoretical posits needed to develop a theory of truth that is to be tested as a whole against the empirical evidence. On this view, then, reference and extension are on a par with unobservable posits like field or chemical bond. Second, he noted that, if any truth theory for a language L is consistent with our evidence, then many are. But if there are many acceptable truth theories for L, then there is no single reference or extension assignment (1984, p. 224): "If there is one way of assigning entities to expressions . . . that yields acceptable results with respect to the truth conditions of sentences, there will be endless other ways that do so as well. There is no reason to call any one of these semantic relations 'reference' or 'satisfaction'". More recently, Stich (1996, chapter 1) has raised epistemological doubts against theories of reference: Noting that judgements about cases play a central role in determining which theory of reference is correct, he raised the possibility that such judgements vary across various demographic groups; if they varied, it would be unclear how to adjudicate which of these judgements, if any, are to be used to develop a theory of reference. As will be clear in what follows, Stich's argument was instrumental in getting cross-cultural experimental semantics going. Finally, deflationists like Horwich (1998) and Field (2001) do not reject the notion of reference itself, but they assert that there is no property to theorize about, and that causal-historical and descriptivist theories of reference are thus misguided. The broad Rylean argument developed in Section 4 of this chapter adds to these arguments against reference.

2. Demographic variation in judgements about the reference of proper names

Influenced by psychologist Richard Nisbett's (2003) important research about cross-cultural variation in cognitive styles, Ron Mallon, Shaun Nichols, Steve Stich, and I hypothesized at the beginning of the 2000s that East Asians may be more likely to make descriptivist judgements (i.e. judgements consistent with descriptivist theories of reference) than Westerners (Machery et al. 2004) about the reference of proper names. To test this hypothesis, we presented participants in Hong Kong and in the United States with cases closely inspired by Kripke's

(1980) Gödel case, such as the following case (for further detail, see Machery et al. 2004):

> Suppose that John has learned in college that Gödel is the man who proved an important mathematical theorem, called the incompleteness of arithmetic. John is quite good at mathematics and he can give an accurate statement of the incompleteness theorem, which he attributes to Gödel as the discoverer. But this is the only thing that he has heard about Gödel. Now suppose that Gödel was not the author of this theorem. A man called "Schmidt," whose body was found in Vienna under mysterious circumstances many years ago, actually did the work in question. His friend Gödel somehow got hold of the manuscript and claimed credit for the work, which was thereafter attributed to Gödel. Thus, he has been known as the man who proved the incompleteness of arithmetic. Most people who have heard the name "Gödel" are like John; the claim that Gödel discovered the incompleteness theorem is the only thing they have ever heard about Gödel. When John uses the name "Gödel," is he talking about:
>
> (A) the person who really discovered the incompleteness of arithmetic? or
> (B) the person who got hold of the manuscript and claimed credit for the work?

Another case, the Tsu Ch'ung Chih case, had the same structure, but used names of Chinese individuals. (I call such cases "Gödel-style cases".)

As we had predicted, Chinese were much more likely to make descriptivist judgements about the Gödel and the Tsu Ch'ung Chih cases than Americans. In fact, most Americans made causal-historical judgements (i.e. judgements consistent with causal-historical theories of reference), whereas most Chinese made descriptivist judgements. That is, Chinese participants tended toward answer A, while American participants tended toward answer B. We also found a substantial amount of within-culture variation (Figure 4.1).

Follow-up studies have provided further empirical support for the hypothesis that judgements about the reference of proper names vary across cultures. Beebe and Undercoffer (2013a) have independently replicated our original finding, and they have shown that it is robust: It is still found when one varies the formulation of the vignettes. They have also provided some suggestive evidence that East Asians are more likely to make descriptivist judgements about reference in Jonah-style cases (i.e. cases in which a proper name is associated with an entirely false description and in which people are asked whether the proper name refers to anything at all). Sytsma and colleagues (forthcoming) have shown that, just like Chinese, Japanese tend to make descriptivist judgements about the reference

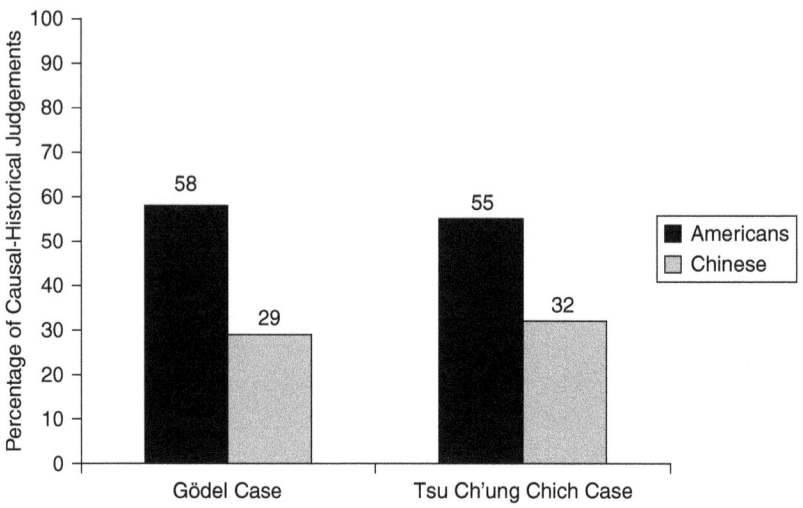

Figure 4.1 Results from Machery et al. (2004)

of proper names in Gödel-style cases, suggesting that the cultural hypothesis put forward in Machery et al. (2004) may well be correct. Finally, against Lam (2010), Machery et al. (2010) have shown that Chinese participants make similar judgements when Gödel-style cases are presented in English (as was originally done in Machery et al. 2004) and in Chinese (see also Machery et al. forthcoming).

Further, Machery and colleagues (2009) have provided evidence that in Gödel-style cases judgements about the reference of proper names and judgements about the truth-value of sentences involving these names are in sync with one another. We presented participants from three countries (Mongolia, India and France) with one of the following two vignettes, and Machery and Olivola have recently done the same thing with American participants (unpublished data):

> Ivy is a high school student in Hong Kong. In her astronomy class, she was taught that Tsu Ch'ung Chih was the man who first determined the precise time of the summer and winter solstices. But, like all her classmates, this is the only thing she has heard about Tsu Ch'ung Chih. Now suppose that Tsu Ch'ung Chih did not really make this discovery. He stole it from an astronomer who died soon after making the discovery. But the theft remained entirely undetected and Tsu Ch'ung Chih became famous for the discovery of the precise times of the solstices. Everybody is like Ivy in this respect; the claim that Tsu Ch'ung Chih determined the solstice times is the only thing people have heard about him.

Having read the above story and accepting that it is true, when Ivy says, "Tsu Ch'ung Chih was a great astronomer," do you think that her claim is: (A) true or (B) false?

The second vignette was identical except for the question, which was:

Having read the above story and accepting that it is true, when Ivy uses the name "Tsu Ch'ung Chih," who do you think she is actually talking about:

(A) the person who (unbeknownst to Ivy) really determined the solstice times?

or

(B) the person who is widely believed to have discovered the solstice times, but actually stole this discovery and claimed credit for it?

Two findings emerged from this study (Figure 4.2). First, in four different countries, which vary tremendously in terms of culture, the proportion of descriptivist judgements was similar when participants were asked about the truth-value of a sentence containing a proper name or about the reference of this name, suggesting that people's judgements about the truth-value of sentences containing proper names track their judgements about the reference of proper names: When someone judges that a proper name x refers to a particular individual y in a fictional case, her judgement about the truth of a sentence containing x in this case seems to depend on what is said about y. Second, the study found further cross-cultural variation in judgements about reference: Americans were less likely to make descriptivist judgements about the reference of proper names than people from Mongolia, India and France, and they were less likely than French to make descriptivist judgements when asked about the truth-value of a sentence containing proper names.

Finally, Machery and colleagues (forthcoming) have provided some evidence that people are genuinely making a judgement about the semantic reference of proper names in Gödel-style cases (roughly, what a proper name refers to according to the language it belongs to) rather than a judgement about the speaker's reference of these names. To show this, we relied on two experimental strategies. First, we wanted to forestall participants from interpreting the question at the end of the vignette as asking for the speaker's reference of "Gödel", but, obviously, we could not simply replace this question with an explicit request to make a judgement about the semantic reference of "Gödel" since "semantic reference" is not a phrase in common English. The task, then, was to find an everyday way to guide participants away from making a judgement about the

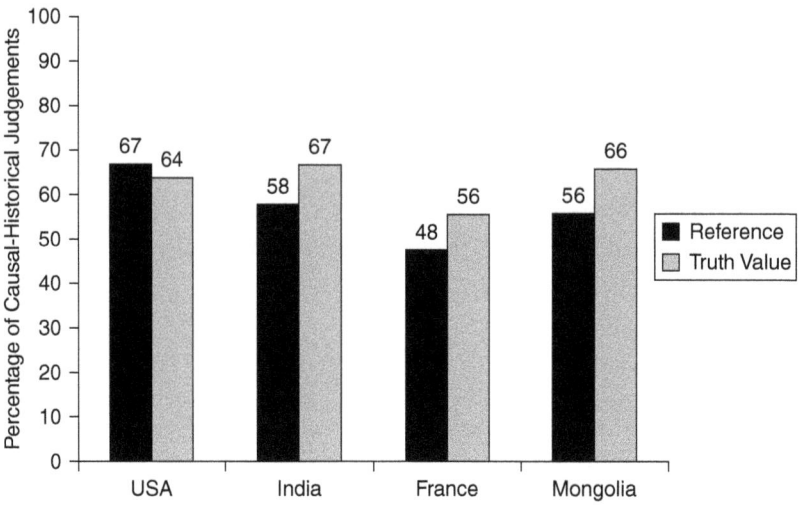

Figure 4.2 Results of Machery et al. (2009) and of Machery and Olivola (unpublished)

speaker's reference of "Gödel". Accordingly, the revised vignette replaced the original question with the following one:

When John uses the name "Gödel," *regardless of who he might intend to be talking about*, he is *actually* talking about:

(A) the person who really discovered the incompleteness of arithmetic;
(B) the person who got hold of the manuscript and claimed credit for the work.

The point of the added clauses, "regardless of who he might intend to be talking about" and "actually", is obviously not that only semantic reference is the actual reference (as if speaker's reference were not actual!); rather, the point of these clauses is to make it clear that participants should ignore the speaker's communicative intention and thus, by contrast, focus on whoever the proper name refers to according to the rules of English. Just like in previous studies, American participants tended to make causal-historical judgements, while Chinese participants tended to make descriptivist judgements.

The second strategy consisted in developing a vignette where the speaker's reference of the proper name is identical to its semantic reference according to causal-historical theories of reference. Anybody who makes a descriptivist judgement, then, must be reporting a judgement about the semantic reference of this proper name. To do so, we added the following paragraph to the end of the Gödel case just before the question:

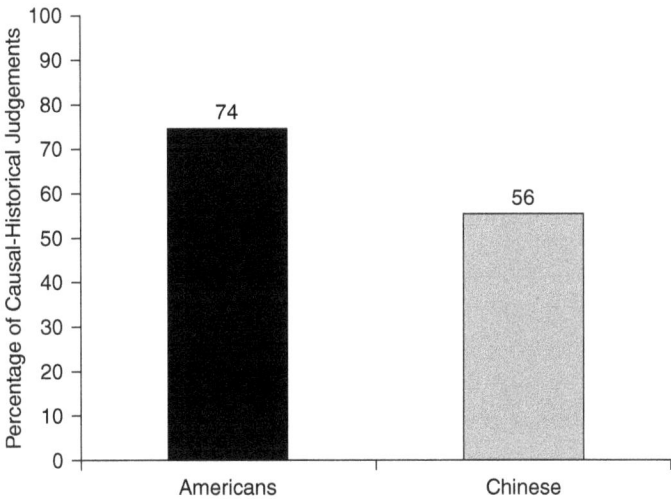

Figure 4.3 Results of Machery et al.'s (forthcoming) Study 5

> One night, John is sitting in his room, reviewing for his mathematics exam by going over the proof of the incompleteness theorem. After a while, he says to his roommate, "Gödel probably got a huge number of awards from mathematical societies!"

This vignette suggests that the speaker intends to be talking about the man who stole the theorem since, given the information provided in the vignette, only the man who stole the theorem can be viewed as having won a huge number of awards from mathematical societies. Americans were again more likely than Chinese to make causal-historical judgements, although the proportion of causal-historical judgements among Chinese participants was higher than in previous studies (Figure 4.3).

The upshot should be clear: Gödel-style cases elicit diverse judgements across cultures, and the same may be true of Jonah-style cases. These cross-cultural results are among the most robust findings of experimental philosophy.

3. Demographic variation in judgements about the extension of natural kind terms

Much of the research in experimental semantics has focused on judgements about the reference of proper names, but there is now an increasing interest in judgements about the extension of natural kind terms. In this section, I review some unpublished work suggesting that these too vary across demographic groups.

The first study of Machery et al. (ms) examines people's judgements about cases inspired by Putnam's (1975) thought experiments. In the lemon scenario, the superficial properties of a fruit (lemons) are modified while its genetic code remains unchanged; participants are asked whether the fruits are still lemons:

> Suppose that following an explosion in a large chemical factory in Brazil, some gases spread all over the world. These gases are innocuous (i.e., harmless) for humans and animals. Although they do not affect the genetic structure of lemons, they react with the pigments in the peel of lemons and with the flesh of lemons. As a result of this reaction, all lemons on Earth turn from yellow to orange and this change is permanent. Moreover, their size increases and they end up being permanently twice as big as they previously were. Their taste is also modified: they now taste exactly like oranges. Would you say that in those conditions there are still lemons?
>
> YES, there are still lemons   NO, there are no more lemons

Participants who answer "Yes" seem to judge, in line with Putnam's externalism, that the extension of natural kind terms is determined by scientifically discoverable properties of the kind *lemon*. I will say that they are making an "externalist" judgement. Participants who answer "No" seem to judge that the extension of natural kind terms is determined by the superficial properties of the kind members, properties they probably view as constitutive of kind membership. I will say that they are making an "internalist" judgement.

In the water case, inspired by Putnam's twin-earth thought experiment, astronauts discover a substance that shares the superficial properties of another substance (water), but not its chemical structure; participants are asked whether the liquid is water:

> Suppose that in the future, astronauts find on a distant, inhabited planet a liquid, called "mantup" by the inhabitants of this planet. The chemical composition of mantup is H_3Sl_2. Although mantup's chemical composition is different from the chemical we call "water" on Earth, this liquid is in all other respects indistinguishable from water. Mantup tastes like water and it quenches thirst like water. Like water, it does not have any specific odor. It freezes at 0 degree Celsius and boils at 100 degrees Celsius. The oceans, seas and lakes on this planet contain this liquid and it also rains this liquid. In brief, mantup interacts with everything in the same way that water does. Would you say that in those conditions, mantup is water? YES   NO

Participants who answer "Yes" make an internalist judgement, while participants who follow Putnam's judgement about the twin-earth thought experiment in answering "No" make an externalist judgement.

We examined people's judgements in 10 different cultures, and we found that the judgements elicited by these vignettes vary substantially across demographic groups (for further detail, see Machery et al. ms). The proportion of externalist judgements about the water case varied from about 30 per cent in India to 75 per cent in Portugal, South Korea, France and Brazil. The proportion of externalist judgements about the lemon case varied from about 15 per cent in Italy to about 65 per cent in Indonesia. The two cases also elicited very different patterns of answers. In most countries, people were much more likely to express externalist judgements when considering the water case than they were when considering the lemon case. Furthermore, we found almost no relationship between the judgements elicited by the two vignettes.

We found other demographic effects too. Gender influenced judgement about the water case, with men being more likely to make externalist judgement, while more educated people were more likely to make an externalist judgement in the water case.

The results presented in Machery et al. (ms) are difficult to interpret. No easily explainable pattern of cultural variation was observed, and no stable distinction between East Asians and Westerners was found. Still, two conclusions emerge from this work: First, there is demographic variation in judgements about the extension of natural kind terms; second, these judgements can easily be framed, and it is possible to push people to make externalist or internalist judgement.

4. A broad Rylean argument against reference

4.1 A tempting response

One could react to the demographic variation in judgements about the reference of proper names and the extension of natural kind terms in various ways (for discussion, see Ludwig 2007; Deutsch 2009, 2010; Jackman 2009; Mallon, Machery, Nichols and Stich 2009; Martí 2009, 2012, 2014; Reimer 2009; Devitt 2011, 2012a, b; Ichikawa, Maitra and Weatherson 2012; Machery and Stich 2012; Machery 2012b, 2014; Maynes 2013; Cohnitz and Haukioja 2013; Machery, Mallon, Nichols and Stich 2013; Maynes and Gross 2013; Ostertag 2013; and Andow 2014), but this chapter isn't the place to review this debate to its full extent (see Genone 2012; Dacey and Mallon forthcoming). Rather, I want to single out an influential and tempting response: Laypeople's judgements about reference and extension can be ignored either because laypeople are unlikely to have the concepts of reference and extension or because, if they have them, their concepts are likely to be confused. Ludwig, for instance, asserts that responding properly to Gödel-style cases requires an understanding of the technical distinction between speaker's reference and semantic reference, which laypeople are unlikely to have mastered (2007, p. 150):

> For anyone at all familiar with work in the philosophy of language, it is immediately evident that the question [in the Gödel case cited above in this chapter] does not clearly distinguish between two things: whom John intends to be talking about (or speaker's reference) and who the name John uses refers to, taken literally in the language he intends to be speaking (semantic reference). Experts may well negotiate this infelicity in the formulation of the question without much difficulty, but that is because they have some relevant expertise about hard-won distinctions developed in the field and will likely understand what is intended. This highlights the importance of the point in section 1 that it is desirable that the subjects of the thought experiment have expertise in the relevant field.

Similar concerns regularly come up in informal discussions regarding the philosophical significance of the demographic variation in judgements about reference.

Let's elaborate on this argument a bit. The concepts of reference and extension are technical concepts (on a par with the concepts of c-command in syntactic theory and of drift in evolutionary biology), and we do not expect laypeople to possess this kind of concept; for example, we do not expect them to possess the physical concept of field or the mathematical concept of a limit. Such concepts must be learned, and learning them may sometimes be quite difficult. So, there is no reason to expect laypeople to have the concepts of reference and extension, and, if they do not, their judgements are not about reference or extension, and as a result do not bear on metasemantical theories of reference and extension. Alternatively, laypeople may have concepts that are related to the technical concepts of reference and extension, but that are confused – that is, when people apply them, they are responding to several distinct phenomena instead of just to reference and extension. Similarly, some people may have a confused concept of temperature: They may be responding to both temperature and to their experience of temperature. If lay concepts of reference and extension are confused, it is unclear whether people are really responding to reference and extension when they apply them, and as a result lay judgements do not bear on the technical theories of reference and extension. Either way, philosophers are justified in ignoring the demographic variation in judgements about reference and extension.

4.2 Is there any such thing as reference and extension?

In what follows, I will take for granted, for the sake of the argument, that the concepts of reference or extension are technical, and that, as a result, laypeople either do not possess them or possess them in at best a confused manner.[4] My goal here is to investigate a troubling consequence of this claim.

Obviously, it does not follow from the fact that the concepts of reference or extension are not possessed by laypeople or are confused that they are empty: The physical concept of field, for instance, does not fail to refer because laypeople do not possess it! But it follows from this fact that we need some justification for believing that the concepts of reference and extension are not empty, that is, for believing that proper names refer and predicates have an extension. We are not allowed to simply assume that people have a pre-theoretical grasp of the phenomena of reference and extension (since, by assumption, laypeople do not have these concepts or may be responding to something else), and that philosophers' job is simply to develop a satisfying account of these independently understood phenomena. If Ludwig and others are right, reference and extension are relations that are introduced theoretically, not phenomena pre-theoretically understood. They are on a par with fields, limits, drift and so on. So, what is our justification for assuming that proper names refer and predicates have an extension?

It is most natural to justify the assumption that proper names refer and predicates have an extension by highlighting the explanatory power of reference and extension (e.g. Devitt 1981). Just as we are justified in positing the existence of fields because of their explanatory power in quantum field theory, we are justified in positing the existence of reference and extension because of their explanatory power in semantics.

But what do reference and extension explain that is not explained by the use of proper names to refer and the use of predicates to single out an extension? Surely not the fact that sentences containing proper names are used to say things about particulars (mutatis mutandis for predicates)! Rather the idea must be that reference and extension are theoretical constructs necessary to develop empirically adequate semantic theories of natural languages (Devitt 1981). More details about the nature of semantic theories and about the function of reference and extension in them are however called for. If a satisfying semantic theory for a given natural language is an empirically adequate truth theory, then Davidson's argument (reviewed in Section 1) suggests that there is no such thing as a unique relation between proper names qua types and particulars. Devitt (1981) rejects this argument on the grounds that Davidson has an instrumentalist conception of reference and that instrumentalism is a dubious position in philosophy of science. Both considerations are problematic. First, attention to actual science and to modelling practices has breathed new life into the idea that at least sometimes, and perhaps often (though not always), theoretical entities are best understood instrumentally. Second, as I read Davidson (1977), Davidson's argument does not rest on instrumentalism about reference, but ends up with something like an instrumentalist view about reference. Davidson is led to this view because semanticists need reference to develop a truth theory and because, if a truth theory is empirically adequate, more than one is. If this reading is correct, then rejecting instrumentalism fails to address Davidson's argument. Instead of following Devitt (1981), one may attempt to distinguish between the many empirically adequate truth theories of a language by arguing that in only one of them do proper names and predicates have natural reference and extension (e.g. Lewis 1983). However, this response will not convince those of us who are reluctant to appeal to metaphysical considerations to adjudicate between empirical theories.

Here is where we seem to stand: The role of reference and extension in developing truth theories of natural languages does not suffice to justify the assumption that proper names refer and predicates have an extension. Of course, reference and extension may be necessary to meet other explanatory purposes in semantics, but it is impossible to assess this idea without detailed proposals about these.

One may wonder whether the sceptical, Rylean conclusion holds whether or not laypeople recognize reference and extension at all: After all, if our best semantic theory does not single out a unique relation of reference or extension, why would it make a difference if laypeople had some relatively clear concept of reference and extension?[5] I would like to resist this suggestion here. If laypeople have some relatively clear concept of reference and extension, then it is at least possible (and it is perhaps even plausible) that reference and extension are real phenomena and that the plurality of semantic relations postulated by the empirically equivalent semantic theories just reveals that looking at what a truth theory for a given language has to say about reference and extension is not the right way to understand their nature.

At this point, it may be tempting to simply note that linguists mention the reference of proper names and the extension of predicates when they theorize about the semantics of natural languages, and that this fact provides us with ample reason to assume that proper names refer and that predicates have an extension. This response suffers from at least two problems. First, it is unclear how to understand linguists' mention of the reference of proper names and the extension of predicates since such mention is consistent with linguists agreeing with Davidson's or with deflationists' position about reference and extension. Consistent with this possibility, linguists are not involved in developing theories of reference – in explaining how proper names refer (mutatis mutandis for predicates). Second, it is something of an exaggeration to refer to a consensus among linguists since some influential linguists have explicitly denied that names have a reference (e.g. Chomsky 1995, 2000; Pietroski 2003). It is particularly notable that scepticism about referential semantics has long been a key theme in Chomsky's work. In *New Horizons in the Study of Language* he writes (2000, p. 17):

> In general, a word, even of the simplest kind, does not pick out an entity of the world, or of our 'belief space'. Conventional assumptions about these matters seem to me very dubious.

Further on in the book Chomsky elaborates on his scepticism (2000, p. 130):

> A good part of contemporary philosophy of language is concerned with analyzing alleged relations between expressions and things, often exploring intuitions about the technical notions "denote," "refer," "true of," etc. said to hold between expressions and something else. But there can be no intuitions about these notions, just as there can be none about "angular velocity" or "protein." These are technical terms of philosophical discourse with a stipulated sense that has no counterpart in ordinary language ... If we rerun the thought experiments with ordinary terms, judgements seem to collapse or, rather, to become so interest-relative as to yield no meaningful results ... [I]t is not at all clear that the theory of natural language and its use involves relations of "denotation," "true of," etc. in anything like the sense of the technical theory of meaning.

Moral: It is unclear what justifies the assumption that proper names refer and predicates have an extension if reference and extension are not pre-theoretically grasped phenomena.

5. Conclusion

It is tempting to respond to the demographic variation in judgements about the reference of proper names and the extension of natural kind terms by holding that laypeople have at best confused concepts of reference and extension, and that as a result philosophers and semanticists can ignore their judgements. However, this response is not costless: When they embrace this response, philosophers cannot anymore assume that they are theorizing about phenomena pre-theoretically grasped, and they commit themselves to providing a justification for the claim that proper names refer and predicates have an extension, as scientists would do for any theoretical entity. But adequately justifying this claim turns out to be particularly challenging, and it becomes at best unclear why we should accept it.

Notes

* I would like to thank Jussi Haukioja, Åsa Wikforss and Sören Häggqvist for their insightful comments.

1. For further research on judgements about the reference of proper names, see Sytsma and Livengood (2011), Machery (2012a), Beebe and Undercoffer (2013b) and Grau and Pury (2014); for further research on judgements about the extension of natural kind terms, see Jylkkä, Railo and Haukioja (2009), Genone and Lombrozo (2012) and Nichols, Pinillos and Mallon (forthcoming).
2. Roughly, according to descriptivist theories of reference, a proper name refers to the individual who satisfies or best satisfies the description it is associated with. By contrast, according to causal-historical theories of reference, a proper name refers to the individual it is associated with by a historical chain of uses.
3. I will ignore mass terms here.
4. However, as Åsa Wikforss and Sören Häggqvist have noted, Ludwig's and others' response is not without difficulty. Judgements using proper names seem to be in sync with metasemantical judgements about the properties of proper names (Machery et al. 2009), and judgements using natural kind terms seem to vary across various demographic groups. If these findings hold up, then experimental philosophers' findings cannot be simply dismissed on the grounds that laypeople do not have the relevant concepts or that they have confused concepts. Ludwig and others would have to claim that people are confused when they *apply* their own language in addition to when they talk about their language, and this claim, though not obviously false, is harder to defend.
5. Thanks to Åsa Wikforss and Sören Häggqvist for pushing this point.

References

Andow, J. (2014), 'Intuitions, disagreement and referential pluralism'. *Review of Philosophy and Psychology*, 5, 223–239.

Beebe, J. R. and Undercoffer, R. J. (2013a), 'Individual and cross-cultural differences in semantic intuitions: New experimental findings'. Manuscript in preparation.

Beebe, J. R. and Undercoffer, R. J. (2013b), 'Moral valence and semantic intuitions'. Manuscript in preparation.

Chomsky, N. (1995), 'Language and nature'. *Mind*, 104, 1–61.

Chomsky, N. (2000), *New Horizons in the Study of Language and Mind*. Cambridge: Cambridge University Press.

Cohnitz, D. and Haukioja, J. (2013), 'Meta-externalism vs. Meta-internalism in the study of reference'. *Australasian Journal of Philosophy*, 91, 475–500.

Dacey, M. and Mallon, R. (forthcoming), 'Reference', in J. Sytsma and W. Buckwalter (eds), *Blackwell Companion to Experimental Philosophy*. Oxford: Blackwell Publishers.

Davidson, D. (1977), 'Reality without reference'. *Dialectica*, 31, 247–258.

Davidson, D. (1979), 'The inscrutability of reference'. *Southwestern Journal of Philosophy*, 10, 7–19.

Davidson, D. (1984), *Inquiries into Truth and Interpretation*. New York: Oxford University Press.

Deutsch, M. (2009), 'Experimental philosophy and the theory of reference'. *Mind & Language*, 24, 445–466.

Deutsch, M. (2010), 'Intuitions, counter-examples, and experimental philosophy'. *Review of Philosophy and Psychology*, 1, 447–460.

Devitt, M. (1981), *Designation*. New York: Columbia University Press.

Devitt, M. (2011), 'Experimental semantics'. *Philosophy and Phenomenological Research*, 82, 418–435.

Devitt, M. (2012a), 'Whither experimental semantics?'. *Theoria*, 73, 5–36.

Devitt, M. (2012b), 'Semantic epistemology: Response to machery'. *Theoria*, 74, 229–233.

Field, H. (2001), *Truth and the Absence of Fact*. Oxford: Oxford University Press.

Genone, J. (2012), 'Theories of reference and experimental philosophy'. *Philosophy Compass*, 7, 152–163.

Genone, J. and Lombrozo, T. (2012), 'Concept possession, experimental semantics, and hybrid theories of reference'. *Philosophical Psychology*, 25, 717–742.

Grau, C. and Pury, C. (2014), 'Attitudes towards reference and replaceability'. *Review of Philosophy and Psychology*, 5, 155–168.

Horwich, P. (1998), *Meaning*. Oxford: Oxford University Press.

Ichikawa, J., Ishani, M. and Weatherson, B. (2012), 'In defense of a Kripkean dogma'. *Philosophy and Phenomenological Research*, 85, 56–68.

Jackman, H. (2009), 'Semantic intuitions, conceptual analysis, and cross-cultural variation'. *Philosophical Studies*, 146, 159–177.

Jackson, F. (1998), 'Reference and description revisited'. *Philosophical Perspectives*, 12, 201–218.

Jylkkä, J., Railo, H. and Haukioja, J. (2009), 'Psychological essentialism and semantic externalism: evidence for externalism in lay speakers' language use'. *Philosophical Psychology*, 22, 37–60.

Kaplan, D. (1990), 'Words'. *Aristotelian Society Supplementary*, 64, 93–119.

Kripke, S. (1977), 'Speaker's reference and semantic reference'. *Midwest Studies in Philosophy*, 2, 255–276.

Kripke, S. (1980), *Naming and Necessity*. Cambridge, MA: Harvard University Press.

Lam, B. (2010), 'Are cantonese speakers really descriptivists? Revisiting cross-cultural semantics'. *Cognition*, 115, 320–329.

Lewis, D. (1983), 'New work for a theory of universals'. *Australasian Journal of Philosophy*, 61, 343–377.

Ludwig, K. (2007), 'The epistemology of thought experiments: First-person approach vs. Third-person approach'. *Midwest Studies in Philosophy*, 31, 128–159.

Machery, E. (2011), 'Variation in intuitions about reference and ontological disagreement', in S. D. Hales (ed.), *A Companion to Relativism*. Malden, MA: Wiley-Blackwell, pp. 118–136.

Machery, E. (2012a), 'Expertise and intuitions about reference'. *Theoria*, 73, 37–54.

Machery E. (2012b), 'Semantic epistemology: a brief response to Devitt'. *Theoria*, 74, 223–227.

Machery, E. (2014), 'What is the significance of the demographic variation in semantic intuitions?' in E. Machery and E. O'Neill (eds), *Current Controversies in experimental Philosophy*. New York: Routledge, pp. 3–16.

Machery, E. and Olivola, C. (unpublished), Unpublished data.

Machery, E. and Stich, S. P. (2012), 'Experimental philosophy of language', in G. Russell and D. Graff Fara (eds), *Routledge Companion to the Philosophy of Language*. New York: Routledge, pp. 495–512.

Machery, E., Olivola, C. and de Blanc, M. (2009), 'Linguistic and metalinguistic intuitions in the philosophy of language'. *Analysis*, 69, 689–694.

Machery, E., Sytsma, S. and Deutsch, M. (forthcoming), 'Speaker's reference and cross-cultural semantics', in A. Bianchi (ed.), *On Reference*. Oxford: Oxford University Press.

Machery, E., Mallon, R., Nichols, S. and Stich, S. P. (2004), 'Semantics, cross-cultural style'. *Cognition*, 92, B1–B12.

Machery, E., Mallon, R., Nichols, S. and Stich, S. P. (2013), 'If intuitions vary, then so what?'. *Philosophy and Phenomenological Research*, 86, 618–635.

Machery, E., Deutsch, M., Mallon, R., Nichols, S., Sytsma, J. and Stich, S. P. (2010), 'Semantic intuitions: Reply to Lam'. *Cognition*, 117, 361–366.

Machery, E., Olivola, C. Y., Cheon, H., Kurniawan, I. T., Mauro, C., Struchiner, N. and Susianto, H. (ms), 'Is folk essentialism a fundamental feature of human cognition?'

Mallon, R., Machery, E., Nichols, S., and Stich, S. P. (2009). 'Against arguments from reference'. *Philosophy and Phenomenological Research*, 79, 332–356.

Martí, G. (2009), 'Against semantic multi-culturalism'. *Analysis*, 69, 42–48.

Martí, G. (2012), 'Empirical data and the theory of reference', in W. P. Kabasenche, M. O'Rourke and M. H. Slate (eds), *Reference and Referring, Topics in Contemporary Philosophy*. Cambridge, MA: MIT Press, pp. 63–82.

Martí, G. (2014), 'Reference and experimental semantics', in E. Machery and E. O'Neill (eds.), *Current Controversies in Experimental Philosophy*. New York: Routledge, pp. 17–26.

Maynes, J. (2013), 'Interpreting intuition: Experimental philosophy of language'. *Philosophical Psychology*, 28, 260–278.

Maynes, J. and Gross, S. (2013), 'Linguistic intuitions'. *Philosophy Compass*, 8, 714–730.

Nichols, S., Pinillos, A. and Mallon, R. (forthcoming). 'Ambiguous reference'. *Mind*.

Nisbett, R. E. (2003), *The Geography of Thought: How Asians and Westerners Think Differently . . . and Why*. New York: Free Press.

Olivola, C. and Machery, E. (2014), 'Is psychological essentialism an inherent feature of human cognition?'. *Behavioral and Brain Sciences*, 37, 499.

Ostertag, G. (2013), 'The "Gödel" effect'. *Philosophical Studies*, 166, 65–82.

Pietroski, P. (2003), 'The character of natural language semantics', in A. Barber (ed.), *Epistemology of Language*. New York: Oxford University Press, pp. 217–256.

Quine, W. V. O. (1960), *Word and Object*. Cambridge, MA: MIT Press.

Reimer, M. (2009), 'Jonah cases', in A. Everett (ed.), *Empty Names*. Oxford: Oxford University Press.

Ryle, G. (1949), *The Concept of Mind*. London: Hutchinson.

Searle, J. (1958), 'Proper names'. *Mind*, 67, 166–173.

Stich, S. P. (1996), *Deconstructing the Mind*. Oxford: Oxford University Press.

Strawson, P. F. (1950), 'On referring'. *Mind*, 59, 320–344.

Sytsma, J. M., and Machery, E. (2010), 'Two conceptions of subjective experience'. *Philosophical Studies*, 151, 299–327.

Sytsma, J. M. and Livengood, J. (2011), 'A new perspective concerning experiments on semantic intuitions'. *The Australasian Journal of Philosophy*, 89, 315–332.

Sytsma, J. M., Livengood, J., Sato, R. and Oguchi, M. (forthcoming), 'Reference in the land of the rising sun: A cross-cultural study on the reference of proper names'. *Review of Philosophy and Psychology*.

5

The Metaphilosophy of Language*

Daniel Cohnitz

1. The dilemma of metaphilosophy

Within the field of philosophy, metaphilosophy has moved to the centre of attention in the past decade.[1] This development was in part provoked by the rise of experimental philosophy as an alleged alternative to standard armchair philosophy.

Of course, the fact that methodological questions in philosophy are now assessed more systematically than they were in the past[2] is a positive development. However, some of the discussions between methodological conservatives and experimental revolutionists appear to be surprisingly naïve. Typically, it seems to be assumed, on both sides of the debate, that there is such a thing as a general methodology of philosophy, which can be discussed and assessed without paying attention to the peculiarities of the different sub-disciplines of philosophy.

But it is easy to show that this is not a terribly plausible assumption. Methodological questions arise relative to the aims or goals one has set for oneself. They are questions of the type "What is the best way to do X?" But it isn't clear at all that all areas of philosophy plausibly involve the same X here at any (even minimally) interesting level of abstraction. Let's take a look why this might be so. Perhaps the best candidate for philosophy's general goal is to find the truth. After all, philosophy is a compound of φιλεῖν and σοφία and translates as Love of Wisdom, so shouldn't we conceive of philosophy's aim in general as cognitive?

First of all, it is not clear that it is even true that all philosophy aims at truth. Is practical philosophy, ethics in particular, an attempt to discover moral truth? If you are a non-cognitivist about ethics, you will dispute such an assumption. Moreover, ethics isn't the only area in which a non-cognitivist attitude can make sense. For example, all areas of philosophy that conceive of their enterprise as one of providing explications in Rudolf Carnap's (1950) sense of the word, the aim of philosophical inquiry might rather be seen as the development of normative proposals (e.g. proposals to use certain concepts in certain refined ways).

Second, even if we agreed that at least large parts of philosophy aim at truth and knowledge, it isn't clear that 'truth and knowledge' alone characterize an aim that could determine a specific methodology. Different kinds of truths might require different methods for their discovery. Is our epistemic access to metaphysical truths the same as our access to conceptual or logical truth? Those who hold on to an analytic/synthetic distinction might doubt that it is. Logical truth is perhaps plausibly accessible a priori, but at least some metaphysical truths might be only a posteriori knowable.

Rejecting the a priori/a posteriori distinction improves the situation only slightly. Sociology, linguistics, history, particle physics and astronomy are all a posteriori disciplines, but they have very different methodologies that display similarities only on a very high level of abstraction. The reason for this is that their subject matter and our epistemic access to that subject matter are very different, even if this access is in all cases a posteriori.

It seems that in order to argue for a general methodology for philosophy as a whole, one would first need to answer a number of substantial philosophical questions in specific ways. Are moral questions cognitive? Are there metaphysical truths that are only a posteriori knowable? Is logic a priori? Are there any analytic truths that are knowable on the basis of linguistic competence alone? When dealing with questions like these, one is already engaging with central topics in first-order philosophy, one is already doing philosophy. But how can one hope to formulate a methodology of philosophy, if that presupposes answers to questions like these?

In this chapter, I will use the example of philosophy of language, and in particular the recent debate concerning the role of intuitions in choosing between alternative theories of reference, to demonstrate which specific assumptions and considerations enter into methodological discussion. Though, as we will see, these assumptions can't plausibly be generalized to other areas of philosophical inquiry.[3]

In Section 2, I will begin with a short summary of the methodological discussion concerning the role of intuitions in philosophy of language, which developed in response to empirical results by experimental philosophers that seemed to indicate a certain cross-cultural variability in intuitions about the reference of proper names. One central question in this debate is which and whose intuitions should count in the first place for theory choice on the standard account that experimental philosophers intend to criticize. As we will see, the experimental philosophers as well as many of their critics seem to assume that the relevant intuitions are certain metalinguistic judgements the reliability of which depends on how correctly they inform us about an independent realm of objective semantic facts.

This realm of semantic fact that a theory of reference is supposed to describe will be the topic of the third section. How should we conceive of the subject matter of theories of reference? Are these semantic facts indeed independent of the intuitive interpretation and production of linguistic items by competent speakers? I will argue that this assumption would be very implausible and at odds with the explanatory aim of philosophical semantics, namely to make a systematic contribution to the explanation of successful linguistic communication. Far from being independent of the intuitive interpretation and production of linguistic items by competent speakers, the realm of semantic facts is instead constituted by it.

Section 4 will discuss how the judgements that seem to play a methodological role in the standard methodology of philosophy of language relate to the intuitive interpretation and production of linguistic items by competent speakers. I will argue that these judgements are best understood as reports of intuitive interpretations or productions. Thus the question of how reliable these judgements are is a question of how reliably they report what they are supposed to report. As we will see, there are good *prima facie* reasons to assume that these reports are reliable.

However, since the reliability of these reports is ultimately an empirical question, Section 5 will sketch how some methods of psycholinguistics could be used to determine their actual reliability empirically.

In the sixth and last section, the results of the discussion of this example will be summarized and the extent to which the results reached can be generalized will be discussed. I will argue that the generalizability of these results is very limited and probably doesn't go beyond philosophy of language (and even within philosophy of language, they don't generalize to all topics or questions).

2. The experimentalist challenge

It is probably fair to say that the recent discussion concerning the role of intuitions in philosophy of language started with the publication of the provocative paper "Semantics, Cross-cultural Style" by Edouard Machery, Ron Mallon, Shaun Nichols and Stephen Stich (2004).[4] In the paper the authors provide reconstructions of two families of theories of reference; that is, theories that are supposed to explain how certain linguistic expressions (e.g. proper names) refer to objects in the world. The two families distinguished are descriptivist theories of reference (characterized by D1 and D2) and causal-historical theories of reference (characterized by C1 and C2):

Descriptivist View

D1. Competent speakers associate a description with every proper name. This description specifies a set of properties.

D2. An object is the referent of a proper name if and only if it uniquely or best satisfies the description associated with it. An object uniquely satisfies a description when the description is true of it and only it. If no object entirely satisfies the description, many philosophers claim that the proper name refers to the unique individual that satisfies most of the description . . . If the description is not satisfied at all or if many individuals satisfy it, the name does not refer.

(Machery et al. 2004, B2)

Causal-Historical View

C1. A name is introduced into a linguistic community for the purpose of referring to an individual. It continues to refer to that individual as long as its uses are linked to the individual via a causal chain of successive users: every user of the name acquired it from another user, who acquired it in turn from someone else, and so on, up to the first user who introduced the name to refer to a specific individual.

C2. Speakers may associate descriptions with names. After a name is introduced, the associated description does not play any role in the fixation of the referent. The referent may entirely fail to satisfy the description.

(Machery et al. 2004, B2–B3)

Machery, Mallon, Nichols and Stich claim that in philosophy theories are chosen if they accord with the intuitions of philosophers when evaluating actual and hypothetical cases in the domain of these theories and theories are rejected if their predictions are in conflict with the intuitive judgements of philosophers. Also in the choice between these two families of theories of reference, a choice was made based on such intuitive judgements. In particular, Saul Kripke had described hypothetical cases in *Naming and Necessity* (1980), the intuitive evaluation of which was compatible with the predictions of a causal-historical theory but contradicted the predictions of descriptivist theories.

Inspired by previous research on cultural variation in cognitive strategies between Westerners (Ws) and East Asians (EAs) (c.f. Nisbett et al. 2001; Nisbett 2003), as well as results about cultural variation (between the same groups) in intuitive judgements about thought experiments in epistemology (Weinberg et al. 2001), Machery et al. conjectured that a similar cultural variation should also be found for the hypothetical cases described by Kripke. Thus, their paper describes two experiments intended to test the following hypothesis:

> When presented with Kripke-style thought experiments, Ws would be more likely to respond in accordance with causal-historical accounts of reference, while EAs would be more likely to respond in accordance with descriptivist accounts of reference.
>
> (Machery et al. 2004, B5)

In order to test this hypothesis Machery et al. formulate four vignettes featuring hypothetical cases that are modelled after the cases discussed by Kripke. One of these, the so-called 'Gödel/Schmidt-case', reads as follows:

> Suppose that John has learned in college that Gödel is the man who proved an important mathematical theorem, called the incompleteness of arithmetic. John is quite good at mathematics and he can give an accurate statement of the incompleteness theorem, which he attributes to Gödel as the discoverer. But this is the only thing that he has heard about Gödel. Now suppose that Gödel was not the author of this theorem. A man called "Schmidt", whose body was found in Vienna under mysterious circumstances many years ago, actually did the work in question. His friend Gödel somehow got hold of the manuscript and claimed credit for the work, which was thereafter attributed to Gödel. Thus, he has been known as the man who proved the incompleteness of arithmetic. Most people who have heard the name "Gödel" are like John; the claim that Gödel discovered the incompleteness theorem is the only thing they have ever heard about Gödel. When John uses the name "Gödel", is he talking about:
>
> (A) the person who really discovered the incompleteness of arithmetic? or
>
> (B) the person who got hold of the manuscript and claimed credit for the work?
>
> (Machery et al. 2004, B6)

Vignettes like this were presented to undergraduate students from Rutgers University and the University of Hong Kong. In response to vignettes modelled after the Gödel/Schmidt-case, about two-thirds of the Ws chose answer (B), while only about one-third of the EAs chose that answer.

Machery et al. draw far-reaching conclusions from this result. In (Machery et al. 2004) they argue that philosophers of language should reconsider their methodology. In a later paper (Mallon et al. 2009) the same authors argue that theorizing about reference should be abandoned completely, since there seem to be no viable methodological alternatives. In other places, experimental philosophers argue that these experiments show that the standard methodology of analytic philosophy (viz. the consideration of hypothetical cases in theory choice) is 'bankrupt'.[5]

These radical claims about philosophy as a whole, and the methodology of philosophy of language in particular, provoked a lively debate. In this debate we find two sets of objections against the argumentation by Machery et al. One set objects to the analysis of standard methodology by Machery et al. The other set objects to details of the experiment:

1. Objections to the characterization of standard methodology
    1.1 Intuitions don't play the special role in philosophy that experimental philosophers assign to it. In particular, intuitions aren't the foundation for philosophical arguments. Therefore the empirical investigation of the possible cultural variation of intuitions is simply irrelevant for philosophical methodology. (Cappelen 2012)
    1.2 Even if the intuitive evaluation of the Gödel/Schmidt-case played some role, Kripke presented many more arguments in *Naming and Necessity* which were much more relevant and significant and which are independent of intuitive judgements about hypothetical cases. (Deutsch 2009, 2011a; Martí 2014)[6]
    1.3 The intuitions of laymen shouldn't play a role in the evaluation of theories of reference. If intuitions should be given an evidential role, then it's the intuitions of experts, that is, professional philosophers of language and perhaps linguists. (Devitt 2011a)[7]

2. Objections to Details of the Experiment
    2.1 The result of the experiment can't inform us about variation in the relevant intuitions, since the answers (A) and (B) were formulated as metalinguistic judgements. However, that people differ in their metalinguistic judgements was obvious from the start. After all that is why there are two different families of theories of reference. (Martí 2009, 2014)[8]

2.2 The result of the experiment can't inform us about variation in the relevant intuitions, because the question at the end of the vignette contains an ambiguity, which can account for the variation in answers. "Who John is talking about" can either mean the speaker meaning (who does John intend to talk about?) or the semantic referent (what does "Gödel" refer to in John's utterance?). (Deutsch 2009; Sytsma and Livengood 2011)[9]

The dissimilitude of these objections already indicates that there is no consensus within philosophy of language on whether semantic intuitions (should) play a significant role, and if so, which and whose intuitions are of relevance. Objection 1.1 denies the relevance of intuitions completely. 1.3 denies the relevance of intuitions of laymen. 2.1 seems to allow intuitions some role but objects that the experiment tested the wrong ones.

Which out of these objections are valid and which should be rejected? As explained in the introduction, methodological questions depend on one's aims. Thus, in order to see what role intuitions should play in our methodology, we should first get clear on what purpose theories of reference are supposed to have. This question will be discussed in the next section. Only after that will Section 4 turn to the question of which and whose intuitions (if any) should be of relevance in choosing between different theories of reference.

3. Meta-Internalism vs. Meta-Externalism

The two families of theories of reference that were introduced in section 2 (viz. descriptivist theories and causal-historical theories) are often also classified as 'internalist' or 'externalist' theories of reference, respectively. A descriptive theory is internalist in this sense because what a proper name in a certain speaker's usage refers to depends partly on her internal states (because it depends on which description, or bundle of descriptions, the speaker associates with the name). A causal-historical theory, in contrast, is externalist in this sense because it depends solely on the existence of a causal chain of name-borrowing between language users that determines what a name refers to, regardless of the speaker's awareness of that chain.

In order to clarify which kind of evidence matters for deciding between these two kinds of theories, we should first inquire into which kinds of facts it could depend on, that is, whether an internalist or an externalist theory is true. When we know this, we can inquire into what is the best way (or at least a good way) to find out about these facts.

As argued in (Cohnitz and Haukioja 2013), we can make progress on the first question by also drawing a distinction between internalism and externalism at a meta-level. We should then distinguish between Meta-Internalism and Meta-Externalism:

> *Meta-Internalism*: How a linguistic expression E in an utterance U by a speaker S refers and which theory of reference is true of E is determined by individual psychological states of S at the time of U.
>
> *Meta-Externalism*: How a linguistic expression E in an utterance U by a speaker S refers and which theory of reference is true of E is independent of the individual psychological states of S at the time of U.

Many theories of reference are meta-internalist: that the referent of, say, a proper name is a matter of the history of its usage within in the linguistic community is usually (though often not explicitly) considered to be so because the speaker in using the name had the (tacit) intention to engage in that tradition of reference borrowing. Thus, on this account, reference is determined via external factors (the history and tradition of using the name) but that it is these external factors is determined by the (tacit) intentions of the speaker.

On a meta-externalist view, it could be that, even if the speaker had no such intentions, nonetheless the reference of proper names in her usage could be determined by the way the name is used in the tradition of her linguistic community, because it is external factors (independent of her intentions, or dispositions or other psychological states) that determine which first-order theory is true of linguistic expressions in her usage.

Hence in this case, semantic facts are independent of the internal facts of speakers, including their dispositions to produce and interpret expressions in certain ways and, consequently, independent of the intuitions speakers might have concerning the semantic properties of the expressions they use. Thus, if we assume that a speaker's intuitive judgements in response to Gödel/Schmidt-cases reveal her dispositions concerning how she'd use or interpret a certain type of expression (an assumption we will scrutinize below), it would be possible that her judgements just don't track the semantic facts (although they'd track her linguistic dispositions). Hence, the meta-externalist response to the found variation between Ws and EAs would be that at least one of the groups is getting the semantic facts wrong. On that account, semantic facts are as independent of intuitions as physical facts are. This view seems[10] to have obvious methodological consequences. Just as we shouldn't have much trust in our intuitions when it comes to matters of physics, we shouldn't have much trust in our intuitions when it comes to semantics.

One philosopher who seems to hold such a meta-externalist view is Michael Devitt. Devitt argues that the subject matter of semantics and linguistics is 'linguistic reality', the study of physical expression tokens and their semantic and grammatical properties (Devitt 2006). This reality should be distinguished from psychological reality. How the expression tokens get their properties seems to be a secondary question for him, and he allows that expression tokens get their semantic properties independently of the psychological states of the speaker at the time of the relevant utterance.

Other, perhaps clearer, examples of meta-externalist positions are theories of reference that assume that objective structures (for example, natural properties) can function as reference magnets for a speaker's expressions and thereby override the intentions of the speaker that pertain to the speaker's use of a term in her repertoire (including the absence of any intentions to use it for whatever the objective structures happen to be).[11]

Although meta-externalism seems to be endorsed by some radical first-order externalists, it is a rather implausible position. As argued in Cohnitz and Haukioja (2013), it leads to the possibility of 'semantic secrets'[12]; expressions might (systematically) 'refer' to objects that are irrelevant to the contents transmitted in communication. But if that can happen, then a theory of reference wouldn't systematically contribute to an explanation of successful linguistic communication. For the latter, it seems that reference must somehow be tied to certain psychological states of speakers, in particular to their dispositions to produce and interpret expressions in certain ways and to revise their usage systematically in light of new information.

Just consider a population like the EAs in the experiment reported by Machery et al. and assume that their judgements (formed in response to the probe) reveal their dispositions to use and interpret proper names and that these dispositions don't align with the semantic facts.[13] In that case, whenever the causal-historical-theory and the descriptivist theory make distinct predictions about the referent of a proper name in an utterance, the content communicated by the utterance (i.e. the content intended to be communicated and the content received) would be systematically different from the content assigned to the utterance by the true theory of reference (in this case, the causal-historical theory). It seems that the semantic properties ascribed by the theory of reference to the utterance tokens would be irrelevant to any explanation of how the content in question got communicated via the utterance. But what would be the point of such a theory?

On the basis of these considerations, the following definition of reference is suggested in (Cohnitz and Haukioja 2013):

> Reference: A token expression E refers in language L to object O iff (i) E is standing in the R-relation to O and (ii) competent speakers of L are disposed to interpret objects (of the type of O) to be the referents of expressions (of the type of E), if they believe these are connected by the R-relation.

If we follow this suggestion (assuming that the causal-historical theory is the correct first-order theory), then a certain token of the name "Angela Merkel" refers in English to the person Angela Merkel because Angela Merkel is at the other end of a causal-historical chain that leads up to the usage of that token, and speakers of English are disposed to interpret persons as the referents of proper names, if they believe that a name-token and a person stand in such a causal-historical relation.

Of course, speakers of English (unless they are particularly nerdy linguists or philosophers of language) do not form any beliefs about the exact causal-historical relations in which people stand to linguistic expression-tokens. What is required is that their usage, including their dispositions to correct their usage, is sensitive to information that happens to be about the causal-historical chain in question.

Thus, when confronted with a Gödel/Schmidt-case, we are disposed to interpret John's usage of the name "Gödel" as referring to the man who stole the manuscript when we learn the facts about the causal historical chain, rather than to interpret him as referring to Schmidt, the man who in fact proved the incompleteness of arithmetic. We are sensitive to information about the causal-historical chain in our interpretation dispositions rather than sensitive to information about the beliefs a person happens to have concerning the (purported) bearer of a name. We don't need to think at any point about any of this in terms of the R-relation, and so on.

Meta-Internalism is a theory about the subject matter of theories of reference and thus about the facts that determine which theory of reference is true. According to Meta-Internalism, these are facts about certain dispositions of competent speakers. Therefore, if we want to know which theory of reference is true, we should try to get information about those facts. That we should endorse Meta-Internalism rather than Meta-Externalism is grounded in our epistemological aim; we are interested in a theory that can make a systematic contribution to an explanation of linguistic communication. A Meta-Externalist theory doesn't seem to be fit for the job.

However, some authors who would agree that this is the role of theories of reference and that these are the facts that determine which theory of reference is true still disagree with the idea that in testing intuitive responses to hypothetical cases in philosophy of language we are studying the relevant intuitions. As explained in Section 2, Genoveva Martí believes that thought experiments in philosophy of language elicit meta-linguistic intuitions. But for all that is said so far, such intuitions shouldn't be very relevant for determining the truth about reference. In the next section we will consider whether Martí is right: what are the relevant intuitions in philosophy of language, and which intuitions are tested with Gödel/Schmidt-type thought experiments?

4. Semantic Intuitions

Let's consider a concrete example: the Gödel/Schmidt case described above and a hypothetical utterance (U) of John:

(U) Gödel was a brilliant mathematician.

What does "Gödel" refer to in this utterance? That's the kind of question that is typically raised in thought experiments in philosophy of language. A typical answer would be

(A) In John's utterance (U), "Gödel" refers to the man who stole the manuscript and claimed credit for the work.

In this case, what is the 'intuition'? An intuitive interpretation of the hypothetical utterance by John that we arrived at thanks to our linguistic competence? Or is it instead a spontaneous meta-linguistic judgement concerning the expression 'Gödel' that we arrived at on the basis of our everyday experience with the usage of proper names by competent speakers of English? Michael Devitt and Genoveva Martí claim that it is the latter (and thus that it is of little value for semantic theorizing). For example, in response to the experimental work by Machery et al., Genoveva Martí offers the following response:

> I think if we focus on the type of data that [the probes used by Machery et al.] are collecting, the 'semantic intuitions' that they elicit, we can see that the responses are not the kind of data that constitutes the input, the raw data that the semanticist relies on in order to start theorizing. Participants in the probes are told a fictional story about a community of speakers . . . Participants are then asked to hand down a judgement as to what the referent of a use of a

name by a hypothetical speaker member of the fictional community is. So, the participants are asked to tell us how they think the hypothetical speaker in question, and the rest of his community, uses names. Is that the evidence that we should rely on to construct a semantic theory? I think the answer is no. (Martí 2014, p. 22)

According to Martí, these intuitive judgements that are elicited by thought experiments like the Gödel case only inform us about how people think that they use language, but not about how they actually use language, and it is only the latter that matters for the semanticist. Therefore, the only real evidence that matters in linguistics and philosophy of language is data about use, collected by observing the theoretician's own linguistic behaviour and that of the linguistic community around her. A judgement like (A) at best informs us about the theoretical preferences of the test subjects:

> The Gödel story invites a reflection on use, it does not collect data on use; it is, hence, a theoretical tool, and Kripke uses it as such. And the responses of subjects to the Gödel story will, at best, tell us what theory they are disposed to find more natural as an explanation of how the hypothetical speaker, or they themselves, use language. But what theory people are more disposed to accept is not the input of the theory itself. (Martí 2014, p. 23)

But how do we know that a judgement like (A) is a theoretical judgement rather than evidence of a relevant bit of language use? How do we know that a response like (A) informs us at best about which theory of reference a speaker is disposed to favour rather than about how she is disposed to interpret an utterance like (U)?

Martí seems to think that this is obvious from the way the probe is phrased (at least she doesn't seem to offer any other evidence). Doesn't the question who John is talking about or the question to whom "Gödel" refers in (U) require reflections on use because, after all, these are questions about how another person uses a name?

This would be right only if interpretation wasn't part of use. But it obviously is. Linguistic competence with proper names isn't only a matter of producing sentences with proper names in the right way. It's also a matter of interpreting the use of proper names in the sentences of others. Presumably production and interpretation are just two sides of the same coin. Therefore the fact that the question asked in the probe concerned the utterance of a third person does not itself establish that the probes were collecting anything other than the relevant 'raw data'.

However, there seem to be two other considerations that speak in favour of the view held by Martí and Devitt. First of all, (A) is a meta-linguistic sentence, since it obviously speaks about language. The sentence contains the word "Gödel" in quotation marks, thus the sentence is (at least in part) about the word "Gödel". Furthermore, the sentence contains an expression from semantics ("refers to"). Therefore it seems plausible to think this sentence, inasmuch as it expresses a judgement, expresses a meta-linguistic judgement.

However, according to Devitt (2006), meta-linguistic judgements are independent of our linguistic competence. They are ordinary judgements that we arrive at on the basis of experience and background-knowledge (in this case, our experience with the way in which proper names are typically used by speakers of English and background knowledge we might perhaps have about linguistics and theories of reference). The only difference between these judgements and others is that the former are made with much greater spontaneity than the latter.

In (Cohnitz and Haukioja forthcoming) this view is discussed in some detail. There it is argued that we need to distinguish, first of all, between the results of dispositional competences and their reports. When we interpret an utterance in a context of utterance, we interpret the utterance and its component expressions intuitively. We are basically doing the same when interpreting (U) in the hypothetical context described above. What enables us to arrive at such interpretations, is our linguistic competence in English. Under certain conditions, we might also be able to report the results of such interpretations. What is required is that (a) the result is available to our consciousness, and (b) we master the concepts and expressions required for making such a report. If both, (a) and (b) are in place, we are able to report our intuitive interpretation of (U) and, in particular, our interpretation of the expression "Gödel" in (U), using the sentence (A).

In the case of semantic interpretations, i.e. our understanding of utterances and their parts, it seems plausible to assume that the results of these interpretations are available to consciousness. After all, these results, that is, our interpretations of what our interlocutors say in their utterances, enter into our inferences about what our interlocutors think and plan.

It also seems plausible that we master the relevant concepts and terms required to report our interpretations. Conversation about what other people have said and about whom they have said things forms a huge part of our everyday communication. Thus requirements (a) and (b) seem to be met for semantic interpretations.

This is already an important result. What seemed to speak in favour of the view championed by Devitt and Martí was that (A) was a metalinguistic sentence because (A) was about the word "Gödel" and (A) included semantic vocabulary. As we have seen now, whether (A) expresses a metalinguistic judgement in their sense is not so much a question of what the sentence is about but rather a matter of what cognitive process leads to the judgement expressed. As we have seen now, (A) could simply be a report of our intuitive interpretation of (U).

(A) could also be the result of a different cognitive process; namely the one described by Devitt and Martí. In this case we'd have a dispositional competence to make generalizations about the reference of expressions based on our observations of the usage of proper names in English. This acquired competence would allow us to make judgements about (U) that we'd report with sentences like (A).

In both cases, in reporting the intuitive interpretation or the metalinguistc judgement, it is possible to make mistakes. In the case of metalinguistic judgements, even if the judgement was reported without mistake, the methodological value and relevance of such judgements for the philosophy of language and linguistics depends on how good we are at making generalizations about linguistic usage based on our everyday experience. One can probably follow Devitt and Martí in thinking that this value is not very high.

For reports of intuitive interpretations, things look different. If the report is accurate and there are no other reasons to assume that our interpretation was not produced by our linguistic competence, then (A) is not only relevant for philosophy of language, but it reports the kind of facts that constitute the very subject matter of theories of reference.

But besides the observation that (A) is a meta-linguistic sentence, Devitt (2011) has a second argument for the claim that (A) expresses a meta-linguistic judgement that doesn't report the output of linguistic competence but instead something independent of it. Devitt cites empirical evidence from developmental psychology that we acquire the relevant meta-linguistic concepts relatively late in our cognitive development and that we are able to make judgements like (A) only a considerable time after we have already acquired (otherwise) complete linguistic competence.

But here Devitt overlooks the fact that this result is entirely compatible with the Meta-Internalist view. Of course, it might well be the case that it is only relatively late in our linguistic and cognitive development that we are able to report our semantic interpretations or parts of them with sentences like (A). But this doesn't provide us with any reason to doubt the view that these reports are reports of the outputs of our linguistic competence rather than reports of an independent observation of our linguistic environment. For example, the ability to visually recognize certain objects in our environment precedes our ability to report what we have recognized. The same could easily hold for our ability to report outputs of our linguistic competence.

Thus, there remains nothing that would speak in favour of Devitt's and Martí's view that the intuitive judgements that serve as evidence in philosophy of language are spontaneous judgements based on linguistic experience. Instead, these judgements are plausibly reports of the interpretation-outputs of linguistic competence.

However, the fact that Devitt and Martí misunderstand these judgements and their proper content is still cause for concern. If there are two distinct processes that can both lead to utterances of (A), and if philosophy of language should really only be interested in one of them, then there is at least the danger that the data (judgements of the form of (A)) are ambiguous. How are we supposed to know that test-subjects would judge that (A) is true on the basis of their linguistic competence, if even experts like Devitt and Martí misunderstand the task?

Moreover, it was speculated above that the reliability with which sentences like (A) report interpretations of sentences like (U) depends in part on how entrenched the relevant metalinguistic concepts and terms are in the idiolect of the test-subject. Perhaps philosophers of language are better at reporting such interpretations than the ordinary folk that Machery et al. tested.

As was said in the beginning, there is also the further problem that (A) can be ambiguous in a second way when it comes to the evaluation of the Gödel/Schmidt-case. It was argued that there might be an ambiguity between the semantic referent of "Gödel" and the speaker referent of John's utterance. In the next section we will look at ways to get around these two problems by refining the standard methodology of philosophy of language.

5. How philosophy could learn from psycholinguistics

Let us first consider possible solutions to the problem of how we could figure out which cognitive process has in fact lead to a certain judgement. *Prima facie* one might think that we are faced with a methodological dilemma. We want to know how competent speakers understand a hypothetical utterance. But we can't just look into their heads, so we need to ask them how they understood it. However, as we have just seen, those questions and their answers seem to be meta-linguistic in the sense that these questions or judgements are about linguistic expressions and in addition make use of semantic vocabulary. Doesn't that lead unavoidably to our methodological problem; namely, that we don't know whether the test person informed us in her answer about her semantic interpretation (which is what we are interested in), or rather about what her lay-theory of proper name reference predicts for this case (which we don't care much about)?

Luckily, this isn't a real dilemma. First of all, we could investigate the interpretations we are interested in without asking the test subjects. For example, we could investigate them indirectly by observing the later behaviour of the test subjects, in particular in situations in which relevant differences in interpretation would lead to observable differences in behaviour. From that, one might be able to infer, under appropriate circumstances, the information (if any) that the test subject extracted from an utterance – either about the world or the speaker.

Of course, it would be even better if we didn't need to use such an indirect methodology (i.e. one that might introduce new ambiguities). In fact, it is indeed possible, at least when it comes to reference, to study the interpretation of linguistic expressions directly. To see how this could be done, we need to look at psycholinguistics and the methods used therein to investigate the resolution of referring expressions.

When psycholinguists investigate, for example, the resolution of anaphoric reference, they often use eye-trackers, that is, instruments that allow experimenters to track the eye-movement of a test subject. Initially this method was used to see how eyes move in reading-comprehension tasks. For our purposes, the more interesting work in psycholinguistics is that performed in studies described by Karabanov et al. (2007). In these experiments, test-subjects are confronted with two stimuli: the auditory stimulus is a spoken text (which contains in this case anaphoric pronouns) and a visual stimulus, in our case a picture of a pseudo-natural market-day situation built up with Playmobil™ toy characters.

In the experiment described by Karabanov et al. (2007), the linguistic stimulus was the following German sentence:

> Heute ist Markt im Dorf. Die Marktfrau streitet mit dem Arbeiter. Sie sagt jetzt gerade, daß er kein' Ärger machen und das neue Fahrrad zurückgeben soll, das er sich geliehen hat. [It's market day in the village. The market woman is quibbling with the worker. She's just saying that he should not make any trouble and should give the new bike back that he borrowed.] (Karabanov et al 2007, p. 211)

There are several theories about the resolution of pronouns that differ with respect to the postulated cognitive processes involved in their interpretation. For example, the theory of Morton Gernsbacher (1989) assumes the interpretation of anaphoric pronouns to be a two-step process. First the antecedent of the pronoun is identified and then, in a second step, the connection to the referent of the antecedent is established. The theory by Lorraine Tyler and William Marslen-Wilson (1982), however, holds that pronouns are immediately interpreted referentially, just like full lexical NPs or proper names. This difference in postulated cognitive processes should (or, in any case, might) lead to empirically testable differences: on the view suggested by Gernsbacher the interpretation of an anaphoric pronoun would seem to require more time than the interpretation of a full lexical NP, while on Tyler and Marslen-Wilson's theory, the resolution of an anaphoric pronoun should take as much time as that of a full lexical NP.

In the eye-tracking experiment by Karabanov et al., it is assumed that eye-movement (or more specifically, the probability by which the eyes of the test-subject will fixate on a certain point in the visual scene) is directly correlated with the interpretation of a heard linguistic item. That makes it possible to compare the times it takes for the fixation probabilities for a certain item in the visual field to increase and relate these times to the type of expression interpreted. Does it take longer for the fixation probability for the referent of an anaphoric pronoun to increase than it does for the referent of a full lexical NP? Karabanov et al. found no time difference (which they took to speak in favour of the theory by Tyler and Marslen-Wilson).

This empirical result itself is (for our purposes) not so interesting. What is interesting about this experiment is the fact that we can use eye-trackers to measure the interpretation of referential expressions without having possible problematic metalinguistic considerations taint the data. Our eye-movements are involuntary and automatic. The causally relevant cognitive process is that of interpreting the sentence. Other potential influences (like the relative salience of an object in the visual field) can be controlled for in the experiment.

That way we possess at least one instrument for measuring the interpretation of referential expressions by competent speakers that is immune to Devitt's methodological worries. Philosophers of language could make use of this tool in two ways. First, one could test theories of reference directly on test subjects, given that these theories make different predictions about the referent of an expression (under certain contextual circumstances). This would presuppose that different theories of reference always make different predictions that can be turned into measurable tasks. This, presumably, is not always the case. However, we could use this methodology also for the calibration of our ordinary armchair methodology. Devitt's worries aren't automatically relevant when cognitive processes other than linguistic interpretation lead to the metalinguistic judgements in question. They are only relevant if these other cognitive processes would lead to different judgements. If it could be shown that our judgements about the reference of a term in a hypothetical utterance and our interpretations as measured by the eye-tracker coincide with high reliability, then Devitt's worries should be simply irrelevant.

The method described could also be helpful in a second sense. We said above (when discussing objection 2.2 against the experiment by Machery et al.) that the responses to the Gödel/Schmidt-probe suffered from a second ambiguity. Consider again the relevant test questions:

> When John uses the name "Gödel", is he talking about: (A) the person who really discovered the incompleteness of arithmetic? or (B) the person who got hold of the manuscript and claimed credit for the work?

It was ambiguous whether the question is about who John intends to refer to with his usage of "Gödel", or instead about who John in fact and objectively refers to with that term.

Indeed, in a later experiment, Justin Sytsma and Jonathan Livengood showed that intra-cultural[14] variation disappears when the final question is changed to the following:

> Clarified Narrator's Perspective: Having read the above story and accepting that it is true, when John uses the name "Gödel", would you take him to actually be talking about: (A) the person who (unbeknownst to John) really discovered the incompleteness of arithmetic? Or, (B) the person who is widely believed to have discovered the incompleteness of arithmetic, but actually got hold of the manuscript and claimed credit for the work? (Sytsma and Livengood 2011, p. 324)

The amount of B-answers increased from 39.4 per cent (for the original question that was used in the study by Machery et al. 2004) to over 73 per cent for the 'clarified narrator's perspective'. This suggests that the variation detected by Machery et al. (at least the intra-cultural one) was due to the ambiguity in perspective in the final question.

However, even the clarified narrator's perspective contains a residual ambiguity. If I know that John believes that Gödel proved the incompleteness of arithmetic and know that John is good at mathematics and knows nothing else about Gödel, then I might think that John intends to (and does) talk about the guy who proved the incompleteness of arithmetic. In order to eliminate this ambiguity one could rephrase the question, using precise semantic vocabulary, thereby again increasing the probability for tainting the data with metalinguistic considerations.

Perhaps the eye-tracking methodology described above could help us also here.[15] As Keysar, Lin and Barr (2003) report, the pragmatic interpretation of an utterance, which takes into account the perspective and knowledge of the speaker/interlocutor, is delayed in comparison to the literal interpretation of an utterance. In one of their experiments, a test situation was arranged such that the test subject (the participant) and a second person (the confederate) were sitting at opposite sides of a table. The test subject could see more items on the table than the other subject and was aware that she could see those other things and that the other person didn't even know these other things were on the table. Nevertheless, when tracking the eye-movements of the participant, it turned out that the fixation probability for those hidden objects increased first when they were better candidates for being the semantic referents of the expressions used by the confederate, while the fixation probabilities for the speaker referents was, by comparison, delayed.

For example, in one instance of such an experiment the participant was asked to secretly hide a roll of tape in a paper bag and to store it at a location visible to her but invisible to the confederate. However, there was a cassette visible to both the confederate and the participant. While monitoring the eye-movements of the participant, Keysar, Lin and Barr found that in many cases in which the confederate instructed the participant to 'move the tape', the eye-movements of the participant revealed that she had first interpreted the referent of "the tape" to be the best semantic candidate (the hidden roll of tape in the box) rather than the only possible speaker referent (the mutually visible cassette). The interpretation of "the tape" as having the intended (speaker) referent occurred with a time delay.

These results suggest that eye-tracking can be used to discriminate between speaker reference and semantic reference, again without involving any problematic meta-linguistic questions or judgements. This interpretation also seems to be consistent with more recent experiments reported in Barr (2008), which show that although listeners in a conversation expect speakers to refer to objects in the common ground (accessible or visible to both), they are unable to reduce interference from 'privileged competitors', that is from better semantic referents that are not in the common ground (Barr 2008). Again, this suggests that eye movement is primarily responsive to semantic interpretation (and only with a delay, is it responsive to the pragmatic integration of knowledge of common ground).[16] To be clear, this interpretation of the experimental results, although consistent with them, hasn't been tested yet (as far as I know). But if this hypothesis holds up, then eye tracking would provide us with a further method to study the relevant 'raw data' (to use Martí's expression) at the level of interpretation in a more reliable way than the usual method wherein test subjects are asked to report their interpretations of hypothetical utterances.

6. Conclusions

We have seen that, if certain assumptions are made about the explanatory aims of philosophy of language and about the nature of reference as it should feature in those explanatory aims, we can investigate philosophical methodology and arrive at recommendations for an improved methodology. We then know what we need to examine, how we could check the reliability of our methods, and consider improvements.

However, the assumptions we started from, (viz. the idea that theories of reference should systematically contribute to explanations of successful linguistic communication) and the consequences these had for Meta-Internalism, are specific to this particular sub-area of philosophy. Perhaps they are even specific to this area of philosophy of language. There might well be another inquiry into 'reference', which doesn't start with a primary interest in communication but perhaps with a primary interest in representation, or perhaps information, and such a project might encumber different methodological commitments.[17]

However that may be, it should be clear that one can't just generalize the methodological insights here described to all other areas of philosophy without first proving that the same assumptions we made about theories of reference also hold for these other areas. As I tried to explain in the introduction, *prima facie*, there is currently no reason to think that they do.

Notes

* I would like to thank Alex Davies, Jussi Haukioja and Edouard Machery for helpful comments on an earlier version of this text. Research for this chapter was supported by the following research grants: SFLFI11085E, ETF9083, SF0180110S08 and IUT20-5.

Some of the ideas presented here are discussed in somewhat more detail in Cohnitz 2014, and a lot of it is based on work that was carried out with Jussi Haukioja, as with our (2013) and (forthcoming). However, the present chapter contains a more careful discussion of Genoveva Martí's recent criticism of experimental philosophy (Martí 2014) and further suggestions pertaining to how empirical methods could be put to use in philosophy of language. Thus readers familiar with the arguments in this earlier work can fast-forward to Sections 4 and 5.

1. Although the notion itself seems to be a rather recent invention, and the discussion has developed systematically only in the past decade, PhilPapers, the most comprehensive index and bibliography of philosophy, already has a top-level category "Metaphilosophy".
2. Of course, there have always been metaphilosophical contributions and discussions. Another unfortunate aspect of the discussion in the past decade is that it appears not to be informed by what has been written on the subject before that decade.
3. Even if we restrict – as I do throughout the chapter – philosophy to analytic philosophy.
4. In this chapter, the focus will be on the discussion of the methodological value of intuitions that resulted from this chapter. For an overview of the development of experimental philosophy of language in general, see Genone (2012) and Hansen (forthcoming).
5. Cf. Stich (in preparation).
6. Cf. Machery et al. (2013) for a response.
7. Cf. Machery (2012) for a response.
8. Cf. Machery et al. (2009) for a response.
9. Cf. Machery et al. (forthcoming) for a response.
10. Of course, the Meta-Externalist view might also be compatible with the reliability of our intuitions, if we assume that we are sufficiently attuned to the linguistic facts. However, in light of the empirical results, the Meta-Externalist would at least have reason to doubt that we (or, in any case, lay speakers) are sufficiently attuned. Thanks to Edouard Machery for pressing me on this.
11. See Schwarz (2013) for a discussion of such views.
12. The term was introduced in Schwarz (2013).
13. On that account, what we should say about the cultural variation found in the study by Machery et al. (2004) is that the Ws get it largely right how proper names work, while the EAs get it largely wrong.
14. However, the inter-cultural variation could be replicated. Cf. Sytsma et al. (forthcoming).
15. I owe the idea that eye-tracking could be used for distinguishing speaker and semantic referent to Manuel Garcia-Carpintero.

16 A curious finding by Wu and Keysar (2007) is that, apparently, listeners from a Chinese background (when listening to Chinese) show less interference from privileged referents than listeners from an English-speaking American background. This is curious, because it would be consistent with the original findings in Machery et al. 2004 and could perhaps (partly) explain the found cultural variation.

17 I don't think that that's in fact the case for reference. But it seems to me that the fact that Devitt's thinking about linguistic meaning departs from considerations about how we can extract information about the world from linguistic items, rather than from considerations about how we manage to communicate with language, explains to some extent why he believes that we can study linguistic reality in ignorance of the psychological basis of reference (cf. Devitt and Sterelny 1999).

References

Barr, D. J. (2008), 'Pragmatic expectations and linguistic evidence: Listeners anticipate but do not integrate common ground'. *Cognition,* 109, 18–40.

Bealer, G. (1996), 'A priori knowledge and the scope of philosophy'. *Philosophical Studies,* 81, 121–142.

Cappelen, H. (2012), *Philosophy without Intuitions*. Oxford: Oxford University Press.

Cappelen, H. and Winblad, D. G. (1999) '"Reference" externalized and the role of intuitions in semantic theory'. *American Philosophical Quarterly,* 36, 337–350.

Carnap, R. (1950), *Logical Foundations of Probability*. Chicago, IL: University of Chicago Press.

Deutsch, M. (2009), 'Experimental philosophy and the theory of reference'. *Mind and Language,* 24, 445–466.

Cohnitz, D. (2014), 'Experimentelle sprachphilosophie', in T. Grundmann, J. Horvath and J. Kipper (eds), *Die Experimentelle Philosophie in der Diskussion*. Berlin: Suhrkamp, pp. 235–258.

Cohnitz, D. and Haukioja, J. (2013), 'Meta-externalism vs meta-internalism in the study of reference'. *Australasian Journal of Philosophy,* 91, 475–500.

Cohnitz, D. and Haukioja, J. (forthcoming), 'Intuitions in philosophical semantics'. *Erkenntnis*.

Devitt, M. (1981), *Designation*. New York: Columbia University Press.

Devitt, M. (2006), *Ignorance of Language*. Oxford: Oxford University Press.

Devitt, M. (2011), 'Whither experimental semantics', *Theoria,* 72, 5–36.

Devitt, M. (2011a), 'Experimental semantics', *Philosophy and Phenomenological Research,* LXXXII, 418–435.

Devitt, M. and Sterelny, K. (1999), *Language and Reality: An Introduction to the Philosophy of Language* (2nd edn). Oxford: Blackwell Publishers.

Genone, J. (2012), 'Theories of reference and experimental philosophy'. *Philosophy Compass*, 7, 152–163.

Gernsbacher, M. A. (1989), 'Mechanisms that improve referential access'. *Cognition*, 32, 99–156.

Hansen, N. (forthcoming), 'Experimental philosophy of language'. *Oxford Handbooks Online*.

Karabanov, A. et al. (2007), 'Eye tracking as a tool to investigate the comprehension of referential expressions', in S. Featherston and W. Sternefeld (eds), *Roots: Linguistics in Search of its Evidential Base*. Berlin: DeGruyter, pp. 207–226.

Keysar, B. et al. (2003), 'Limits on theory of mind use in adults'. *Cognition*, 89, 25–41.

Kripke, S. (1980), *Naming and Necessity*. Boston, MA: Harvard University Press.

Machery, E. (2012), 'Expertise and intuitions about reference'. *Theoria*, 73, 37–54.

Machery, E. (2014), 'What is the significance of the demographic variation in semantic intuitions?', in E. O'Neill and E. Machery (eds), *Current Controversies in Experimental Philosophy*. New York and London: Routledge, pp. 3–16.

Machery, E. et al. (2004), 'Semantics, cross-cultural style'. *Cognition*, 92, B1–B12.

Machery, E. et al. (2009), 'Linguistic and metalinguistic intuitions in the philosophy of language'. *Analysis*, 69, 689–694.

Machery, E. et al. (2013), 'If intuitions vary, then so what?'. *Philosophy and Phenomenological Research*, 86, 618–635.

Machery, E., et al. (forthcoming), 'Speaker's reference and cross-cultural semantics', in A. Bianchi (ed.), *On Reference*. Oxford: Oxford University Press.

Mallon, R. et al. (2009), 'Against arguments from reference'. *Philosophy and Phenomenological Research*, LXXIX, 332–356.

Marslen-Wilson, W. and Tyler. L. K. (1987), 'Against modularity', in J. L. Garfield (ed.), *Modularity in Knowledge Representation and Natural Language Understanding*, Boston, MA: MIT Press, pp. 37–62.

Martí, G. (2014), 'Reference and experimental semantics', in E. O'Neill and E. Machery (eds), *Current Controversies in Experimental Philosophy*. New York and London: Routledge, pp. 17–26.

Martí, G. (2009), 'Against semantic multi-culturalism'. *Analysis*, 69, 42–48.

Nisbett, R. (2003), *The Geography of Thought: How Asians and Westerners Think Differently . . . and Why*. New York: Free Press.

Nisbett, R. et al. (2001), 'Culture and systems of thought: Holistic vs. analytic cognition'. *Psychological Review*, 108, 291–310.

Schwarz, W. (2013), 'Against magnetism'. *Australasian Journal of Philosophy*, 92, 17–36.

Stich, S. (in preparation), 'Experimental philosophy and the bankruptcy of the great tradition'.

Sytsma, J. and Livengood, J. (2011), 'A new perspective concerning experiments on semantic intuitions'. *Australasian Journal of Philosophy*, 89, 315–332.

Sytsma, J. M. et al. (forthcoming), 'Gödel in the land of the rising sun'. *Review of Philosophy and Psychology*.

Weinberg, J. (2007), 'How to challenge intuitions empirically without risking skepticism'. *Midwest Studies in Philosophy,* XXXI, 318–343.
Williamson, T. (2007), *The Philosophy of Philosophy*. Oxford: Oxford University Press.
Wu, S. and Keysar, B. (2007), 'The effect of culture on perspective taking'. *Psychological Science,* 18, 600–606.

6

Experimental Semantics: The Case of Natural Kind Terms[*]

Sören Häggqvist and Åsa Wikforss

Introduction

Recent experimental work on judgements about reference has given rise to wide-ranging debates. But these debates have focused almost exclusively on the putative impact on theorizing about names. Natural kind terms have by and large received what might be called the 'Cinderella treatment'. One principal aim here is to redress this neglect and see which, if any, conclusions should be drawn concerning them from experimental work so far. Another, connected, aim is to assess when and where different sorts of empirical evidence properly enter in semantic theorizing. Finally, we shall briefly consider (and lament) the status of the armchair case for current orthodoxy regarding natural kind terms.

The paper has three parts. In the first, we briefly try to sort out the general dialectic surrounding semantics and experimental philosophy established by Machery, Mallon, Nichols and Stich (2004) – hereafter "MMNS 2004". In the second part, we attempt to disentangle certain ambiguities of the label "semantic theory" and discuss the extent to which different kinds of empirical evidence are relevant for different levels of theorizing. The final section first considers the armchair arguments motivating Kripke's rejection of descriptivism, as a semantic theory for natural kind terms; then we consider the empirical evidence concerning such terms – both from the experimental literature and from history of science. In our estimate, available empirical evidence poses a serious challenge to Kripke's account of the semantics of natural kind terms and lends some support to cluster theories for these terms.

1. The origins of recent debates

MMNS 2004 offered tentative evidence that intuitions about reference vary with culture.[1] It suggested that this is true for intuitions of professional philosophers as well as for the participants in the study (MMNS 2004, p. B9). And it attempted to stir philosophers of language out of methodological complacency: instead of relying on their own, partly culture-induced and non-universal, intuitions, they should get out of the armchair. At the same time, MMNS 2004 assumed that philosophy of language relies on evidence consisting precisely of intuitions concerning reference in cases like those used in their study:

> There is widespread agreement among philosophers on the methodology for developing an adequate theory of reference. The project is to construct theories of reference that are consistent with our intuitions about the correct application of terms in fictional (and non-fictional) situations. (MMNS 2004, p. B3)

Now although the paper's target is obviously methodological, it is not clear that the method described above is really under attack. The authors suggest that results of the type they predicted (and found) "would raise questions about whose intuitions are going to count, putting in jeopardy philosophers' methodology" (p. B4). But what is jeopardized, it seems, is the assumption of universality rather than the basic method – which itself, one might note, seems sketched almost to the point of caricature: mere *consistency* with intuitions appears a remarkably low standard for a "theory of reference".

In Mallon, Machery, Nichols and Stich (2009) – henceforth "MMNS 2009" – the methodology to which they hold philosophers of language committed is called "the method of cases":

> *The method of cases:* The correct theory of reference for a class of terms T is the theory which is best supported by the intuitions competent users of T have about the reference of members of T across actual and possible cases. (MMNS 2009, p. 338)

Here the bar is, more plausibly, raised from mere consistency to actual support. But in this paper, the principal target are so-called arguments from reference: attempts to 'derive philosophically significant conclusions from the assumption of one or another theory of reference' (MMNS 2009, p. 332). Although the authors list – as one option open to philosophers in light of their results – the possibility of downplaying or giving up the method of cases, they don't advocate this but on the contrary "remain skeptical of the proposal to downplay the role of the method of cases in choosing a theory of reference" (MMNS 2009, p. 343). Moreover, they state that "we have no idea what other considerations philosophers of language might appeal to" (MMNS 2009, p. 343).[2] So if their aim all along was, as reported in Machery, Mallon, Nichols and Stich (2013, p. 621), to condemn the method of cases, they were somewhat coy about this. And insofar as they wanted to condemn it while simultaneously insisting on its unavoidability, they would surely be guilty of inflicting an odd double bind on theorists.

Below, we'll try to sort out what methodological elbow room may be open on various construals of "theory of reference". We shall suggest that while some construals make the theory more immediately amenable to empirical testing, along the lines of 'the method of cases', all construals require a mix of empirical and theoretical considerations.

2. Experimental semantics

2.1 The theory of reference

What, precisely, is 'the theory of reference'? In what sense is it an empirical theory? It is important, here, to keep distinct different types of semantic theories, sometimes conflated in the literature.

The first important distinction concerns that between *descriptive semantics* and *metasemantics* (sometimes called "foundational semantics").[3] Descriptive semantics tells us something about the *semantic content* of a term: whether it is equivalent to a set of descriptions, or whether it is directly referential, etc. Semantic theories in this sense include traditional descriptivism, the cluster theory, versions of two-dimensionalism and Millianism (among others). Metasemantic theories, by contrast, tell us something about *the facts in virtue of which* a term has a certain semantic value. Use theories of meaning, causal theories, social externalism and internalism are all metasemantic theories in this sense. Thus, a use theory appeals to the individual speaker's dispositions to use a term, whereas social externalism emphasizes the practice of the linguistic community and causal theories the role of the physical environment in the determination of meaning and reference.

Although descriptive semantics and meta-semantics are related there is no one-one relation. For instance, even if descriptivism is typically coupled with some version of a metasemantic use theory, it is quite possible to combine a descriptivist semantics with an externalist metasemantics.[4] And while

Millianism may invite some sort of causal metasemantic theory (which perhaps explains why Millianism and causal theories are so often conflated), the details of this metasemantic theory are up for grabs. Is a purely causal theory required? Or do we need a mixed version, in which speaker intentions contribute to determining reference? This illustrates that metasemantic theories are more theoretically committed than descriptive semantics, a point we shall stress below.

With this distinction in place, we can address the central question what role, if any, empirical evidence does play. Construed as a descriptive semantic theory, the theory of reference is a straightforwardly empirical theory. After all, construed that way, it is a theory concerning the semantic content of a given language L, as used by a speaker (or a group of speakers) at a given time. To determine which such theory is true of L empirical evidence is required. However, even within descriptive semantics it is useful to distinguish between a less theoretically committed version and a more theoretically committed one.

The less committed theory, let us call it a 'weak semantic theory', is simply one that tries to get the referents and extensions of singular and general terms in L straight. Such a theory is obviously closely tied to the relevant evidence (such as facts about use), but even here there is a gap between the evidence and the theory. After all, people make mistakes, and the theory has to take this into account. Therefore, some apparent evidence provided by use may have to be written off. The task of the philosopher, then, is to provide some principle that serves to map facts about use on to meanings, allowing us to determine what counts as an error and what does not.[5] Even when it comes to weak semantic theories, therefore, there are important theoretical commitments involved. Nevertheless, the theory as a whole must be based on empirical facts about the speaker use.

A more committed version of descriptive semantics – 'strong semantic theory' – goes further, and assigns semantic content in accordance with theories such as the Millian theory or some version of descriptivism. This is one more step removed from the evidence, since it is possible for both Millians and descriptivists to accept the same weak semantics. That is, they may agree on the truth conditions of sentences as used by a speaker (even 'across possible worlds') but disagree on what semantic theory best accounts for these truth conditions. Indeed, the versions of descriptivism that emerged after Kripke typically tried to accommodate his claims about the reference of proper names, for instance by appealing to rigidified descriptions.[6] It should be clear that this is a kind of disagreement that cannot be settled by further evidence from speaker use. Other types of considerations have to be marshalled here, such as various theories' explanatory power vis-a-vis phenomena like co-referring or empty names. Arguably, other sorts of empirical evidence are also relevant, such as findings within developmental psychology or cognitive science.

Next, moving on to metasemantics, we are one step further removed from the empirical evidence. Since the correct semantic theory (weak and strong) does not by itself dictate a certain metasemantic theory, general epistemological and metaphysical considerations will play an important role here. One example is the debate concerning self-knowledge and semantic externalism, where many philosophers accept that if they are incompatible, we should question the externalist metasemantics. Nevertheless, metasemantics too must be considered an empirical theory, constrained by speakers' application of terms, both to actual and hypothetical cases (such as Twin Earth cases). So while metasemantic theories are less directly connected to the empirical evidence, and more dependent on general philosophical considerations, they are clearly empirical theories, subject to falsification.[7]

How do MMNS construe "theory of reference"? Are they testing weak semantic theories, strong semantic theories or metasemantic theories? This, unfortunately, is not clear. The talk about descriptivism and the focus on Kripke's Gödel-case suggests that their concern is with weak and strong semantic theories. After all, Kripke appeals to intuitions concerning the counterfactual story about Gödel, in order to show that proper names are rigid and to provide evidence against descriptivism in support of Millianism. At the same time, MMNS claim to be testing the *causal-historical view*, not Millianism (2004, pp. B4–B5); and this, as we saw, is a metasemantic theory.[8] However, as stressed above, there is only a loose connection between Gödel-style intuitions and the causal-historical theory. Before a purely causal theory could be said to be supported, for instance, it would first have to be shown that the semantic theory that best accounts for the Gödel-intuition is Millianism, rather than some version of rigidified descriptivism or two-dimensionalism. Then it would have to be shown that the metasemantic theory that best accounts for Millianism is a pure causal-historical theory, rather than some mixed theory (appealing to speaker intentions in addition to causal links). The connection between the empirical evidence and the theory of reference, understood as a metasemantic theory, is therefore less close than MMNS (2004) and MMNS (2009) appear to hold.

This unclarity underlies some of the current disputes over their experiments. Thus, Martí (2009) has argued that the experiments carried out are flawed and do not prove what they purport to prove, since they test subjects' meta-linguistic judgements.[9] Martí is surely right to draw attention to the fact that MMNS are asking speakers to make meta-linguistic judgements concerning what they think a term refers to. If the aim is to determine the correct semantic theory for a class of terms, it would seem more relevant to consider how speakers in fact apply these terms. But, as noted above, the aim of MMNS (2004) was to examine judgements supposed to be indicative of people's theories of how their terms refer, their 'folk-psychological metasemantics'. To this extent, Martí's objection misfires, as Devitt (2011, p. 428, n. 8) notes. At the same time, there is something strange about the project understood this way. Why should we expect ordinary people to have views, even implicit ones, on *how their terms refer*? The parallel with Chomskian theory tentatively broached by MMNS (2004, p. 88) does not hold up: even if it is accepted that ordinary speakers have an implicit semantic theory, guiding their use of language, it is quite different to claim that ordinary speakers have an implicit *metasemantic* theory.

If MMNS really aimed to test *semantic* theories (as they sometimes seem to claim), then Martí's objection would be justified: to test semantic theories (weak and strong), what would seem to be needed is the whole artillery of tests that linguists employ, including corpus studies and elicited production. As for judgements, we should rely simply on first-order judgements involving the application of proper names to individuals and the use of general terms in categorization tasks, not reflexive judgements *about* the use of terms.[10]

Another objection to MMNS (2004) can be found in Deutsch (2009). According to Deutsch, the very idea that intuitions play an important role in semantics is simply a mistake: What matters is philosophical *theorizing*, not intuitions.[11] Kripke's arguments against descriptivism, Deutsch argues, simply rely on counterexamples, not on intuitions. For instance, that "Gödel" refers to Gödel, not to Schmidt, is a counterexample to this theory since descriptivism predicts that "Gödel" applies to Schmidt (in these circumstances). But when Deutsch suggests that the philosopher can take for granted facts about reference, he is in effect suggesting that she needn't worry at all about the first step, that of determining the weak semantic theory. The problem here is that even if some meta-linguistic claims may seem too trivial to require any empirical evidence – such as the statement that "Gödel" refers to Gödel – they are nevertheless empirical claims and as such they do, ultimately, depend on empirical evidence.[12] And when we move to general terms, including natural kind terms, this step is more controversial as well as more theoretically involved. For example, the claim that "water" only has H_2O in its extension cannot be presented as a counterexample to descriptivism unless we have already been given some reasons to think that "water" only has H_2O in its extension. This is far from trivial.

2.2 The expertise defence

Much of the evidence adduced by experimental philosophers (including MMNS 2004) concerns lay persons, not philosophers. Hence the claim that it threatens traditional philosophical methodology is vulnerable to the objection that responses, intuitions or opinions of laypeople are not the relevant evidence in the first place. This objection, made by several writers, often uses analogies with other disciplines. For instance, Devitt writes: "We don't do physics, biology, or economics simply by consulting people's intuitions. Why should semantics be different?" (Devitt 2011, p. 424).[13]

We have stressed that doing semantics is never a matter simply of constructing a theory "consistent with our intuitions about the correct application of terms", as MMNS (2004, p. B3) suggest. Even when it comes to weak semantics, theoretical virtues and general philosophical considerations must be brought to bear. This arguably takes expertise. However, it is one thing to recognize this point, quite another to suggest that ordinary intuitions are irrelevant or less weighty than expert intuitions. Since semantic theories are *empirical* theories, contingently true of a group of speakers at a time, there is simply no possibility of doing semantics without evidence provided by speaker use. Whatever the merits of the expertise defence in other areas, it is of limited value when it comes to semantics.

It is sometimes suggested that the trouble with the expertise defence in the case of semantics concerns the assumption that expert intuitions are more reliable because they are the product of better theories. *Linguistic* intuitions, it is argued, reflect the linguistic competence of the speaker and it makes no sense to assume that the philosopher has a greater linguistic competence than the ordinary speaker (MMNS 2013, p. 627). However, we do not think it is very helpful to speak of linguistic intuitions as merely reflecting the linguistic competence of the speaker. How we apply our terms is of course in part a reflection of our linguistic competence but equally a reflection of our general knowledge and background beliefs, and it does not seem possible to peel off a part of this use as being an expression specifically of the speaker's 'linguistic competence'. For this reason, it is quite possible that the better one's theory in a particular area, the more reliable are one's 'intuitions' about how the relevant term applies. Thus, the philosophers have a greater competence when it comes to philosophical terminology, just as the biologists do when it comes to biological terminology; for instance, in order to understand the semantics of 'tiger', as used in the common language, it makes sense to pay attention to how biologists use this term in biological classification.

This is not to deny that there may be semantically relevant variation between the lay use of kind terms and the experts' use of these terms. However, the very point of the Kripke-Putnam account of natural kind terms is precisely that our everyday use of these terms is *continuous* with their use within science, and that what the terms ultimately "pick out", supposedly determined by the essence of the kind, is a matter for science to adjudicate.[14] If so, the intuitions that carry weight are those of the relevant scientists, not of the philosophers.

It might be suggested that even if this is so, there is reason, when it comes to certain types of semantic intuitions, to trust the philosophers more than the layperson. Devitt (2011), for example, suggests that when it comes to *modal* intuitions, these are likely to be more reliable if the subject has reflected on metaphysical matters, such as the essence of individuals or the essence of natural kinds, and so "the intuitions we need are ones from people with some expertise in these matters, presumably metaphysicians and other philosophers" (Devitt 2011, p. 427). Since arguments for or against Millianism depend crucially on evidence provided by intuitions about what is possible, what is necessary, and what would be the case in various hypothetical scenarios, expert intuitions will play a decisive role, if Devitt is right.

Now, it is clear that it is an open question to what extent the modal intuitions of non-experts are reliable. But the fact that there is a great deal of variation in important modal intuitions among philosophers suggests that these intuitions are not entirely reliable when held by experts either (assuming the language is shared).[15] Moreover, to the extent that Devitt is right and we need to have done metaphysics in order to have modal intuitions, the value of these intuitions as evidence for the semantic theory decreases. For example, if my modal intuitions about gold or water require a theory concerning the essences of natural kinds, then these intuitions run a real risk of being theory driven, as Devitt explicitly thinks they are. If so, we should handle modal intuitions with care rather than accepting them as theory independent evidence for semantics.[16]

Again, none of this is to deny that general philosophical considerations matter when doing semantics. For the same reason, the mere fact that there is variation in speaker judgements does not immediately imply that there is a semantic variation. Philosophical theory plays a central role when constructing the semantic theory (even a weak one) out of the materials provided by speaker use. What is wrong with the expertise defence, it seems to us, is not the idea that expertise matters, but the idea that when it comes to basic applications of terms, the philosopher's intuitions carry greater evidential weight than those of the non-experts. We now turn to the case of natural kind terms, where it has been widely assumed that we can do semantics from the armchair.

3. Natural kind terms and empirical evidence

3.1 Kripke's armchair intuitions

Kripke's main target in the case of proper names was the cluster theory. He does not merely argue against definitionalist versions of descriptivism, but follows Mill and argues against the very idea that proper names have descriptive content. Unlike Mill, he applies the same strategy in the case of natural kind terms, arguing against the cluster theory and in support of a Millian semantics.[17] In this, Kripke departs radically from his contemporaries. After Quine, there was widespread scepticism about traditional, definitionalist accounts of general terms and versions of the cluster theory were suggested to take its place.[18] Kripke breaks with all this, arguing that natural kind terms are semantically akin to proper names and lack all descriptive content.

One would expect a radical claim of this sort to require substantial support. However, Kripke's defence of the Millian account of natural kind terms is sketchy and brief (covering barely 25 pages of the book). It raises a number of questions. In particular, why should natural kind terms, being general terms, be treated like proper names? And what does it mean for a kind term to be a rigid designator? The latter question has been much debated since Soames (2002), but there is little consensus on how it is to be answered. We shall leave it here and simply consider the underlying question: Why should natural kind terms be given the same Millian semantics as proper names (assuming that is the correct semantics for the latter terms)? What is Kripke's evidence for taking this radical step?

Kripke starts the discussion of natural kind terms by criticizing Kant's claim that the judgement "Gold is a yellow metal" is analytic and a priori. Kripke imagines a scenario in which it is discovered that the yellow appearance of gold is merely an illusion, and argues that if this were to happen we would conclude not that gold does not exists, but simply that it has turned out that gold is not yellow. This is an empirical claim about how we would respond, but Kripke's armchair guess seems prima facie plausible. After all, we have accepted that some gold is white. But this type of scenario merely provides evidence against *definitionalist* versions of descriptivism, not against the cluster theory. Kripke is aware of this and quickly moves on to make two much more radical claims:

(i) Something could have *all* the properties normally associated with gold and not be gold.
(ii) Something may have *none* of the properties associated with gold and still belong to the kind.

It is clear that (i) and (ii) are needed to support Millianism since the central Millian contention is that natural kind terms lack all descriptive content: whatever descriptions we associate with these terms, their function is merely to *fix* reference (i.e. the metasemantic function of fixing the term onto a property in the actual world), not to *determine* reference (i.e. the semantic function of determining reference and extension across all possible worlds). Instead, the 'underlying' property itself (however that is to be understood) somehow provides necessary and sufficient conditions, whether or not speakers have any knowledge of this property.

Thesis (i) concerns the possibility of 'twin cases', of the sort discussed by Putnam. To support (i) Kripke suggests that if there were a substance that had all the identifying marks of gold but which is not the same substance, we would say that "though it has all the appearances we initially used to identify gold, it is not gold" (1980, p. 119). This seems true, but trivially so. If something is a *different substance*, and we are aware of this fact, we would not call it "gold". Less trivially, Kripke appeals to a real-life example, that of fool's gold, which, he claims, has all the appearances we initially used to identify gold (1980, pp. 119, 124). The trouble with this example, as many have pointed out, is that fool's gold does *not* have all the appearances of gold. On the contrary, the substances have been seen as distinct long before the development of modern chemistry and knowledge of atomic numbers.[19] Consequently, even if widely shared, the intuition that fool's gold is not gold does not support the claim that something may have *all* the normal properties of gold and not be gold. Indeed, any difference in underlying properties appears bound to cause differences in macro-level properties as well.[20] It is therefore no accident that philosophers have taken recourse to thought experiments to test thesis (i).

Like Putnam, Kripke proposes such a thought experiment. He imagines a tiger that has all the characteristics typically associated with tigers, all the external appearances of a tiger, but with an internal structure completely different from that of the tiger, the structure typical of reptiles. Raising the question whether we would conclude that some tigers are reptiles, he responds: "We don't. We would rather conclude that these animals, though they have the external marks by which we originally identified tigers, are not in fact tigers, because they are not of the same species which we called 'the species of tigers'" (Kripke 1980, p. 120). This claim about what we would conclude in such a scenario, clearly, is a strong empirical claim. If indeed the aim is to determine the semantics of natural kind terms, as used by ordinary speakers, the claim would have to be tested: Kripke's armchair judgements cannot by themselves be decisive.[21]

Moreover, Kripke's judgements are in conflict with what the experts – i.e. biologists – say about the individuation of species. Kripke associates forming a natural kind with having a particular internal structure. But the notion of internal structure makes little sense in the case of species, and however it is construed, few biologists would take it as criterial.[22] Kripke therefore has to choose: Either he can insist that species terms track 'internal structure' (in accordance with his intuitions) or he can hold on to the idea that the extension of natural kind terms is ultimately determined by science.

Similar worries apply to thesis (ii), which is by far the stronger thesis. In the case of proper names, Kripke appeals to modal intuitions, such as the intuition that Aristotle might not have had *any* of the properties commonly attributed to him (Kripke 1980, p. 75). In the case of natural kind terms, similarly, Kripke appeals to the intuition that tigers might have had none of the properties by which we originally identified them. It is possible, he says, that tigers lacked all the properties we commonly attribute to them, such as being tawny yellow, striped, carnivorous, four-legged, and so on. For instance, Kripke suggests, we might find out that all of these properties had been mistakenly attributed to tigers due to "optical illusions or other errors". From this Kripke concludes that "gold" and "tiger" do not mark out a cluster concept in which most of the properties used to identify the kind must be satisfied: "On the contrary, possession of most of these properties need not be a necessary condition for membership in the kind, nor need it be a sufficient condition" (Kripke 1980, p. 121).

In support of thesis (ii), therefore, Kripke simply appeals to his intuition that tigers could lack all of the properties normally attributed to them, without spelling out any details. Is this a widely shared intuition?[23] Do we even know what we are supposed to imagine – a creature that does not have four legs, is not tawny yellow and striped, does not have large teeth, is not a carnivore, and is not a mammal? One without fur, skin and eyes? And how does this proposal square with the classifications employed by biologists? Kripke, no doubt, is driven to this conclusion by his assumption that natural kind terms are semantically more similar to proper names than to other kind terms. But, again, what is needed is precisely some empirical evidence, or at least argument, to support this claim, which for over four decades has shaped much of what philosophers of language have said about natural kind terms.

Kripke's assimilation of natural kind terms to names has been momentous, despite his caution when suggesting it (1980, pp. 127–128). On the one hand, it has led to attempts to construe natural kind terms simply as singular (for a recent attempt, see Bird 2009; for a rebuttal, see Needham 2012) or at least as rigid (for rebuttals, see Soames 2002). On the other, it has more insidiously invited the thought that *something* must confer on kinds the sort of metaphysical unity across possible worlds intuitively had by individuals. Many have found it tempting to think of microstrucure as offering such unity; hence the allure of (micro)essentialism. Kripke's discussion certainly seems informed by something like this idea and as we shall see shortly, it is easily made even when it shouldn't. We think that the semantic thesis underlying it – that natural kind terms function in a way completely different from other general terms – is mistaken.

We have not ourselves carried out any experiments, so we don't have any new data to offer here. Instead, we shall survey the available experimental data and other evidence. The extant data suggest that Kripke's picture of how natural kind terms function does not cohere with ordinary use of these terms (within or outside science) and that a much more complex picture is required, one that does not fit with the Millian proposal.

3.2 Empirical evidence from experiments

Experimental psychologists have been interested in natural kind concepts since the 1970s, in part as a result of the work of Kripke and Putnam. The primary concern of the psychological literature, naturally, is not semantics but 'concepts', the psychological states and processes that guide people's categorization judgements.[24] A main goal has been to test *psychological essentialism*, the thesis that people take objects to have deep-lying, 'invisible' essences determining categorization.[25] Early experiments provided initial support for psychological essentialism (Keil 1989; Rips 1989; Gelman and Wellman 1991), suggesting that people categorize not only on the basis of similarity but also on the basis of assumed deep-lying causal features, such as chromosomes. However, later experiments have shown the results to be less robust and actually highly contextual (Hampton 1995; Kalish 1995; Hampton, Estes and Simmons 2007).

The relation between psychological essentialism and Kripke's semantics is not straightforward, since the former is a psychological thesis, not a semantic one. Nevertheless, the experiments carried out by psychologists are relevant to semantics, since they focus on categorization tasks and typically involve term application. Many involve 'name appropriate judgements', where participants face a 'forced choice' of applying or withholding a term in accordance with one feature rather than another (for instance, in accordance with deep-lying features or observable features); other experiments involve 'free naming', where people apply a term in spontaneous discourse.

Of particular interest, from our point of view, are psychological experiments explicitly designed to test the essentialist approach to the meaning of natural kind terms. Thus, Braisby, Franks and Hampton (1996) set out to "evaluate the intuitions about word use that Kripke and Putnam deploy in support of essentialism, by putting them to empirical test" (1996, p. 248). 'Essentialism' is here construed as the claim that essential properties determine reference independently of people's beliefs, and the experiments test the extent to which people allow underlying features to govern their use of natural kind terms such as "cat", "water", "tiger" and "gold". The experimental results, Braisby et al. argue, do not support essentialism of the Kripke-Putnam sort. Although in some scenarios the majority (73%) took underlying features to play an important role, a substantial minority did not, and the experiments do not support the conclusion that *only* underlying features play a decisive role (as Millianism suggests).[26]

Clearly, results of this sort are relevant when we try to determine the proper semantics of natural kind terms, and it is surprising that philosophers have largely ignored the findings of experimental psychologists. If a substantial group of people do not apply their terms in the ways predicted by Kripke and Putnam, then this poses a difficulty for their semantics. Naturally, it might be possible to explain away the divergencies – either as resulting from error or as indicating that people use terms with different meanings. However, there is one type of explanation that does not seem very promising in the context: the claim that people are mistaken in their modal intuitions, since they are not philosophers and therefore ignorant about essences of natural kinds. As we've stressed, philosophers are not the experts when it comes to natural kinds: scientists are. And even if a particular philosophical theory about natural kind essences were accepted, it would not tell us anything about the *semantics* of terms such as "water", "gold" and "tiger". Rather, if people do not use these terms to track "underlying" properties only, then it follows that they do not use them to track natural kinds of the sort envisaged by Kripke or Putnam.[27, 28]

In experimental philosophy, so far only a small fraction of studies have focused on natural kind terms, compared to names. Here we shall briefly summarize the findings of two interesting studies – Jylkkä, Railo and Haukioja (2009), from now on referred to as "JRH"; and Genone and Lombrozo (2012) – and their implications.

JRH set out to test what they label 'externalistic essentialism'. This is the thesis of psychological essentialism, combined with the semantic claim that "the speakers take possessing E [the essence] to be a necessary and sufficient condition for belonging in the extension of C" (2009, p. 41). Their starting point is the experiments reported in Braisby, Franks and Hampton (1996), and they argue that the study's evidence against externalism is weaker than the authors suggest and even lends some support for externalism. Moreover, JRH suggest, the internalistic answers could be explained away, perhaps as a result of the fact that the participants relied on pre-discovery identificatory knowledge associated with the kind (i.e. on the descriptions that serve to fix the extension of the term).

JRH therefore proceed to design their own experiments, hoping to secure more decisive evidence for or against externalist essentialism. The first experiment has two different stages, using a set of scenarios involving six fictive natural kinds. In the first stage, subjects read descriptions of a natural kind having certain macro-level properties, believed by scientists to be a certain compound (2009, p. 49). Thus in one scenario the subjects read about a yellowish, bitter-smelling, fragile mineral common in Siberia, 'zircaum', which scientists believe to be the compound ACB. They are then told that in Norway a deposit of a mineral with the same macro-level features is found, and after examining its deep structure scientists conclude that it is ACB too. Participants are asked whether they considered the novel sample as falling under 'zircaum' as well, and by and large people answered yes to this question. At the second stage subjects are presented with a scenario where it turns out that the scientists had been wrong about the mineral in Norway and that it is in fact a different substance, KML. Participants are then asked to answer two different questions: Whether they consider the earlier categorization judgement to be *justified*, and whether they consider it to be *correct*. According to JRH (2009), strict externalistic essentialism predicts that while subjects may consider the judgement to be justified, they will not consider it correct, whereas internalism predicts that the participant considers her earlier judgement unambiguously correct (since the Norwegian mineral fits all the descriptions concerning the macro-level properties of zircaum).[29] The authors suggest that externalism was largely confirmed: 69 per cent of the answers were externalistic (out of which 33% gave purely externalistic answers), 28 per cent were internalistic, and 3 per cent were compromises (JRH 2009, p. 52).

JRH (2009) comment on the need to explain the substantial number of internalist answers. One hypothesis is that natural kind terms are ambiguous and have two senses – one internalistic, another externalistic – as suggested by hybrid theories. The authors therefore designed a second experiment, intended to test the hybrid theory more directly, also reported in JRH (2009). The scenarios were similar, but participants were given the option of giving an ambiguous answer ("yes on the one hand, but . . ."), which is what a hybrid theory would predict. Again, participants were asked whether the earlier categorization judgement was correct and whether it was justified. In this experiment too, the results were rather mixed: 48 per cent externalistic answers, 22 per cent internalistic, 17 per cent ambiguous ("yes on the one hand . . ."), and 12 per cent were "cannot say" answers. Since ambiguous answers and internalistic answers contradict one another, the latter cannot be explained away as an expression of natural kind terms having two senses, an internalistic and an externalistic. A quarter of the answers, therefore, support pure internalism. Nevertheless, JRH (2009) conclude that since the majority of the judgements were in accordance with the predictions of externalistic essentialism this experiment also supports externalism and that, therefore, the two experiments support the claim that "category membership is determined by the hidden, external essence or deep structure *even if nobody knows about it*" (JRH 2009, p. 58).

In conducting these experiments Jylkkä, Railo and Haukioja have provided a very important contribution to semantics. They have taken seriously the fact that externalist essentialism is an empirical thesis and set out to test it. However, we think that there is some reason to question their conclusion that the experiments provide support for externalist essentialism.

First, there is a problem with how the scenarios are described. Consider the following description of what happens when the scientists examine the Siberian substance more closely:

> Using methods and instruments more exact than previously available, they find out that they were wrong about the deep structure of the substance: the substance is KML instead of ACB. However, the substance found in Northern Norway was indeed ACB, just as the scientists thought it was. (2009, p. 49)

By talking about the substance *being* KML, rather than ACB, it is implied that chemical substances are *identical* to their molecular composition. However, if so, it would seem to follow rather trivially that the substances are distinct: if the first substance is identical to ACB then it must be distinct from the substance, which is identical to KML (assuming, as stipulated, that ACB≠KML). Subjects therefore appear *primed* to conclude that the Norwegian mineral samples do not belong to the extension of "zircaum". Hence, the description of the scenario is problematic in just the same way that Kripke's description of twin-gold is, when he describes it as a substance which has all the appearances of gold but which is not the same substance.

Moreover, there are problems with the interpretation of the results of the experiments. The first, and most obvious, difficulty concerns the fact that even if the majority of the answers comply with the predictions of externalism, a substantial minority complies with internalism, and as the second experiment shows, this cannot be explained away by appealing to a hybrid theory. In the end, the authors appear to fall back on a version of the expertise defense: "Lay speakers' intuitions towards or against externalism may be very implicit, and fuzzy, which could result in significant deviation in the answers. In contrast, philosophers have spent lots of time reflecting their intuitions and formed a very explicit opinion about the subject matter" (JRH 2009, p. 58). This suggests that what is decisive is not so much how non-experts judge these cases but how philosophers judge them and that since the majority of philosophers are externalists that provides evidence in support of externalism. This would be a step back from the empirical approach motivating the authors, and since the terms here are natural kind terms, there is – as we noted – no special reason to think that philosophers are particularly adept at using these. Indeed, many claims made by philosophers about natural kinds are simply incorrect (such as the claim that biological species are individuated by genetic structure) or disputed by philosophers of science (like the claim that chemical substances are individuated by molecular composition).

The second worry concerns the description of internalism. It is said that internalism predicts that underlying composition does not matter to categorization and that "internalism has no way of accounting for any significant number of externalist answers" (JRH 2009, p. 48), but this is incorrect. Consider the zircaum scenarios again. The subjects have been told that the scenarios involve substances, natural kinds, with a certain chemical composition. It has also been made clear that these kinds are important to scientists (the chemical composition is examined by them) and, therefore, that they belong to scientific categorizations and not just to everyday categorizations. Given all this, one can account for the participants' reactions simply by appealing to a version of the cluster theory. After all, if "kind K is a substance", or "kind K is a natural kind" belongs to the cluster of descriptions, and the subjects are assumed to believe that substances are not *merely* individuated in terms of their macro-level properties, then the cluster theory predicts that if the mineral in Norway has a distinct composition, a number of subjects will judge the mineral not to be zircaum. This is so even if the subject does not have any belief about the precise nature of the chemical composition.

Indeed, it seems to us, the cluster theory gives a *better* account of the mixed results of the experiments than either externalism or the hybrid theory (which, again, predicts ambiguity). According to the theory a sample falls in the extension of a kind term if it fits the weighted majority of the associated properties (this is how Kripke characterizes the cluster theory), which implies that both macro-level properties and underlying features, such as chemical composition, play a role. The precise role played by these different components, however, will depend on how individual speakers *weight* them, and it is likely that some speakers will consider the underlying component to be more decisive than others – hence, the theory predicts that some people will judge the Norwegian samples not to belong to the kind zircaum whereas others will judge them to belong to this kind.

The results reported in JRH (2009) thus illustrate an important point pressed earlier. To refute the cluster theory it is not sufficient to show that 'underlying' properties *matter*: it also has to be shown that *only* underlying properties matter, as suggested by Millianism. This, however, isn't shown by the experiments reported in JRH (2009). What is being tested is only the first part of the Millian theory, thesis (i); that is, the thesis that two samples may share all the same observable properties and yet not belong to the same kind as a result of a difference in underlying properties. Even if we ignore the above objections to the experiments, therefore, they simply do not test externalistic essentialism, that is, the thesis that "the speakers take possessing E [the essence] to be a necessary and sufficient condition for belonging in the extension of C" (2009, p. 41). To test this thesis, one has to determine whether subjects would grant that a sample may belong to a category even if not only one (or some) of the ordinary descriptions fail to hold of the sample but they *all* fail, as in Kripke's reptile-tiger case.

A similar reading is invited by the second study, Genone and Lombrozo (2012). They conducted two experiments; both concerned with kind terms for fictive natural kinds (diseases, minerals) and nominal kinds (artefacts, legal documents). In this study, undergraduates were asked to judge whether two fictional persons in various scenarios are thinking about the same disease/mineral/artefact/legal document (2012, pp. 724–725).[30] In the first experiments, participants were asked to judge simply whether or not reference was shared; in the second, they were asked to indicate degree of agreement with a claim about shared reference on a seven-point scale (2012, pp. 728–729).

For each term, four vignettes were used, in which the characters had variously matching – and variously erroneous – descriptive information associated with the term and where they were either linked to a common causal chain or not. The central finding, replicated in the second experiment, was that speakers do not consistently rely on either causal or descriptive information.[31] Moreover, experiment 1 found that willingness to attribute shared reference decreased as a function of number of false beliefs on one character's part; experiment 2 confirmed this finding (2012, p. 730).[32] If Kripkean Millianism were correct for kind terms, there should be no reason to expect this. For according to Millianism, members of a kind may lack *all* properties speakers believe that they have. Certainly, the properties that were varied in these experiments – conductivity, shininess, hardness and colour – are exactly the sort that Kripke held speakers may be massively in error about *in toto*. Hence, Genone and Lombrozo may also be read as providing tentative evidence against Millian kind term semantics.

Genone and Lombrozo suggest that individual variation may be explained by different individual strategies for weighting or combining causal and descriptive information in reaching reference judgements and even applying different strategies on different occasions due to contextual factors. On this suggestion, statistical differences between cultures might be explained by differing, and partly culturally induced, ways of filling in unspecified contextual assumptions about presented scenarios (2012, pp. 732–733). We think that, albeit speculative, this hypothesis is promising (perhaps more so than the speculation, inspired by Nesbitt, about wholesale cultural differences in causal thinking broached in MMNS 2004). We note that it is quite compatible with a cluster theory for kind terms.

3.3 Evidence from history of science

The broader empirical evidence for evaluating the semantics of natural kind terms is not limited to surveys using cases. Other relevant evidence includes history of science. The relevant literature here is too vast to summarize or even list, of course, but many particularly interesting data are gathered and discussed in LaPorte (2004). LaPorte writes:

> Putnam and Kripke prompt intuitions about the proper use of a term in counterfactual scenarios by asking *what we would say* were we presented with this or that scenario. This procedure seems reasonable. Speakers' dispositions indicate the proper use of a term. (LaPorte 2004, p. 97; italics in original)

Now irrespective of the propriety of the method of cases in general, it seems right to impute use of it to Putnam and Kripke, as MMNS (2004) did and as LaPorte does here. Invoking, as Putnam (1975) did, the parallels between H_2O and XYZ, on the one hand, and jadeite and nephrite, on the other, LaPorte immediately continues:

> And Chinese speakers have indicated by their actions *what they would say* were they presented with a new substance like what they had called "jade" except in its microstructure. These speakers have been presented with such a substance, and they have displayed a strong disposition to count it "jade". Therefore, speakers' dispositions can hardly be said to make a case for the position that [the newly discovered substance of] jadeite would clearly have failed to belong in the extension of "jade". (LaPorte 2004, pp. 97–98)

LaPorte's claim, which we endorse, is that this carries evidential weight for claims about what speakers would be disposed to say, were they presented with XYZ. It suggests that they would not go with microstructure, as assumed by Putnam (1975).[33] In fact the convoluted history of "jade" also suggests that speakers would not go with observable characteristics. The historical evidence suggests that neither counterfactual about 'what we would say' is warranted, and indeed, that both are false. What the case – and others studied by LaPorte – indicates is something rather different: that both microstructural and observable properties are important, though neither is decisive, and that when they are discovered to come apart, resulting usage may follow either and hence will be hard to predict. This is just what would be expected on a cluster semantics for kind terms, when microproperties are allowed to partake in the cluster of descriptions.

LaPorte is chiefly interested in biological kind terms. Consider terms for species, or higher taxa such as "mammal". If "mammal" has only "live-bearing" as its sole, criterial description, inclusion of egg-laying monotremes will indeed have drastic consequences (LaPorte 2004, pp. 114–116). Insisting on applying such a single criterion would be to overzealously apply a crude definitionalist descriptivism. But happily, it is not what scientists do, or have done. As LaPorte notes, cluster descriptivist theories allow "some needed conceptual continuity" (2004, p. 117). They also allow some referential continuity or stability, unlike simple description theories. Key to seeing this is accepting some negotiability – and vagueness – in what the extension of a kind term includes. When Putnam, and other causal theorists, discuss reference of natural kind terms by first using the term or the generic definite description "the kind" and then moving on to anaphora like "it", they in effect exclude the possibility of open texture.[34]

LaPorte argues forcefully that the causal theory is, "contrary to wide acclaim, useless in blocking instability" (2004, p. 118). This is so because even if terms are introduced via baptisms of samples supposedly fixing reference conditions, *and* samples of enough foils to deflect some of the so-called *qua* problem (avoiding reference to metals or elements in general, rather than to gold; or to mammals or vertebrates rather than to horses), the speakers performing the baptisms cannot foresee how new discoveries will force refinements in usage affecting the extensions of the terms. As LaPorte stresses, open texture cannot be avoided even if it is agreed that kinds have essences and what, in general, constitutes the essence of (say) species and substances. The refinement of the extension of "mammal" that resulted upon the discovery of monotremes, for instance, was not dictated by acceptance of cladistic essences for biological taxa (2004, p. 119). Neither was the refinement in how the term "water" came to be used after the discovery of deuterium and heavy water. Such developments always contain an element of stipulation and so are, in effect, decisions rather than discoveries – pace Putnam and Kripke.

LaPorte attributes the causal theory's inability to guarantee referential stability to the fact that, on this theory, "baptisms... are performed by speakers whose conceptual development is not yet sophisticated enough to allow the speakers to coin a term in such a way as to preclude the possibility of open texture, or vague application not yet recognized" (2004, p. 118). But this observation, while sensible, overlooks a more general point, namely that no amount of conceptual sophistication will endow speakers with an ability to – somehow – anticipate and resolve in advance potential vagueness laid bare only with future empirical discoveries. Open texture appears to be endemic. Further illustration is offered by the historical vicissitudes of virtually any putative natural kind term.

Take 'acid', whose trajectory from Boyle in the seventeenth century until the mid-1950s is traced in Stanford and Kitcher (2000, pp. 115–118), from whom we'll borrow in this paragraph. Boyle characterized acids via descriptions of observable properties: they are sour, corrosive, and precipitate sulphur from sulphide solutions. Subsequent refinements were principally due to, in turn, Arrhenius in the 1880s, Brønsted and Lowry in the 1920s (Brønsted 1928) and G. N. Lewis in the 1920s and 1930s (Lewis 1938). Lewis characterized acids as electron pair receptors, dropping earlier theorists' restriction to hydrogen compounds. His chief motivation was that this characterization captures four phenomenological criteria: (i) rapid combination with bases, (ii) replacement of weaker acids, (iii) characteristic effects on coloured indicators [like Litmus paper], and (iv) characteristic catalytic action. This rationale was defended by

Luder and Zuffanti (1946, p. 3, quoted in Stanford and Kitcher 2000, p. 117): "a substance that exhibits the properties of an acid should be called an acid, regardless of preconceived notions about the dependence of acidic properties on a particular element". Lewis himself appears to have regarded the microlevel characterization in terms of electron pairs as incidental, albeit handy: "it is possible . . . to discuss and define acids and bases merely from their behavior in chemical reactions without any theory of molecular structure" (Lewis 1938, p. 293, quoted in Stanford and Kitcher 2000, p. 116).

This offers a good illustration of what happens with a term as scientific knowledge matures. A kind term is first associated with descriptions, and if the term is introduced at a stage of relative scientific underdevelopment, these descriptions typically concern observable properties. What happens with accumulated discoveries and increasing scientific sophistication, however, is *not* that microstructural characterizations are first found and then explicitly appointed to the office of determining reference or extension. What happens is rather that simple, observational descriptions are replaced by increasingly sophisticated, theoretical ones, and that microstructural descriptions enter if they are deemed economical explanantia of other properties. Microstructure[35] may be made 'criterial', but that status depends on which other properties are held to need explanation and are retained (like Lewis's four phenomenological properties) and which are deemed expendible (like Boyle's sour taste), and this – as LaPorte stresses – is highly contingent and involves some negotiation and decision-making. It is not a matter of simply "discovering that some members of a natural kind lack properties originally used in picking out a kind", as Stanford and Kitcher suggest (2000, p. 117). Of course, if a fairly stable characterization of a kind is in place, and "pick out" just means that some property is thought to be a reliable indicator of a kind, is seems fair to call this simple discovery of certain kind members' lacking this property – say, that not swans are white or not all zebras striped. But dropping the hydrogen requirement, in the case of "acid", was not a matter of simple discovery – to judge from the records, the transition from Brønsted-Lowry to Lewis didn't even have a phenomenology of simple discovery to the chemists involved.

Moreover, microstructural criteria may not emerge for natural kind terms, either because no candidate is found or because suggested candidates are contested, due to disagreement over the importance of other descriptions.[36] The history of science is, as we said, replete with illustrations of both sorts of cases.[37] However, this matters a great deal less for science than would often seem assumed by philosophers of language. First, kinds may be defined satisfactorily without appeal to microstructure, as Lewis argued in the case of acids.[38] Second, when there is controversy over the extension of a kind term due to disagreement about what is central, such disagreement is often partly due to shifting assessments of how much promise not-yet-explored hypotheses and research agendas hold. Since science wouldn't be better off without the latter sort of disagreement, it is hard to see how it would be better off without open texture. And in fact, history of science offers several examples of prolonged conceptual disputes between experts over different characterizations, due to open texture. Such dispute, it seems, hasn't hindered or even necessarily hurt communication, understanding or progress (cf. Cowie 2009, pp. 90–97).

Thus it appears that open texture is simply an ineliminable by-product of how terms are used, both in science and elsewhere. Hence, it shouldn't be surprising that neither causal nor cluster description theories are successful in blocking it, which LaPorte notes – however, it is not clear why it should be, as LaPorte says, "unwelcome" (2004, p. 118). To us it seems a feature rather than a bug. In any case, its pervasiveness fits naturally with a cluster theory for kind terms.

The last few paragraphs were concerned with extensions of kind terms in the actual world. When the issue concerns extensions at all possible worlds, as in the modal arguments of Kripke, the morals still apply. If the earlier use of a term fails to dictate how the term will apply after discoveries revealing inherent vagueness, clearly it doesn't determine application at all possible worlds either. In discussing a different but related topic (modal epistemology), Yablo comments that "grasp of meaning is not a normative crystal ball telling us what modal conclusions are to be drawn from every new empirical finding, however unforeseen or unforeseeable" (Yablo 2000, p. 120). We concur: applying or refusing to apply a kind term (say, "water") to a hypothetical scenario (Twin Earth) need not betray lack of understanding of the term.

4. Concluding remarks

We have argued that experimental semantics provides an important source of evidence for semantic theory – in particular when it comes to descriptive semantics, which are clearly empirical theories, but also when it comes to the more theoretically committed metasemantics. Although semantics requires philosophical expertise, the experts cannot ignore the empirical evidence provided by speaker use. Nor can they exclusively rely on their own dispositions to use terms – not, at any rate, if they are interested in the semantics of the shared language.

Although the role of empirical evidence has recently received attention when it comes to proper names, it has received much less attention when it comes to natural kind terms. Instead, it has generally been assumed that the considerations that apply to proper names apply equally to natural kind terms, and that the intuitive evidence against descriptivism is equally strong. We have questioned this orthodoxy, and argued that the extant empirical evidence does not support a Kripkean semantics for these terms. No doubt, the experimental evidence is still too scant to draw any firm conclusions. However, we have argued, it is safe to conclude that the widely endorsed assumption that natural kind terms cannot be given a descriptivist semantics is nothing but armchair semantics – an empirical theory driven by prior philosophical commitments without support in the available empirical data.

Notes

* Thanks to Max Deutsch and Nat Hansen for valuable comments on a draft of this chapter.

1 The study involved undergraduate participants from Rutgers and The University of Hong Kong, all fluent in English. Among other probes, they were presented with this vignette and question, modelled on Kripke's example of "Gödel" and "Schmidt" in *Naming and Necessity* (Kripke 1980, pp. 83–92):

   Suppose that John has learned in college that Gödel is the man who proved an important mathematical theorem, called the incompleteness of arithmetic. John is quite good at mathematics and he can give an accurate statement of the incompleteness theorem, which he attributes to Gödel as the discoverer. But this is the only thing that he has heard about Gödel. Now suppose that Gödel was not the author of this theorem. A man called "Schmidt", whose body was found in Vienna under mysterious circumstances many years ago, actually did the work in question. His friend Gödel somehow got hold of the manuscript and claimed credit for the work, which was thereafter attributed to Gödel. Thus, he has been known as the man who proved the incompleteness of arithmetic. Most people who have heard the name "Gödel" are like John; the claim that Gödel discovered the incompleteness theorem is the only thing they have ever heard about Gödel. When John uses the name "Gödel", is he talking about:

   (A) the person who really discovered the incompleteness of arithmetic? or
   (B) the person who got hold of the manuscript and claimed credit for the work?
   (MMNS 2004, B6)

Answers consonant with (B) were scored as 1; answers consonant with (A) as 0; the mean score for 'Western' participants was 1.13 (SD = 0.88) and for Chinese participants 0.63 (SD = 0.84). Similar results were obtained for a Gödel case involving a historical Chinese astronomer (MMNS 2004, B9–B10).

2 The closest MMNS (2009) gets to outright rejection of the method is this passage: "Our data seem to show that two individuals can belong to two distinct intuition groups despite evidently speaking the same dialect (because they speak the same language, belong to the same culture and have much the same socio-economic status). Faced with this variation, it is very tempting to abandon the assumption that intuitions about reference provide evidence about reference all together [sic]" (MMNS 2009, p. 345). This passage occurs in the context of an extended attack on "referential pluralism" – the idea that "differences in intuitions about the reference of a word t (or a class of words T) indicate that t (or every member of T) refers differently for different groups" (MMNS 2009, p. 343). What the authors call pluralism thus incorporates the method of cases, but their attack seems more concerned with pluralism itself than with its method, and ends with a plea to abandon it, rather than the method of cases. We are not sure how to reconcile the quoted passage with the authors' stated reluctance to drop that method. Moreover, Machery has recently explicitly argued that laypeople "are likely to produce true judgements about the reference of proper names in actual and possible cases" and that therefore, "the resulting judgements plausibly constitute evidence" (Machery 2014, p. 14). This looks like a defence of the method of cases.

3 For discussion, see Stalnaker (1997, pp. 535–536).

4 Burge's metasemantics, for example, is externalist and yet he rejects Millian semantics and endorses what seems to be a version of traditional descriptivism (see Burge 1986 and 2007, pp. 1–31). For a discussion of externalism and the relation between semantics and metasemantics, see Wikforss (2008).

5 For example, one might appeal to a principle of 'best fit' (such as Davidson's principle of charity) or to the principle that provides the best teleological explanation (as Millikan does) or to asymmetric-dependency considerations (as Fodor does), and so on.

6 See for instance Stanley (1997). Stanley stresses that the discovery that proper names are rigid designators can be accommodated by some versions of descriptivism, such as the 'actualized' description theory, and that Kripke does not conclude, from rigidity alone, that Millianism is correct. The philosophical significance of the discovery that names are rigid designators, Stanley argues, should therefore be a matter of controversy. That is, in our terminology, even if the weak semantic theory is not a matter of controversy (such as names being rigid designators) the strong semantic theory is, bringing to bear all sorts of philosophical considerations.

7 Moreover, the thesis is hostage to empirical assumptions about the kinds in question, (cf. Häggqvist and Wikforss 2008). We return to this below.

8   See also Machery (2011, p. 38), where he stresses that theories of reference 'belong squarely to metasemantics'.
9   In the initial experiment the participants are invited to respond to questions concerning what the speaker, in the story, uses the name "Gödel" to refer to. The trouble with this way of asking the question, Martí argues, is that it does not test the right kind of intuitions. By making the question explicitly meta-linguistic, asking *what the term refers to*, what is tested is not how the participants use their names, but which theory of reference they think is correct: "MMNS test people's intuitions about *theories* of reference, not about the *use* of names. But what we think the correct theory of reference determination is, and how we use names to talk about things are two very different issues" (Martí 2009, p. 44).
10 Of course, it is an empirical question to what extent the meta-linguistic judgements of speakers track their first-order use. Thus, in a response to Martí's criticisms, Machery, Olivola and De Blanc (2009) have carried out experiments testing whether meta-linguistic intuitions are in agreement with linguistic intuitions. They conclude that these intuitions are in agreement and that the variation between cultures and within cultures remains when the test questions are not meta-linguistic. However, Martí (forthcoming) argues that that new experiments still do not collect the right kind of data since they too prompt the subjects to *reflect* on their use of "Gödel", rather than require them to *use* the name.
11 For a similar line of reasoning, see Cappelen (2012).
12 The same holds for Evans's famous "Madagascar" counterexample to the causal-historical theory. Since it is common knowledge that "Madagascar" refers to the island, and not to a portion of the African mainland, Evans did not need to provide evidence for the counterexample, but it is nevertheless an empirical fact that "Madagascar" has this reference. For a related point, see Machery's response to Deutsch (2014, p. 9).
13 Cf. Ichikawa: "Suppose someone did a survey and discovered that the distribution of people who believed the earth was more than one million years old correlated with certain demographic variables . . . I think that the obvious thing to say is that we've discovered that members of a certain demographic group are not reliable judges about the age of the Earth" (2009, pp. 110–111). And Williamson: "[W]e do not expect physicists to suspend their current projects . . . on the basis of evidence that undergraduates untrained in physics are bad at conducting laboratory experiments" (2011, p. 217).
14 This is why semantics involves metaphysics in the Putnam-Kripke theory. Since both hold that the extension of "tiger" across possible worlds is determined not by the psychological states of the speakers, but by the underlying nature of the actual animals picked out, an answer to the metaphysical question (what is the essence of tigers?) is required for an answer to the semantic question (what is the extension of "tiger"?).

15 This is not to deny that there may be any number of modal propositions that experts as well as non-experts do agree on.
16 Cf. Machery (2011). Machery appeals to experimental data suggesting that philosophers are more likely to have Kripkean intuitions than linguists working in discourse analysis, historical linguistics and sociolinguistics (2011, p. 48).
17 As is often noted, Kripke denies defending any real theory, and so he may not in fact endorse the Millian theory. However, he explicitly states that he agrees with Mill on proper names but disagrees with him on general terms, since he thinks that proper names and general terms should be understood along the same lines (Kripke 1980, p. 127).
18 See, for instance, Putnam (1962).
19 See Ben-Yami (1991, p. 161), who notes that "iron pyrites only have a *faint* resemblance to gold". See also LaPorte (2004, p. 161).
20 For a fuller discussion of this point, see Stanford and Kitcher (2000, esp. p. 105).
21 It might be suggested, as Max Deutsch did to us, that Kripke's claim here is not an empirical claim but rather the metaphysical claim that the tiger-looking things are a different species. However, the metaphysical claim, in itself, does not support the semantic claim that Kripke wishes to make, that is, the claim that the tiger-looking things are not in the extension of our term "tiger". In order to support the semantic claim, Kripke needs evidence that "tiger" is used in such a way that it tracks underlying features rather than observable features; this is precisely why he makes a claim about what 'we would conclude' – an empirical claim about our reactions which, in fact, does not seem supported by the empirical evidence (see Section 3.2).
22 And although the notion does make sense in the case of substances, it is utterly unclear what Kripke, Putnam or subsequent semantic theorists mean by the term (Needham 2010).
23 Dummett was early to reject it, writing that "Kripke's efforts to show that that by which we originally identify the species or the substance might not be true of it at all ... are bizarre and quite unconvincing" (1981, p. 146).
24 Precisely what is meant by "concept" varies, and it is a matter of dispute how the psychological notions relate to the philosophical notion of a concept (cf. Machery 2009).
25 The type of psychological essentialism that is often tested is so-called "placeholder essentialism", according to which subjects need not have any specific beliefs about the actual essence of the kind, but merely the belief that the kind has some essence or other, consisting of deep properties that cause the macro-level properties that are typical of the category.
26 For further experiments that show similar results see Malt (1994) and Hampton, Estes and Simmons (2007). In the latter experiment the support for essentialism

was even weaker, where only 7 out of 110 participants categorized fully in accordance with essentialism.

27   Indeed, as we shall suggest below, there are reasons to think that the scientists do not use kind terms this way either.
28   Hacking (2007) notes that there are differences between Kripke's and Putnam's theories, but these are small enough to be finessed here (as they usually are in the literature).
29   JRH (2009) also use a third-person version of the scenario, asking the participant to answer the same two questions concerning the expert's judgements. Moreover, there was a positive version of each scenario, where an instance first thought of as not belonging to a kind turns out to belong to it, after all. The description here is simplified in several respects in order to focus on the central issues.
30   Genone and Lombrozo say that "participants were asked whether or not the concepts two characters associate with a common word share the same reference" (2012, p. 723). This way of glossing their question may be problematic, but there is not room to discuss this here.
31   The second experiment also tested whether information about the learning history of the characters influenced judgements – it didn't, which, as Genone and Lombrozo note, "suggests that the findings in experiment 1 were not an artefact of having failed to specify a learning history" (2012, p. 730).
32   The beliefs at issue were always four, and experiment 1 tested for falsity of one, two, three and four false beliefs separately; experiment 2 tested for falsity of one and four false beliefs. In both cases, a character's having four false beliefs was thus tantamount to being wrong about everything stipulated to hold of the kind in question.
33   LaPorte points out that speaker dispositions were supposed to motivate "the conviction that microstructure trumps superficial properties is reference" (2004, p. 98), and that it would be ad hoc to disregard the evidence provided by the case of "jade". As we have noted in Section 2, dispositions constitute important evidence for semantic theories (at least when manifested), but error, and even dispositions to err, must be allowed for.
34   This is the term LaPorte, following Waismann (1945), uses for hidden and unforeseeable vagueness in a general term.
35   Or other properties thought to serve a unifying role, such as geneaology in the case of cladistic taxonomy.
36   As Stanford and Kitcher admit, "some natural kind terms have their references fixed through the use of descriptions that are not attempts to pick out 'inner constitution' or 'underlying structure'" (2000, p. 124).
37   For "gene", see Sarkar (1996); Griffiths and Neumann-Held (1999).
38   For an extended argument that even chemical kinds are in fact perfectly well individuated in terms of macroscopic properties, see Needham (2010).

References

Ben-Yami, H. (1991), 'The semantics of natural kind terms', *Philosophical Studies*, 102, 155–184.

Bird, A. (2009), 'Are natural kinds reducible?', in A. Hieke and H. Leitgeb (eds), *Reduction – Abstraction – Analysis*. Frankfurt: Ontos, pp. 127–136.

Braisby, N., Franks, B. and Hampton, J. (1996), 'Essentialism, word use, and concepts', *Cognition*, 59, 247–274.

Brønsted, J. (1928), 'Acid and base catalysis', in K. H. Sandved and V. K. LaMer (trans.), *Chemical Reviews*, V, 231–338.

Burge, T. (1986), 'Individualism and psychology', *Philosophical Review*, 45, 3–45.

Burge, T. (2007), 'Introduction', in T. Burge (ed.), *Foundations of Mind*. Oxford: Oxford University Press, pp. 1–31.

Cappelen, H. (2012), *Philosophy without Intuitions*. Oxford: Oxford University Press.

Cowie, F. (2009), 'Why isn't Stich an elimiNativist?', in D. Murphy and M. Bishop (eds), *Stich and His Critics*. Malden, MA: Wiley-Blackwell, pp. 74–100.

Deutsch, M. (2009), 'Experimental philosophy and the theory of reference', *Mind and Language*, 24 (4), 445–466.

Devitt, M. (2011), 'Experimental semantics', *Philosophy and Phenomenological Research*, LXXXII, 418–435.

Dummett, M. (1981), *Frege: Philosophy of Language*. Cambridge, MA: Harvard University Press.

Gelman, S. A. and Wellman, H. M. (1991), 'Insides and essences: early understandings of the non-obvious', *Cognition*, 38, 213–244.

Genone, J. and Lombrozo, T. (2012), 'Concepts possession, experimental semantics, and hybrid theories of reference', *Philosophical Psychology*, 25, 717–742.

Griffiths, P. and Neumann-Held, E. (1999), 'The many faces of the gene', *BioScience*, 49 (8), 656–662.

Hacking, I. (2007), 'Putnam's theory of natural kinds and their names is not the same as Kripke's', *Principia* 11, 1–24.

Häggqvist, S. and Wikforss, Å. (2008), 'Externalism and a posteriori semantics', *Erkenntnis* 67, 373–386.

Hampton, J. (1995), 'Testing the prototype theory of concepts', *Journal of Memory and Language*, 34, 686–708.

Hampton, J., Estes, Z. and Simmons (2007), 'Metamorphosis: essence, appearance, and behavior in the categorization of natural kinds', *Memory and Cognition*, 35, 1785–1800.

Horvath, J. (2010), 'How (not) to react to experimental philosophy', *Philosophical Psychology*, 23, 447–480.

Ichikawa, J. (2009), 'Explaining away intuitions', *Studia Philosophica Estonica*, 2 (2), 94–116.

Jylkkä J., Railo, H. and Haukioja, J. (2009), 'Psychological essentialism and semantic externalism: evidence for externalism in lay speakers' language use', *Philosophical Psychology*, 22, 37–60.

Kalish, C. W. (1995), 'Essentialism and graded membership in animal and artifact categories', *Memory and Cognition,* 23, 335–353.
Keil, F. (1989), *Concepts, Kinds and Cognitive Development.* Cambridge, MA: MIT Press.
Kripke, S. (1980), *Naming and Necessity.* Cambridge, MA: Harvard University Press.
LaPorte, J. (2004), *Natural Kinds and Conceptual Change.* Cambridge: Cambridge University Press.
Lewis, G. (1938), 'Acids and bases', *Journal of the Franklin Institute,* 226, 293–313.
Luder, W. and Zuffanti, S. (1946), *The Electronic Theory of Acids and Bases.* New York: John Wiley & Sons.
Machery, E. (2009), *Doing without Concepts.* Oxford: Oxford University Press.
Machery, E. (2011), 'Expertise and intuitions about reference', *Theoria,* 73, 37–54.
Machery, E. (2014), 'What is the significance of the demographic variation in semantic intuitions?', in E. Machery and E. O'Neill (eds), *Current Controversies in Experimental Philosophy.* New York: Routledge, pp. 3–16.
Machery, E., Mallon, R., Nichols, S. and Stich, S. (2004), 'Semantics, cross-cultural style', *Cognition,* 92, B1–B12.
Machery, E., Mallon, R., Nichols, S. and Stich, S. (2013), 'If folk intuitions vary, then what?', *Philosophy and Phenomenological Research,* LXXXVI, 618–635.
Machery, E., Olivola, C. and De Blanc, M. (2009), 'Linguistic and metalinguistic intuitions in the philosophy of language', *Analysis,* 69, 689–694.
Mallon, R., Machery, E., Nichols, S. and Stich, S. (2009), 'Against arguments from reference', *Philosophy and Phenomenological Research,* LXXIX, 332–356.
Malt, B. (1994), 'Water is not H_2O', *Cognitive Psychology,* 27, 41–70.
Martí, G. (2009), 'Against semantic multiculturalism', *Analysis,* 69, 42–48.
Needham, P. (2010), 'Microessentialism: What is the argument?', *Noûs,* 45, 1–21.
Needham, P. (2012), 'Natural kind thingamajigs', *International Studies in the Philosophy of Science,* 26, 97–101.
Putnam, H. (1962), 'The analytic and the synthetic', in H. Feigl and G. Maxwell (eds), *Minnesota Studies in the Philosophy of Science,* Vol. 3. Minneapolis: University of Minnesota Press, pp. 358–397.
Putnam, H. (1975), 'The meaning of "meaning"', *Philosophical Papers Vol. 2: Mind, Language, and Reality.* Cambridge: Cambridge University Press.
Rips, L. (1989), 'Similarity, typicality and categorisation', in S. Vosniadou and A. Ortony (eds), *Similarity and Analogical Reasoning.* Cambridge: Cambridge University Press, pp. 21–59.
Sarkar, S. (1996), 'Biological information: A skeptical look at some central dogmas of molecular biology', in S. Sarkar (ed.), *The Philosophy and History of Molecular Biology: New Perspectives.* Dordrecht: Kluwer, pp. 187–231.
Soames, S. (2002), *Beyond Rigidity: The Unfinished Semantic Agenda of Naming and Necessity.* Oxford: Oxford University Press.
Stalnaker, R. (1997), 'Reference and necessity', in B. Hale and C. Wright (eds), *A Companion to the Philosophy of Language.* Oxford: Blackwell, pp. 534–554.

Stanford, K. and Kitcher, P. (2000), 'Refining the causal theory of reference for natural kind terms', *Philosophical Studies*, 97, 99–129.

Stanley, J. (1997), 'Names and rigid designation', in B. Hale and C. Wright (eds), *A Companion to the Philosophy of Language*. Oxford: Blackwell, pp. 555–585.

Waismann, F. (1945), 'Verifiability', *Proceedings of the Aristotelian Society* (supplementary volume 19), 119–150.

Wikforss, Å. (2008), 'Semantic externalism and psychological externalism', *Philosophy Compass*, 3 (1), 151–181.

Williamson, T. (2011), 'Philosophical expertise and the burden of proof', *Metaphilosophy*, 42, 215–229.

Yablo, S. (2000), 'Textbook Kripkeanism and the open texture of concepts', *Pacific Philosophical Quarterly*, 81, 98–122.

7

Ambiguity and Referential Machinery

Ángel Pinillos

1. Introduction

One the most important debates in the philosophy of language concerns the question of how proper names and natural kind terms manage to refer to things in the world. According to the descriptivist account, championed by Bertrand Russell and Gottlob Frege, the referent of a name or natural kind word N is just whatever satisfies some description competent users associate with N and believe about the referent of N.[1] In contrast, the causal-historical view focuses on the causal history of uses of the word. According to a very simple version of this position, championed by Saul Kripke, N refers to some object only if uses of N lead back, via a chain of communication, to a dubbing or some appropriate grounding of the term to its referent.[2] Crucially, there is no requirement that speakers have a description in mind that must be satisfied by the referent and that determines the referent of the term. The debate between the two camps has been intense, but in my view, it has obscured the possibility that both sides could be right. In particular, I am attracted to the thesis that names and natural kind terms are ambiguous between causal-historical and descriptive interpretations. An argument for the ambiguity of natural kind terms has already been put forward by Philip Kitcher (1978, 1983) and Nichols, Pinillos and Mallon (forthcoming). In this paper I raise some further considerations for the thesis and sketch how it might be extended to proper names. Although I report on two original experiments which give partial support for the thesis applied to proper names, these studies are modest and extremely limited. The main purpose of this paper is to lay conceptual room for the thesis. Much more work needs to be done, but I think the possibility should be taken seriously.

2. Lewisian cluster view

Let me start by discussing the thesis as it applies to natural kind terms, using "water" as an example. According to classic descriptivism, the term "water" refers to whatever substance fits the description competent agents associate with the term and believe of the substance. If we consider a time before modern chemistry, the description associated with the word might be something like "The liquid that is clear, drinkable, and runs in rivers, streams and oceans". Any liquid that satisfies the description will count as water, even if it is not H_2O. For example, suppose there is a far away planet, "Twin Earth", that is just like Earth except that a certain molecule, XYZ, replaces H_2O. This liquid, XYZ, counts as "water" (on the descriptivist account). In contrast, according to the causal-historical account, "water" will refer to the liquid that is causally connected to our uses of "water". This would only be H_2O and not XYZ. Here's a case then where the competing views make distinct predictions. The sentence "Some water is XYZ" would be true on the descriptivist reading and false on the causal-historical view. In contrast, according to the ambiguity hypothesis, some uses of that sentence are true and some uses are false, depending on the disambiguation of "water".

In order to clarify the thesis, I want to discuss David Lewis' (1994) view on the matter where according to him, natural kind terms are associated with a cluster of descriptions. Although he doesn't defend an ambiguity view of natural kind terms, his view resembles the ambiguity view (as I construe it) in certain important respects:

> When we hear that XYZ off on Twin Earth fits many of the conditions in the cluster we are in a state of indecision about whether it deserves the name "water". When in a state of semantic indecision, we are often glad to go either way, and accommodate our usage temporarily to the whims of our conversational partners . . . So if some philosopher, call him Schmutnam, invites us to join him in saying that the water on Twin Earth differs in chemical composition from the water here, we will happily follow his lead. And if another philosopher, Putnam (1975), invites us to say that the stuff on Twin Earth is not water – and hence that Twoscar does not believe that water falls from the clouds – we just as happily follow his lead. We should have followed Putnam's lead only for the duration of that conversation, then lapsed back into our accommodating state of indecision. But, sad to say, we thought that instead of playing along with a whim, we were settling a question once and for all. And so we came away lastingly misled. (Lewis 1994, p. 424)

I want to focus on two important features of this passage. The first is that the interpretation of "water" is undecided or unsettled between the causal-historical and descriptive reading. For Lewis, the indeterminacy (for a token of the word) arises when we are asked to consider a place like Twin Earth, which fits many but not all conditions in the cluster. (In my view, the indeterminacy is more prevalent, as we will see.) The second is that the precisification is subtle in the sense that we may precisify (say by following Putnam or Schmutnam) without being consciously aware that the word needs precisifying or being consciously aware that one is precisifying (this is the situation for most philosophers according to Lewis).

I accept both of these ideas, though I disagree with Lewis about the semantic mechanism that explains the phenomenon. Lewis accepts a cluster theory:

> I think that "water" is a cluster concept. Among the conditions in the cluster are: it is liquid, it is colourless, it is odourless, it supports life . . . but . . . there is more to the cluster than that. Another condition in the cluster is: it is a natural kind. Another condition is indexical: it is abundant hereabouts. Another is metalinguistic: many call it "water". Another is both metalinguistic and indexical: *I* have heard of it under the name "water". (Lewis 1994, 424)

A cluster theory is not an ambiguity theory. I do not endorse Lewis' theory for the following reason. There doesn't seem to be much room for a causal-historical theory of reference. Saying that a term's cluster contains a description with a relevant indexical ("it is abundant hereabout"), or a description specifying that the denotation is a natural kind, is different from saying that a term's cluster contains a description that must be satisfied by an object at the end of the causal-chain of communication. So I see no way that, in general, Lewis' theory can accommodate certain uses where the causal-historical theory seems to get it right. Let us look at this in more detail.

The point can be made more vivid by focusing our attention on proper names. The descriptions most people associate with the biblical character Jonah are all mistaken, and yet, as Kripke (1980) pointed out, there are at least some uses of "Jonah" that refer to a historical individual. If the best explanation of how the referent of *those* uses are fixed appeals to the causal-historical theory of reference, then this couldn't be accommodated on the cluster view unless the cluster contained a description that mentioned the causal-historical chain (Ackerman 1979; Kroon 1987; Jackson 1998; Garcia Carpintero 2000). The problems with this view have been dealt with in detail by other philosophers (Devitt and Sterelny 1999; Soames 2002), and so I won't go into details here. One problem is that it is not plausible that one of the descriptions typical competent speakers associate with Jonah is a description of the causal-chain mechanism (Devitt and Sterelny 1999). The causal-chain theory is at best an implicitly held theory and not specified by a name's descriptive content. To see this, note that an important motivation behind descriptivism is that the descriptions associated with a name provide the cognitive content of that name. As such, these descriptions often specify a person's mental content when that content is described using the name. But it is not plausible that ordinarily, these contents involve a specification of the causal-historical chain. For example, it doesn't seem like typical uses of "Smith thinks Jonah lived in a whale" attribute to Smith a belief directly about a causal-historical chain of communication from uses of "Jonah" tracing back to a dubbing or grounding on the historical figure. This belief is too theoretical for ordinary people to have. In addition, this account predicts that Smith's belief (that Jonah lived in a whale) is partially about the word "Jonah". But this is too strong a requirement since Smith might have forgotten Jonah's name. So Smith could still believe that Jonah lived in a whale, even if he failed to recall that the guy's name was "Jonah". This possibility would be ruled out by the view we are now considering.[3]

For these reasons, I do not believe that descriptive theories can accommodate many uses of proper names where the reference is fixed via a causal-historical chain. Of course, it is beyond the scope of this paper to fully argue that the descriptivist doesn't get it right in all cases. I refer the interested reader to Soames (2002) for detailed arguments against various descriptivist approaches. However, I do not conclude from this that the causal-historical account is fully correct. The ambiguity theory also vindicates the descriptivist account.

3. Indeterminacy and ambiguity

As I mentioned earlier, what I think is right, or approximately right, about Lewis' view is that there is indeterminacy with respect to the semantics of "water", and that it can be made determinate by subtle changes in context. However, the indeterminacy in meaning for a token instance of "water" is not generated just in conversations where the substance being described (XYZ) only partially satisfies the description cluster associated with the word (as Lewis seems to suggest). Rather, in my view, the indeterminacy is the default setting for the word. This is very similar to how Lewis (1999) thinks about a different topic: vagueness. The word "house" is vague. The extension is indeterminate between the set determined by the condition expressed by "... is a main structure minus a garage" and the set determined by the condition expressed by "... is a main structure plus a garage". Nothing in our practices settles that "house" means one thing as opposed to another. In addition, there doesn't seem to be great obstacle to adopting one or another interpretation depending on the interests and goals of conversational participants.

Lewis' treatment of vagueness is naturally seen as a type of (massive) ambiguity. I think the same phenomenon is at play with proper names and natural kind terms. Moreover, both phenomena arguably have similar roots: the conventions of language fail to settle on one interpretation over the other. We may call the phenomenon concerning names and natural kind terms "vagueness" but I prefer "ambiguity". The reason is that, typically, when a word is vague, it often admits of multiple candidate extensions, but the phenomenon I have in mind restricts the interpretations to two: causal-historical and descriptivist.

The type of ambiguity at issue is not at all like that found for homonyms like "bank" (between river bank and financial institution). With the latter type of ambiguity (but not for names, natural kind terms or Lewis' "house") the candidate meanings may be wholly unrelated. In addition, while we expect the disambiguation of "bank" to have distinct lexicalizations across languages, we do not have the same expectation for names or natural kind terms, just as we do not have the same expectation for "house".

It is important to clarify that the ambiguity view I am presenting is incomplete. I will not be providing the specification of the candidate meanings corresponding to the disambiguations of proper names and natural kind terms. Instead, I will just be arguing that these terms must have at least two meanings corresponding to either the causal-historical or the descriptive reference fixing mechanism. Reference fixing mechanisms are not meanings, nor do they uniquely determine meanings. For example, a causal-historical account of names can be combined with a Millian semantics for proper names or a view under which the cognitive content of a name is a description.[4] Of course, if we accept the latter, we will reject the idea that the referent of the name is just what satisfies the description associated with the term. The descriptivist account is also neutral with respect to a theory of meaning. Although the description which fixes the referent is normally taken to be or correspond to the meaning of the term (or a component of the meaning), there is no requirement that this be so.

So although the meaning of a term and its reference fixing mechanisms must be kept separate, the notions are intimately connected. If two reference fixing mechanisms predict different referents (or extensions) for a term, then they predict different meanings. For reference is certainly either a component of meaning or is determined by it. Hence, if we find that a term is ambiguous in reference or referential mechanisms, then there should be ambiguity in meaning. This is the strategy that I employ in this paper. I do not go further and specify what these meanings are.

4. The character of the data

Why do we think that 'bank' is ambiguous? Here's one important consideration. We can use the word to mean financial institution and we can also use it to mean riverside. At the very least, this type of consideration is sufficient to take the possibility of ambiguity seriously.

I submit that similar considerations can be raised in favor of the thesis that names and natural kind terms are ambiguous. I find David Lewis's suggestion that speakers could go either way with the interpretation of "water" extremely plausible. Another example is "fruit". I think "fruit" is ambiguous between a meaning that includes tomatoes and cucumbers in its extension and a meaning that excludes them. I also hold that "Jonah", the name of the biblical character whose generally associated descriptions are mostly false, can get either a descriptive or causal-historical interpretation. For example, if someone where to insist that Jonah wasn't a real person on account of the descriptions associated with the term not being satisfied by a real person, then I would be happy to agree and go along with her. And if someone else were to insist that Jonah was a real person on account of the causal-historical chain leading to a real person, I would be happy to agree and go along with her as well.

Admittedly, examples of ambiguity for names and natural kind terms are more difficult to find and are less readily available than for words like "bank". Why is that? The reason is that the distinct interpretations for names and natural kinds are normally in harmony.[5] That is, normally, the distinct reference-fixing mechanisms yield the same extensions in the actual world (or at least in our immediate environment). The differences are subtle and often appear only when we focus on remote possible worlds or faraway places. With ordinary ambiguity, the distinct interpretations are normally well represented in our environment.

Of course, simple judgements about dual uses can only take us so far. There are a number of ways that the initial data may not signify ambiguity. There are alternative explanations that appeal instead to pragmatic effects, performance errors, context sensitivity or polysemy. I do not believe appealing to these ideas is promising. Or at least, they are less promising that the ambiguity view. I will revisit these ideas one by one after I present some initial data.

To end this section, I would like to make a remark about how the debate between descriptivists and causal-historical theorists is understood from the perspective of the ambiguity theory. A philosopher defending one of the two theories will often draw our attention to a sentence or linguistic construction that is then evaluated with respect to some possible scenario, and then the case is made that the resulting intuitive judgement favors one theory over the other. From the perspective of the ambiguity view, the conclusion is hasty. This datum does not favor one theory over the other. Instead, it merely indicates that in certain situations, a particular disambiguation is preferred.

5. Experimental data for natural kind terms

I want to begin my discussion with some recent work I have done in collaboration with Shaun Nichols and Ron Mallon.[6] This research supports the ambiguity view of natural kind terms. One experiment we ran was designed so that exposure to or absence of a subtle cue about scientists misdescribing a kind would push subjects back and forth between causal-historical and descriptive interpretations of a term. We gave the following motivation for this experiment:

> The basic idea is that often in the history of science, as we come to discover that earlier views implicating a kind are mistaken, we retain the kind term and revise the description. It is commonly taken to be an advantage of causal-historical theories that they can accommodate this practice (since they do not presume the description – now falsified – plays a role in determining the referent of the term). Thus, in devising our first experiment, we predicted that descriptivist intuitions would be deflated if we exposed participants to a case in the history of science in which scientists mischaracterized a kind, even though we in fact presume a continuity in reference. The idea is that such examples naturally induce a causal-historical way of thinking about reference, and our prediction is that by bringing such an interpretation to mind, this will make participants less inclined to give a descriptivist interpretation to a subsequent example. (Nichols et al. forthcoming, p. 11)

In fact, when Putnam argued against descriptivism for natural kind terms, he focused on hypothetical cases where a familiar kind was mischaracterized (gold, cats, etc.). From the perspective of the ambiguity theory, Putnam was merely pushing one interpretation. Our experiment exploits this insight.

In the neutral condition, we gave subjects this prompt:

> Neutral Condition
>
> The dinosaur Triceratops has a giant bony structure, a "frill", behind the head. As scientists have accumulated more fossils, they have learned much more about his dinosaur. For instance, as the Triceratops ages, the frill becomes much longer. The frill also develops giant holes and these holes become covered with keratin, which is a key component in human skin. Researchers have argued about different ways that the frill might become longer and develop holes. This remains an issue of discussion in dinosaur research.

and in the experimental condition subjects got the following:

> Mischaracterization condition:
>
> The Triceratops is a large dinosaur with a giant bony structure, a "frill", behind the head. However, our understanding of the Triceratops has changed dramatically over the last century. As scientists have accumulated more fossils, they have come to recognize that there were many mistakes made in the initial description of this dinosaur. For instance, scientists thought that the Triceratops had skin like an elephant, but it turns out that it really had scales like an alligator. They that Triceratopswas exclusively a plant eater, but now hold that the Triceratops was at least partly a meat-eater. And most strikingly when scientists first named Triceratops, they thought it was an ancient bison. Only later did they realize that it was really a dinosaur.

Both groups were then given the following passage based on medieval bestiaries (Pliny the elder 1940 book 8 from Isidore of Seville 2006). One benefit of using this passage is that it involves an unfamiliar term, and hence it is less likely that subjects would import prior information about the kind to the experiment which can distort the results.

> In the Middle Ages, animal researchers described a distinctive kind of mammal. They called it catoblepas. The catoblepas was said to be like a bull but with a head so heavy that the animal has to keep its head down at all times. It was also thought that the catoblepas had scales on its back. In addition, the researchers said that looking into the animal's eyes causes immediate death. Of course there is nothing that meets this description, but researchers think that it was based on reports of encounters with wildebeest.

Subjects were then asked whether they agreed with the sentence "Catoblepas exist". What we found was that subjects were swayed by the misdescription cue. They were more likely to say that Catoblepas existed when they were given the misdescription cue about Triceratops prior to the vignette. The ambiguity view can help explain this result since on the causal-historical reading, "Catoblepas" should refer to wildebeests and on the descriptivist account, it should fail to refer (because the associated description is not satisfied by anything). The subtle cue about misdescriptions shift interpretations from one reading to another.

We explored this idea further in another experiment. This time, we deleted the priming material and just focused on the Catoblepas vignette (we modified it somewhat to make the causal-historical path to wildebeests clearer). We then asked participants to record their agreement or disagreement with the following statements (both in a "between" and a "within subjects" study):

(1) Catoblepas exist
(2) Catoblepas are wildebeests

What we found was that subjects rejected (1) (in accordance with the descriptivist account) but accepted (2) (in accordance with the causal-historical account). This is hard to explain on a univocal account of natural kind terms. This is because, on that view, if you are committed to (2), then you should also be committed to (1), precisely what was not found. This result is especially difficult to explain for the "within subjects" condition where subjects saw (1) and (2) back to back. If there was an easy inconsistency to catch between them, our subjects should have detected it.

Although the ambiguity theory has the flexibility to account for the divergent responses to (1) and (2), there is still a need to give a more specific explanation about why subjects are more attracted to the causal-historical interpretation for (2) than for (1). In the article, we argued that this result can be explained in part by appealing to presupposition accommodation. Arguably, sentence (2) presupposes that Catoblepas exist. Therefore, subjects search for an interpretation of "Catoblepas" that can accommodate this. The interpretation that achieves this is the causal-historical one linking the term to wildebeests. Crucially, the descriptive interpretation does not achieve this. In contrast, sentence (1) does not carry the presupposition of existence (since this is what the sentence says). Subjects in this condition then are less likely to give a causal-historical response.

There are a couple of alternative explanations to the data, which can be pursued by univocal theorists. I want to discuss them here since they were not addressed in detail in the paper. First, it might be thought that (2) should be read as a universally quantified sentence "$\forall x(Cx \supset Wx)$" where "C" abbreviates "Catoblepas" and "W" "Wildebeests". This sentence is vacuously true in the cases in which the extension of "C" is empty. Hence, this interpretation predicts the results we got. However, I do not think that the universally quantified sentence is a plausible interpretation of (1). That interpretation predicts subjects will judge that a replacement of the second predicate "W" with any other would yield a judgement of truth. Thus, it would predict that "Catoblepas are squirrels" and "Catoblepas are triangles" are both true. Although we didn't experimentally test these cases, we find it implausible that subjects would agree with these sentences.

A second, more plausible alternative explanation can be raised by the defender of the univocal theory. It might be thought that our subjects surmise that catoblepas are a non-existing type or subspecies of wildebeest. Consider an analogy. Intuitively, we may agree with the claim that unicorns are four legged but reject that unicorns exist. Perhaps whatever explains this about unicorns can explain our data about catoblepas.

There are a number of things to say about this proposal. First, the view doesn't seem to be predicted by the causal historical view (at least a simple version of it). This is because if the causal chain of "Catoblepas" really leads back to wildebeests (which exist), then Catoblepas should exist. Second, there is an important difference between "Unicorns are four legged" and "Catoblepas are wildebeests". The predicate in the latter can denote a natural kind while the predicate in the former cannot do so. This difference is important. Suppose we learn, for instance, that talk of unicorns was based on horses with branches stuck to their heads (just as talk of catoblepas was based on sightings of wildebeests). If we were tempted to say that unicorns were horses, we wouldn't also be tempted to say that unicorns do not exist. Hence, it is not clear that the analogy with unicorns will be very helpful.

Third, the idea that catoblepas are a non-existing kind or subspecies of wildebeests could be interpreted in a variety of ways: (a) Catoblepas no longer exist but they used to (have gone extinct), (b) Catoblepas are a non-existing mythical creature and they are wildebeests, and (c) there is a myth according to which Cateblopas are wildebeests. Each of these interpretations is problematic and would saddle our subjects with serious confusion. We can rule out (a) since there is nothing in the vignette that suggests that Catoblepas used to roam earth but have now died off. We can rule out (b) because mythical creatures are not a type of mammal, so mythical creatures cannot be a type of wildebeest. Finally, (c) is problematic because it is not clear that even according to the myth, catoblepas belongs to an actual species (and, for instance, is a mammal). Rather, what seems plausible is that according to the myth, catoblepas are a magical animal and that discussion of catoblepas was inspired by wildebeests. Consider mermaids: supposedly talk of mermaids was based on sightings of sea lions. It wouldn't be correct to say that in the mermaid myth, mermaids were sea lions. In the myth, they were hybrid fish-human creatures, not sea lions.

Of course, I cannot rule out the possibility that the subjects are confused, so it may be that our subjects accept (a), (b) or (c) (despite their implausibility). Absent some evidence that our subjects are going for (a-c), it is preferable not to attribute to them confused notions.

There are, then, a number of problems with the alternative explanations of why responses to (1) and (2) diverge. I think the ambiguity hypothesis gives the most plausible account.

6. Experimental data for proper names

Based on the previous experiment, I developed a vignette concerning a goblin named "Benjaminus" with associated descriptions that aren't satisfied by anything. However, the causal-historical chain does lead back to a real person named "Benjamin Smith". So if descriptivism is right, "Benjaminus" would fail to refer, but if the causal historical theory is right, then "Benjaminus" would refer to Benjamin Smith. Here's the vignette:

> The medievals used to believe in a goblin named Benjaminus. Benjaminus was widely thought to fly around the night sky and also thought to have the power to read people's minds. According to legend, Benjaminus liked to scare the local population by going in their houses and moving objects around. Of course, we know now that nothing in fact ever met the description associated with "Benjaminus". However, historians in Germany have discovered that the tales of Benjaminus were based on a real person, Benjamin Smith, who was a skillful night thief in medieval London.

After the vignette, I asked participants to record their level of agreement with (a) "Benjaminus existed", (b) "Benjamin Smith existed" and either (c1) "Benjaminus is Benjamin Smith" or (c2) "Benjamin Smith was Benjaminus" (there were two conditions which differed only with respect to [c1]/[c2]). For each question, subjects marked their answer on a 5 point Likert scale (1=strongly disagree, 2=somewhat disagree, 3=neutral, 4=somewhat agree, 5=strongly agree).

I found no differences between the (c1) and (c2) responses, $t(35)=0.28$, $p>0.05$, so the following data collapses the two groups. In accordance with the descriptivist theory, subjects tended to disagree with "Benjaminus exists", M=2.13 (3=neutral) SD=1.22. This number was below the neutral point, t(29)=3.90 and the difference was statistically significant, t(29)=3.90, p<0.01.

Now, the large majority subjects tended to agree that Benjamin Smith existed. This information is explicit in the passage, so I excluded the eight subjects who failed to agree for failing to comprehend the passage. The mean for the identity statements "Benjaminus was Benjamin Smith" /"Benjamin Smith was Benjaminus" (recall there was no difference between these) was 3.41, N=30, SD=1.35. And the difference between responses to the identity statements and the existence claim was statistically significant, p<0.001, t(28)=5.38 (paired t-test). The difference between responses to the identity statement and the neutral point (3) was not statistically significant, t(29)=1.66, p>0.05.

These result are difficult for the univocal theorist to explain. If people disagree that Benjaminus existed, and agree that Benjamin Smith existed, then they should disagree that they are one and the same. But this is not what was found. It was found instead that our subjects are neutral on this question. Moreover, as I mentioned above, the difference between these responses was statistically significant.

To see how puzzling these results really are, suppose that while people thought that Santa Claus didn't exist and that Bill Clinton existed, they were ambivalent about whether Santa Claus and Bill Clinton were one and the same. This type of result would be puzzling, though a natural response is to wonder whether subjects were using "Santa Claus" (or "Bill Clinton") in a uniform way across the questions. Similarly, I think that positing ambiguity can help explain the data.

The ambiguity theory has the resources to explain these results. When subjects consider (and disagree with) "Benjaminus exists", they are using the descriptive disambiguation of the name, and when they consider "Benjaminus is Benjamin Smith/Benjamin Smith is Benjaminus", they are more likely to invoke the causal-historical disambiguation.

So far so good, but why do subjects tend more toward the descriptive interpretation for the existence prompt than for the identity prompt? Perhaps the identity claim makes an interpretation of "Benjaminus" that refers to Benjamin Smith salient. That interpretation is less salient when agents consider the existence claim. Hence, the identity prompt is more likely to elicit the causal-historical disambiguation of "Benjaminus"

There is an important disanalogy between the Benjaminus and the Catoblepas vignettes. In the Catoblepas vignettes, uses of "Catoblepas" were perceptually grounded to sightings of wildebeests. In the Benjaminus case, uses of "Benjaminus" were presumably not perceptually linked to Benjamin Smith. Instead, the passage suggests that the causal chain links back from uses of "Benjaminus" to uses of "Benjamin Smith" which are in turn perceptually linked to Benjamin Smith. As such, the sentence our subjects were asked about, "Benjaminus is Benjamin Smith", involve two occurrences in the same causal chain of names. In sharp contrast, "Catoblepas are wildebeests" do not involve occurrences in the same chain of communication. Rather, the occurrences belong to different chains but both grounded on wildebeests (On David Kaplan's account of words, "Benjaminus is Benjamin Smith" involves occurrences of the same name or word whereas "Catoblepas are wildebeests" does not).[7]

It might be thought that this could make a difference to judgements about identity. To be precise, it might be thought that the strength of a judgement about "a=b" where "a" and "b" are in the same causal-historical chain will be different from judgements when they are not (leaving all else the same as much as possible). To test this hypothesis, I developed a vignette just like the one for Benjaminus except that instead of saying that stories of Benjaminus were based on Benjamin Smith, I said they were based on Karl Gustavson. The idea here is that it is unlikely that "Karl Gustavson" would be seen as belonging to the same chain of communication as "Benjaminus".

As reported earlier, the mean response for "Benjaminus was Benjamin Smith/Benjamin Smith was Benjaminus" (recall also that which name goes first in the sentence made no statistically significant difference) was a 3.41 (where 1 is strongly disagree, 3 is neutral and 5 is strongly agree). The mean response to "Benjaminus was Karl Gustavson/Karl Gustavson was Benjaminus" was 2.97, SD=1.17, N=31 (the order of the names did not matter, p=0.45, t(29)=0.75). Although this number is trending more toward the disagreement end of the spectrum than responses to the first set of identity claims, the difference between them is not statistically significant, p=0.178, t(59)=1.36. This means that we failed to confirm the hypothesis that identity statements with names in the same causal chain are more likely to be seen as true. However, I think further investigation in this direction might bear some fruit.

7. Alternative explanations

I have said that a reason to accept the ambiguity view is that we have an initial impression that a name or a natural kind term can be used to mean different things. In addition, I have provided some modest experimental evidence for the position. But this initial data may not hold up to further scrutiny. Here are some alternative explanations. I do not believe these options are compelling.

7.1 Speaker's reference

Sometimes we use a name with the intention to refer to someone who is not the conventional bearer of the name. If Bob is about to spill his beer at a crowded bar and I mistake him for Juan, I will warn him "Hey Juan, watch your beer". In this situation, I intend to refer to Bob (speaker's reference) using "Juan". But the semantic referent of the name will still be Juan. Here's a type of case where we could get data about names having double uses but where we don't want to posit ambiguity. It might be thought that the data I presented earlier here can be explained by appealing to the distinction between speaker's reference and semantic reference.[8]

In response, note that the paradigm instances of speaker and semantic reference divergence involve the user of the name making a mistake about some feature of their environment. In the case we just saw, I confused Bob and Juan. But our experiments (Catoblepas and Benjaminus) do not have this feature. Our agents are given all the information about the subject matter (which is assumed to be accurate). Moreover, by design, the terms used are ones that they probably never encountered before, so it is unlikely that they would import prior confounding information about "Benjaminus" or "Catoblepas" to the case.

7.2 Conversational implicature

Sometimes we use sentences to convey propositions that go beyond what is semantically expressed by a sentence. Paul Grice (1975), through his theory of conversational implicatures, gave an explanation of how this can happen for rational and cooperative agents. Crucially, the explanation of how an implicature arises normally involves the apparent violation or flouting of a maxim by uttering S, which is resolved as being merely apparent by assuming the speaker is attempting to communicate something beyond the semantic content of S.

Grice laid out four maxims that he hoped could do the work in explaining how implicatures arise: Quality (speak truthfully and backed up by evidence), Quantity (be as informative as required but no more), Relation (be relevant) and Manner (be orderly, clear and avoid obfuscation). Here's an example of Quality at work. If someone says sarcastically to you, "you look great" in a situation when you obviously look terrible, you would take your interlocutor to want to communicate something that is not the semantic content of the sentence uttered (that you look bad). Otherwise, the interlocutor would be violating Quality.

It is not obvious to me how appealing to implicatures can help explain the conflicting uses of names and natural kind terms we have seen in this chapter. To be specific, it is not clear what feature of the vignettes would lead subjects to interpret questions about the level of agreement with sentences such as "Benjaminus exists" or "Catoblepas are wildebeests" to be questions about other sentences or questions that are not about the semantic referents of "Benjaminus" or "Catoblepas".

It might help to think about a case where there is a referential shift for names, and it is plausible that implicature is at play. I make use here of interesting work by Jennifer Saul (2007). Consider a use of the sentence "Superman leaps more tall buildings that Clark Kent". This may strike one as true even if one is aware that Clark Kent is Superman: if "Superman" and "Clark Kent" corefer, then the sentence cannot be true under standard assumptions of compositionality. One way of accounting for the intuition that the sentence is true is that uses of that false sentence implicate a true proposition: that the person stage of Superman/Clark Kent associated with wearing a cape and tights leaps more buildings than the person stage associated with being a reporter and wearing glasses. The implicature is triggered, presumably, by flouting the maxim of quality (which requires, among other things, that speakers not say obviously false things).[9]

Something similar may be said about the existence prompts in our studies. Perhaps the causal-historical theory is correct and it is just obvious that Catoblepas and Benjaminus exist and so the question about existence is taken to implicate a question about whether the descriptions associated with those terms are satisfied.

One possible response to this alternative explanation is that in surveys participants are often asked obvious (and non-obvious) questions as checks to ensure they are not blindly responding to the material. Most subjects get these questions right, signifying that quality implicatures are not often triggered. In addition, in the Benjaminus prompts, I asked subjects about whether Benjamin Smith existed (which should be obvious given the vignettes), but the subjects overwhelmingly agreed that he did exist. If this question did not trigger an implication through a Quality violation, it is not likely that the question about whether Benjaminus exists did either. As far as I can tell, then, I do not see a way that appealing to conversational implicatures can explain the dual use data.

7.3 Context sensitivity and polysemy

Some terms shift their extensions from conversation to conversation. For example, "I" will refer to different people depending on who is speaking. Ever since David Kaplan (1989), it has been common to say that paradigm instances of context sensitive terms have a stable meaning, a "character", which can be modeled as a function from contexts of utterance to intensions. For example, the meaning of "I" is a function that takes as input a conversational context and returns a constant function from worlds to the speaker of the context. In this sense, we can say that pronouns and other indexicals are context sensitive.

But not all terms with shifty extensions work like this. Polysemy does not work like paradigm cases of context sensitivity. A word is polysemous whenever it admits of different meanings that are nonetheless related. Sometimes the relatedness of the meanings is systematic in the sense that there are general rules that can transform one meaning to another. In other cases, there aren't such rules. An example of the former is "cup" which can be used to mean a container or else a quantity ("I filled the cup with vinegar" and "there are twenty cups of butter in that batch of cookies"). Evidence that the meanings are systematically connected is that we see other words that admit of similar ambiguity ("bag", "box" etc.), and we also see that their translations to other languages preserve the polysemy. Unsystematic polysemy lacks these features. For instance, "glasses" can be used to talk about a eyewear or a drinking containers (which are related), but the relation between these two meanings is not also present between other words and is not preserved under translation.

I think that context sensitivity is not the right way to understand the dual use of names or natural kind terms (at the very least they don't work like paradigm cases of context sensitivity). First, with many indexicals like "I" and "you" and demonstratives like "this" and "that" we can readily come up with an approximation for the meaning (character) associated with those terms ("refers to the speaker" for "I", "refers to the audience" for "you", "refers to a nearby object demonstrated" for "this", "refers to a distant object demonstrated" for "that" etc.), but we draw a blank if asked to produce a meaning that would determine which disambiguation is invoked on a particular occasion for names and natural kind terms. To return to our old example, we wouldn't expect an interesting meaning for "water" (that gives us the dual use) any more than we would expect one for Lewis's "house".[10]

Second, the various extensions of context sensitive terms are normally sets or objects that are disjoint or non-overlapping. For instance, the various referents of "I" are distinct individuals and so on for "you", "this" etc. Of course, there can be overlap as when "this" is used to refer to the leg of a chair and later to the chair itself. But this is the exception rather than the norm. In contrast, as mentioned earlier, the disambiguations for natural kind terms are often in harmony and will wholly overlap in the actual world as well as nearby worlds. Very often, we have to come up with far-fetched scenarios to tease apart descriptivist and causal-historical interpretations.

The phenomenon under investigation seems to have more in common with systematic polysemy. The candidate extensions of "water" are related, and the ambiguity expected can also be expected for many words (all names and natural kind terms) and across languages. However, it fails to pattern with polysemy in that (as I emphasized earlier) the candidate extensions for names and natural kind terms are overlapping.

A worry about categorizing our phenomenon as polysemy is that we would also need to include Lewis's "house" and countless other vague terms in the category. Ultimately, lumping these terms alongside ordinary cases of polysemy may not be fruitful. But even if so, a subcategorization just capturing the dual uses of names and natural kind terms would have to be reified.

Notes

1 Frege (1893/1952), Russell (1919).
2 Kripke (1980).
3 Diana Ackerman (1979) defends a view where the description correlated with a name is sometimes a specification of the causal-historical chain. However, she does not endorse the idea that this description provides the cognitive content of the name or enters into the content of belief ascriptions, which may be the chief advantage of descriptivism. The view does not count as descriptivist on the criterion I proposed (which follows Kripke's).
4 Evans' (1973) hybrid view is causal-historical but posits a descriptive content.
5 I thank a referee for the "Ambiguous Reference" paper for the term "Harmony".
6 Nichols, Pinillos and Mallon (forthcoming).
7 Kaplan (1990).
8 Kripke (1977).
9 Saul considers the implicature account, but she does not endorse it.
10 Even if a term is not context sensitive, it will still have a default character that will just be a constant function from contexts to the term's intension.

References

Ackerman, D. (1979), 'Proper names, propositional attitudes and non descriptive connotations'. *Philosophical Studies,* 35 (1), 55–69.

Devitt, M. and Sterelny, K. (1999), *Language and Reality*. Oxford: Blackwell.

Evans, G. (1973), 'The causal theory of names'. *Proceedings of the Aristotelian Society,* Supplementary Volume 47, 187–208. Reprinted in *Collected Papers*. Oxford: Oxford University Press, 1985, page references to reprinted version.

Frege. G. (1893/1952), 'On sense and reference', in P. Geach and M. Black (eds), *Translations from the Philosophical Writings of Gottlob Frege*. Oxford: Blackwell.

Garcia-Carpintero, M. (2000), 'a presuppositional account of reference fixing'. *Journal of Philosophy,* 97 (3), 109–147.

Grice, H. P. (1975), 'Logic and conversation', in P. Cole and J. Morgan (eds), *Syntax and Semantics*, Vol.3. New York: Academic Press.

Isidore of Seville (2006), *The Etymologies of Isidore of Seville*. Trans. S. Barney, W. Lewis, J. Beach and O. Berghof. Cambridge: Cambridge University Press.

Kaplan, D. (1989), 'Demonstratives', in D. Kaplan, J. Almog, J. Perry and H. Wettstein (eds), *Themes From Kaplan*, Oxford: Oxford University Press, pp. 481–563.

Kaplan, D. (1990), 'Words'. *Proceedings of the Aristotelian Society,* Supplementary Volume 64, 93–119.

Kitcher, P. (1978), 'Theories, theorists and theoretical change'. *The Philosophical Review,* 87, 519–547.

Kitcher, P. (1993), *The Advancement of Science: Science without Legend, Objectivity without Illusions*. Oxford: Oxford University Press.

Kripke, S. (1980), *Naming and Necessity*. Cambridge: Harvard University Press.

Kroon, F. (1987), 'Causal descriptivism'. *Australasian Journal of Philosophy,* 65, 1–17.

Lewis, D. (1994), 'Reduction of mind', in S. Guttenplan (ed.), *A Companion to the Philosophy of Mind*. Oxford: Blackwell, pp. 412–431.

Lewis, D. (1999), 'Many, but almost one', *Papers in Metaphysics and Epistemology*. Cambridge: Cambridge University Press, pp. 164–182.

Nichols S., Pinillos A. and Mallon R. (forthcoming), 'Ambiguous reference'. *Mind*.

Russell, B. (1919), 'Knowledge by acquaintance and knowledge by description', in *Mysticism and Logic*: London: George Allen and Unwin.

Saul, J. (2007), *Simple Sentences, Substitution and Intuitions*. Oxford: Oxford University Press.

Soames, S. (2002), *Beyond Rigidity: The Unfinished Semantic Agenda of 'Naming and Necessity'*. New York: Oxford University Press.

8

General Terms, Hybrid Theories and Ambiguity: A Discussion of Some Experimental Results[*]

Genoveva Martí

1. Introduction

In their 2004 paper "Semantics, cross-cultural style", Machery, Mallon, Nichols and Stich (MMNS), concluded that there are wide variations in intuitions with regard to how the reference of proper names is determined. Some speakers tend to give descriptivist or internalist answers[1] when asked who the referent of a certain use of a name is, whereas other speakers are more inclined to give externalist answers, answers that are in line with the chain of communication picture.[2] The results of MMNS (2004) were established on the basis of probes run in the United States and in Hong Kong, using vignettes very similar to Saul Kripke's fictional Gödel case from *Naming and Necessity*.[3]

Two aspects of MMNS' discussion are worth noticing for our purposes here. First, MMNS were motivated by Richard Nisbett and colleagues' work on a wide variety of cognitive differences between Westerners and East Asians (Nisbett, Peng, Choi and Norenzayan 2001). MMNS' probes are geared toward testing if there are also such cultural differences in the responses to questions about the referential link between a use of a name and what that use refers to. On the basis of the results, MMNS conclude that there is a tendency toward descriptivism among East Asians and a tendency toward the so-called causal-historical picture among Westerners, and they suggest that the intuitions that give support to the theory of reference are relative to culture.

It is not clear that the differences MMNS found are linked to culture since, as further work suggests, there is also wide intracultural variation in the responses to cases like the ones posed by MMNS. In fact, some authors suggest that the variations can be found even at an individual level, as the same person may be inclined toward different responses in different situations.

The second aspect to notice is that MMNS focused on the debate between classical descriptivism and the so-called causal-historical picture in regards to proper names. However, both approaches to reference provide also different explanations of the connection between general terms (natural and artefactual) and the things and samples those terms apply to. Other authors (Braisby, Franks and Hampton 1996 and Jylkkä, Railo and Haukioja 2009) have brought the debate initiated by MMNS to bear on general terms.

In the past (Marti 2009, 2012), I have criticized MMNS and a subsequent piece by Machery, Olivola and, DeBlanc (2009) that follows a similar strategy. In a nutshell, I have argued that the questions asked in the MMNS (2004) probes, as well as in Machery, Olivola and DeBlanc (2009), ask the participants to express an opinion regarding how the reference of a particular use of a name is determined, a question whose answer requires reflection on practice and does not capture what the participants' practice really is, that is, how they themselves use names.[4] I still have the same criticism, but for the purposes of this chapter I will set these concerns mostly aside to focus on other aspects of the debate. My purpose in this chapter is to examine two proposals by James Genone and Tania Lombrozo (GL) (2012) and by Shaun Nichols, Ángel Pinillos and Ron Mallon (NPM) (forthcoming).[5] In their papers GL and NPM focus on general terms and away from the cross-cultural issues. Both sets of authors set out to test the tendencies toward descriptivism and the causal-historical picture among the population. They both conclude that there are wide variations among speakers, that those variations are intracultural and that they affect even individuals' responses depending on the situation. However, they differ in their assessment of what kind of theory would be supported by their results. Whereas GL favour some sort of hybrid theory, one incorporating elements of descriptivism and elements of the historical account, NPM defend the virtues of an account according to which general terms, or some general terms, are ambiguous: on some occasions of use the connection between an utterance of a general term and its domain of application follows a descriptivist recipe, whereas on other occasions the connection can be traced via a causal-historical chain of communication.

The discussion of these two proposals will lead to a reflection on the differences between the postulation of hybrid theories and the endorsement of pervasive ambiguity, as well as to an assessment of the kind of theory that the data collected by GL and NPM support.[6]

2. The two studies and their conclusions

GL (2012) extend MMNS' (2004) line of inquiry to general terms, both natural and artefactual. GL presented participants with stories that are similar to the Gödel case exploited by MMNS. In each one of the stories there were slight variations depending on the degree of fit of the definite descriptions that two different hypothetical speakers associated to a kind term, and depending also on the causal-historical connection of the term to the kind. The participants in GL's study were asked whether the two protagonists of the vignette were thinking and talking about the same kind under four sets of conditions: (i) different description and same causal origin, (ii) same description and same causal origin, (iii) same description and different causal origin, and (iv) different description and different causal origin.

As expected, cases (ii) and (iv) were unsurprising, but the data collected about (i) and (iii) revealed that there is an important split among participants. When the description associated with a term by the protagonists of the vignette was different but the kind at the end of the chain of communication was the same,[7] 44 per cent of the participants gave a positive answer to the question as to whether the two protagonists in the story were thinking about and referring to the same kind. When the causal connection of terms used by two protagonists in the vignettes led to different kinds but the description in their minds was the same[8] 53 per cent of the speakers responded affirmatively to the question as to whether the two protagonists were thinking and referring to the same kind. GL conducted their experiment using terms for diseases, minerals, artefacts and legal documents, and their results are consistent. On the basis of the data GL also concluded that the split among participants was not due to their being unsure about the answer or to lack of comprehension. More importantly, GL conducted further probes to determine if the divergences could be attributed to the fact that different groups of participants had and expressed different intuitions, some of them more descriptivist, and some of them more in line with the chain of communication picture. GL observed that the responses to (i) and (iii) type of questions were not correlated, so they concluded that the strategies pursued by participants "did not take the form of consistent reliance on a single factor" (2012, p. 728), namely they were not consistent with a purely descriptivist or a purely historical approach. This, according to GL shows that "the findings support the hypothesis that reference judgements are a function of both descriptive and causal factors" (2012, p. 728), that "individuals utilize both descriptive and causal information in making judgements about reference, and that mixed patterns do not reflect . . . a heterogeneous population with some 'intuitive descriptive theorists' and some 'intuitive causal theorists,' as suggested by Machery et al.'s studies" (2012, p. 731).

GL conclude that the account of reference determination should take into account that both causal connections and descriptive information figure in the explanation of what constitutes the domain of application of a kind term and they suggest that a hybrid theory, one that incorporates both causal and descriptive elements, may provide the right sort of account. GL mention Gareth Evans' (1985) approach as the kind of hybrid theory that would be supported by the data collected, although they also express some doubts that the details of Evans' theory really do fit the data. I discuss below Evans' theory in the context of GL's arguments, but for the moment it is worth noting that GL do not make a specific commitment to a specific theory of reference determination. Their claim is just that speakers' judgements about reference, in particular the judgements about what certain general terms apply to, are swayed by both descriptive factors and causal factors, and they advance the tentative hypothesis that a theory that combines both kinds of factors may be supported by the data, without exploring in their paper the form that such a theory might take. The kind of vignettes presented by GL are very similar to MMNS's (2004) and Machery, Olivola and DeBlanc's (2009) vignettes. The questions that GL ask are questions that require the participants to reflect on what hypothetical speakers are thinking about or referring to. They are, thus, questions that invite theoretical reflection about practice and do not collect, in my view, data about practice. So, I would direct to GL the same objections I expressed in Marti (2009) and (2012).[9]

The situation is slightly different as regards NPM (forthcoming). NPM do not construct fictional stories that test participants' intuitions as regards counterfactual use scenarios; instead, they use real cases in the history of science in which experts misdescribed a kind. For instance, in the Middle Ages the catoblepas was described as "an animal said to be like a bull but with a head so heavy that the animal had to keep its head down at all times. It was also thought that the catoblepas had scales on its back" (NPM forthcoming).[10] Of course, Middle Age descriptions of the catoblepas are not satisfied by any real animal (it is worth noting that the descriptions of the alleged animal also mention that looking into the animal's eyes would cause immediate death).

Nevertheless, as NPM note, researchers believe that the introduction of the term "catoblepas" was connected to sightings of wildebeest. Some of the choices NPM present to their subjects do prompt theoretical reflection. For instance, on several occasions participants are asked to judge the truth value of

"'Catoblepas' refers to wildebeest". However, other questions are closer, in my view, to capturing the participants' dispositions to use the terms in question. For instance, subjects were asked to indicate their level of agreement with statements such as "Catoblepast exist" or "Catoblepas are wildebeest".

NPM hypothesized that if participants in their experiment were primed to stress the continuity of application of a term in spite of the presence of radical misinformation, by reading, for instance, about the story of the continued use of "triceratops" in spite of the extreme original mischaracterizations of the dinosaur, they would make choices in line with the causal-historical picture, whereas subjects exposed to a story that heavily highlighted the radically erroneous nature of the characterization of the catoblepas (for instance, the inclusion of the statement that looking into a catoblepas' eyes would cause immediate death) would be more inclined to respond in ways more sensitive to the fact that the descriptive information associated with 'catoblepas' is not satisfied by any existing kind. By and large, the results support NPM's hypothesis.

The choice of the catoblepas story is, in my view, unfortunate. The description of the catoblepas, in particular the attribution of the property of causing death with its sight, makes it almost a mythical character. And in such cases the fact that some rather unspecified alleged connection to some real animal, the wildebeest in this case, figures in the story may not be sufficient to push speakers to accept that the word does indeed refer to those real animals. Kripke has pointed out that "if the story of the unicorns were historically connected to some genuine and ordinary kind of animal . . ., and the mythical traits attributed to it gradually evolved, we would probably not say that it turned out that unicorns really existed after all" (Kripke 2013, p. 50, n. 18). Thus, the tendency NPM observe among speakers to deny that the catoblepas existed when the erroneous nature of the Middle Age experts description was highlighted, may not be driven by descriptivism but simply by the presumption that 'catoblepas' refers to a mythical animal. Nevertheless, although I will refrain here from discussing the details, some of the speakers' reactions reported by NMP are indeed surprising[11] and they reveal variations among speakers' reactions, even if it is not entirely clear what the cause of the variations is.

If we concede that NPM's hypothesis is corroborated, the interesting point for our purposes is that NPM's results appear to be approximately in line with GL's. Nevertheless, NPM put forward a different conclusion as regards the semantic explanation supported by the data. Instead of endorsing a unified hybrid theory of reference, NPM suggest that kind terms are ambiguous between a descriptivist and a causal-historical reading. Depending on the conversational setting, speakers will be inclined either toward responses consistent with a descriptivist disambiguation or toward responses consistent with a causal-historical approach.

NPM argue that a hybrid theory would not account for the data presented, and their target in such argument is the kind of theory suggested in Evans 1985. So, both in GL's and in NPM's case the discussion revolves around the adequacy of a hybrid theory like Evans'. Before assessing GL's and NPM's recommendations, it is worth stopping to reflect on the nature of Evans' proposal and the sense in which it can be considered to be a hybrid approach.

3. Hybridity and Evans's approach

Right off the bat, it is hard to see what a unified theory that incorporated elements of classical descriptivism – the kind of descriptivism Kripke, Donnellan and others were arguing against, which happens to be also the sort of descriptivism GL, NPM, as well as MMNS focus on – together with elements of the causal-historical approach would consist in.

This is not because the causal-historical approach is an alternative to a theory of the determination of reference such as classical descriptivism. The chain of communication picture, or causal-historical picture, is not a theory of the determination of reference. What *makes* a use of "Aristotle" refer to Aristotle is not the fact that the use is connected to previous uses of the word, since that connection at most will lead to the first use of the name, not to the referent.[12] The picture presented by Kripke (1980) and Donnellan (1970) is rather an intuitive explanation of the transmission of names – of words, in general, and the preservation of their semantic function.[13]

As an aside, let me point out that it is unfortunate that the chain of communication picture continues to be presented as a theory of determination of reference, and experimental philosophers, although not the origin of the confusion, are contributing to it.

In fact, a classical descriptivist could incorporate the causal-historical chain into their approach. All a descriptivist would need to argue is that names are bestowed by being linked to definite descriptions that are then passed from user to user, from link to link of a chain of communication. From this point of view, what makes a speaker a new link in the chain of communication would be the acquisition of the definite description associated with the name, a definite description that determines the reference of each use of the name. Of course, a theory of this sort would be a descriptivist theory through and through and not the kind of theory contemplated by GL, NMP, and Machery and colleagues.

What makes classical descriptivism and any approach to reference consistent with Kripke's approach so difficult to combine in a hybrid theory is precisely the fact that Kripke's argument is essentially a negative argument. What emerges from Kripke's considerations, and in particular from the crucial semantic arguments – the ignorance and error arguments – is that reference does not have to be established via the satisfaction of descriptive information. And this amounts to the denial of classical descriptivism.[14]

An approach to reference that is, arguably, hybrid is the sort of causal descriptivism proposed by Frederick Kroon (1987), a view according to which reference is determined by a description such as "the individual at the end of the chain that leads to this use of N," or "the person that the members of my community from which I inherit my use of N refer to", or something similar. This could count as a hybrid view, since it claims that reference is determined by the satisfaction of a definite description a speaker associates with N, as classical descriptivism urged, while at the same time incorporating the chain of communication into the descriptive content. But this is not the kind of theory that the data collected by GL, nor by NPM, appear to underwrite, since the descriptive information used in the vignettes does not include mention of the chain of communication and it is closer to the type of descriptive information contemplated by classical descriptivists such as Bertrand Russell.

Both GL and NPM take issue with the approach endorsed in Evans 1987, characterizing it as a sort of hybrid theory. But it is not clear at all that Evans defends a hybrid of the classical descriptivist approach tested by GL and NPM and the chain of communication picture.

It is, to begin with, doubtful that Evans would incorporate elements of classical descriptivism as reference determiners, or partial determiners. For one of the features of Evans' positive view is precisely that reference is not determined by the satisfaction of descriptive information and that it is a mistake to interpret Fregean senses as descriptive and as determiners of reference by fit. According to Evans, "there is absolutely nothing in the texts to support the claim that he [Frege] held that the way of thinking of any object *must* exploit the subject's knowledge of some description uniquely true of it" (Evans 1982, p. 18).

Evans' view is often characterized as a hybrid theory. Thus, for instance, according to M. Reimer (2010):

> Evans provides several examples of uses of proper names that are most naturally accounted for via a hybrid theory... Like description accounts, [Evans' approach]

accounts for cognitive significance . . . as well as reference; like causal accounts, it preserves the intuition that one cannot refer to something with which one has no causal link whatsoever.

And Evans himself argues that the approach he proposes in some sense vindicates both descriptivism and the causal-historical picture, but it is far from clear that the approach he endorses can be characterized as a hybrid or as providing support for classical descriptivism.[15]

For Evans' vindication of descriptivism does not afford definite descriptions a role in fixing the reference: even in the midst of his avowals of vindication Evans insists that "the fix is by causal origin and not by fit" (1987, p. 23). As GL put it:

> Evans . . . proposed that each use of a name is associated with a file of information that an individual stores about the referent of the name. While some of the information in the file can be false (by not being generated by the appropriate source), reference will be tied to whatever is the dominant causal source of the information in the file. (GL 2012, p. 720)

Descriptive information plays an undeniably important cognitive role in Evans' approach. But this is something that neither Kripke nor Donnellan, nor even a true causal theorist of reference such as Devitt need deny.

As a theory of reference determination, Evans' theory is fundamentally causal, for the referent of a name is the causal origin of the descriptive information that speakers have in their minds. The information might be erroneous. The information that Aristotle was born in Stagira or that he tutored Alexander the Great may well be mistaken, even if Aristotle himself is the source of that information. So, as Reimer (2010) puts it: "Evans' theory avoids the problem of ignorance and error". But this is precisely because the description plays no role in determining the reference. The descriptive information associated with a name can be erroneous, and this is immaterial for Evans precisely because, *contra* classical descriptivism, the associated attributes do not determine reference. If there is massive error in the descriptive information associated with a name, we may of course conclude that the name does not refer or that a kind term does not apply to anything. But this conclusion would not, according to Evans, be based on the fact that no object satisfied the descriptive information; it would simply be because the massive error would be taken as an indication that nothing could plausibly be the source of such radically wrong information. So, for example, the claim that experts believed catoblepas to cause instant death to those who looked into their eyes makes if very doubtful that any real animal could be the source of such a wild attribution.

Evans' theory is, in a sense, more causal than Kripke's and Donnellan's picture for it gives more of an explanation of the causal elements at work, something that Kripke and Donnellan do not do. In fact, there is little in Kripke's and Donnellan's remarks about the chain of communication that justify calling the theory 'causal'. Kripke himself stresses the social character of the picture (the fact that what we refer to depends not on what is in our minds but on our connections to other members of our speakers' community), over and above the causal factors, and he as often uses "causal chain" (1980, pp. 93, 96) as "'causal' chain of communication" (1980, p. 59, n. 22, with quotes around "causal"), "historical chain" (1980, p. 8, n. 9), and "chain of communication" (pp. 91–93).

Some of the cases that Evans discusses are meant to highlight the differences between his approach and a naive chain of communication picture inspired by Kripke's and Donnellan's remarks. Among those the "Madagascar" and the "Ibn Kahn" case stand out. In these two cases, the naive picture presented by Kripke and Donnellan appears to give the wrong results as to what uses of those names refer to: a portion of the mainland and not the island, in the case of "Madagascar", and the scribe who wrote his name in the document, not the mathematician that did the proof, in the case of "Ibn Kahn". Part of the reason to suppose that the picture presented by Kripke and Donnellan gives the wrong results, is precisely the fact that the picture they present is so under-described. Kripke and Donnellan describe a very simplified and idealized picture of how names are bestowed and how their use is transmitted from speaker to speaker. The dubbing ceremony that is supposed to account for a name bestowal is acknowledged to be just a portrayal of a typical way in which names get tied to their bearers, but it is clearly not essential to the picture. There are other ways in which names are introduced: by description, for instance, or by a direct use without the mediation of a metalinguistic ceremony. The picture is flexible enough to allow for the bestowal of a name in the kinds of circumstances that are contemplated in the "Madagascar" and the "Ibn Kahn" case. Speakers may, simply by mistake, start using a name with the intention to speak about a certain object and the practice may catch on. As Michael Devitt has suggested, a mistake can function as the initiation of a chain of communication, by grounding reference in a new object, even when the intention to dub is absent (Devitt 1981; see also Devitt and Sterelny 1999). According to Evans in such cases uses of the name refer to the causal origin of an attributive file, and one may disagree with his explanation, pointing rather, for instance, to the existence of a systematic practice that connects use to use even in the absence of a common file. But no matter what, and even if we accept Evans' account, the point is that the role of the file is not to determine the reference by searching and finding an object that satisfies the, or most of the, attributes associated, as classical descriptivism would have it.

Thus, it is not surprising that Evans' approach would not be a good match for the kind of data GL or NPM collect, as GL themselves acknowledge (GL 2012, p. 733). The data appear to point toward the reliance, on occasion, on definite descriptions as reference determiners, something not contemplated by Evans.

4. Ambiguity and the causal-historical approach

As far as I can tell both sets of data – supposing them to portray actual speakers' use – reveal that individual speakers are in some occasions inclined to produce judgements that are in line with classical descriptivism whereas in some other occasions their judgements give prominence to the continuity of reference and reliance on previous uses that is highlighted by the chain of communication picture. Rather than suggesting a unified theory of reference that combines in each use some descriptivist and some causal elements, the explanation of speakers' responses suggests, in my view, the kind of approach NPM endorse, a form of ambiguity according to which in some cases the descriptive information associated with a term is dominant in determining what the term applies to, whereas in some other occasions the chain that leads back to the introduction of the term takes precedence.

The kind of ambiguity postulated by NPM is different, as they themselves point out, from typical cases of lexical ambiguity. But, if NPM are right, the data point towards different uses of terms on different occasions. In spite of the differences with other cases of lexical ambiguity, it would not be entirely surprising if, on occasion, the file of information that a speaker associates with a term was taken to be that which determines what she is speaking about, for after all the file does play a cognitive role, and it is a file of things we think we know about the things we refer to. It is not unnatural to think that the information we possess applies to whatever it is that we are talking about. Whether this should be treated as a semantic or as a pragmatic phenomenon is a different issue, and it is not one that NPM have addressed, but it is something that needs to be elucidated, perhaps by designing tests that can provide evidence on this regard.

There is, certainly, a long-standing tradition in semantics that recommends resisting the postulation of ambiguities, springing from the presumption that a unified theory is in general preferable to the endorsement of different explanations. Nevertheless, the resistance is to be taken as a recommendation and in fact, the possibility that in certain conversational settings different factors, causal or descriptive, may take prominence is not far-fetched.[16] For instance, in cases where the descriptive information associated with a term is wildly implausible or off the mark, the judgement of non-existence is entirely natural, and in fact there are plenty of historical examples: we say that there is no phlogiston, not that phlogiston turned out to be O_2 and that we were wrong in, for instance, attributing to it negative mass.[17]

An important question is what those variations show as regards semantic theory. NPM, for instance, argue that their results "put pressure on a univocal theory of reference along the lines of the causal-historical theory" (NPM forthcoming). And the impetus for the debate around experimental semantics comes from MMNS (2004) who viewed their results as a threat to a universal theory of reference, specifically the kind of anti-descriptivist theory endorsed by Kripke.

Experimental semanticists argue against the adequacy of Kripke's approach to reference on the basis of arguments about the apparent descriptivist semantics of some terms. The assumption, I believe, is that an argument to the effect that a set of terms have a descriptivist semantics, or that some uses of terms follow a descriptivist mode of reference determination, constitutes an objection to Kripke's stance. It is worth reflecting on the structure of the dialectic, for it seems to me that there are deep confusions underlying the debate.

First of all, it is important to distinguish between intuitions about how reference is determined from data that is meant to collect actual usage. I have already argued (Marti 2009, 2012) that the former are not relevant to semantic theorizing. So, I am focusing here on results that can plausibly be interpreted as reflecting usage, such as NPM's, and the issue to elucidate is whether the results and observations constitute counterexamples to the chain of communication picture. In order to see that they do not, it is important to remember the crux of the disagreement between classical descriptivism and the chain of communication picture. According to classical descriptivism reference is mediated, always mediated. From this perspective, it is impossible to establish reference unless it is via descriptive material. Kripke's arguments open the door to a view according to which reference is established directly, by convention and without the mediation of definite descriptions, a view according to which the conditions of correct application of a term, be a singular or a general term, are to be found outside of the speakers' minds. The kind of semantics that emerges from Kripke and Donnellan and from Putnam's considerations about natural kind terms (Putnam 1973) contemplates direct reference. Their cases and examples are meant to show that reference can be direct, that it does not have to be established via a definite description and this is accompanied by arguments directed toward showing that proper names, in general, and natural kind terms, in general, do refer without the mediation of definite descriptions. To argue that the use of some terms is arguably guided by an associated definite description, is not to disprove the Kripke-Donnellan-Putnam approach, whereas showing that some terms refer or apply without the mediation of semantic mechanisms such as descriptions, does disprove descriptivism. It is not, and it should not be, part of the Kripke-Donnellan-Putnam approach to show that no term can have its reference or domain of application determined by associated descriptive material.

Nothing, as Kripke himself noted, prevents speakers from introducing a term and deciding to use it as a real abbreviation of a definite description. Of course, whenever a non-structured, tag-like term is introduced in a language, the potential for the associated reference-fixing description to stop operating is there. Speakers often do not pass along the chain of communication the descriptions that are supposed to determine reference, erroneous information is easily added to the original reference fixing attributes and uniquely identifying properties may be lost, giving rise to ignorance and error and leaving speakers with a file whose role is undoubtedly cognitive, but non-operational at the level of fixing reference, even though the chain that connects use to use and leads back to the introduction of the term is still present and guarantees the appropriate connections that keep usage uniform. Name-like expressions have a tendency to be used as standard proper names.

None of this is a threat to the chain of communication, or causal-historical picture.

Of course, according to NPM, their results point in the direction of something stronger: it is not just that some terms are semantically connected with definite descriptions. Their point is that individual speakers do use terms descriptively and non-descriptively depending on the conversation setting. But even that is no threat to the chain of communication view. In fact, it is something that has been pointed out by one of the staunchest defenders of a causal theory of reference. Michael Devitt (1981, pp. 157–160) has often pointed out that proper names are used descriptively in some contexts. Literary historians, for instance, use "Shakespeare", bypassing anti-Stratfordian concerns, to talk about whoever wrote the famous plays, when their focus is the discussion of the plays and their contents

> the names of authors . . . can have a double life. In claims about where "Shakespeare" lived, was educated, and so on, the name seems to function as

a designational name. In critical assessments of "the works of Shakespeare", however, it often seems to function as a descriptive name, so that it would not matter to the truth of these assessments if the work was actually written by Bacon. (Devitt forthcoming)

Again, that names, or other expressions, can be used in a way that gives prominence to associated descriptive information in the determination of reference is no threat to the anti-descriptivist arguments by Kripke, Donnellan and others.

It is tempting here to engage in an argument as regards how extended the Kripkean uses, vs. the descriptivist uses are, as if the statistical distribution of different uses was relevant in order to establish one theory over another. In my view, arguing in these terms amounts to misunderstanding the dialectic of the Kripke-Donnellan stance against descriptivism. Kripke and Donnellan are arguing against a conception of reference according to which reference *has to be* mediated; the reference of an expression has to be established via an associated mechanism, a description that determines the reference on each occasion of use. The gist of Donnellan's and Kripke's arguments is that this is not so, and that speakers refer in the absence of such mechanism. The issue of contention is about the possibility of reference: the descriptivist claims it is not possible to refer without the mediation of a description; Donnellan's and Kripke's arguments and the examples they use to illustrate them are meant to show that it is, and it is also worth noticing, that the examples used by anti-descriptivists to make their case, cover a pretty substantial number of expressions and kinds of expressions.

If NPM are right, individual speakers, in certain conversational contexts, use terms to refer to whatever fits an associated descriptive file. This should not provoke changes in the chain of communication approach, although certainly would be interesting to continue to investigate what kinds of conversational contexts prompt one or another usage and whether the phenomenon is really a semantic phenomenon or a purely pragmatic one.

Notes

* I am grateful to Ángel Pinillos for comments on a previous version. The research for this paper has been partly funded by the Spanish MICINN, under grant 2011FFI25626. I acknowledge also the support of the AGAUR of the Generalitat de Catalunya (2014-SGR-81).

1. Internalist, because the referent of a use of a name is determined by a description that the speaker has in mind and associates with the name.
2. Externalist, because what the use of the name refers to depends on the objective position of the speaker in a network of users.
3. See Kripke (1980), pages 83–84.
4. See Devitt (2011) for similar concerns.
5. Pinillos's chapter in this book discusses and develops the view further.
6. Two clarifications: (i) the concerns I expressed about MMNS's work apply also to some of the probes conducted by GL and NMP. More on this below, although for the purposes of the discussion here I will be setting these issues aside and I will proceed on the assumption that the data collected provides evidence about the use of terms by speakers. (ii) a recent discussion on hybrid theories of concepts is related to the issues discussed here (see Machery and Seppälä 2009/2010). Nevertheless, in this chapter I concentrate exclusively on semantic issues.
7. For instance, one of the speakers (an expert) associates with "tyleritis" the descriptive information "disease that affects muscles" whereas the other associates "disease that affects the joints" to a disease that is at the end of a chain that ends with the introduction of the term for the disease that affects muscles.
8. For instance, in a story about Alex and Bob, speakers in two different communities that use the word "tyleritis", a term that in each community is historically connected with the dubbing of two different diseases.
9. GL acknowledge this (GL 2012, p. 735), and for the purposes of the discussion in the present chapter it should play no role in the argument.
10. I am told that in Greek "cato" means "down" and "blepas" means "looking".
11. For instance, participants do not react consistently to the pair of sentences "Catoblepas are wildebeest" and "Wildebeest are catoblepas". See NPM (forthcoming) for discussion.
12. What positive story of how reference is established is compatible or suggested by Kripke and Donnellan's arguments is an important issue but not one we need to discuss in this chapter. See Marti (forthcoming) for discussion.
13. It was Michael Devitt (1974 and 1981) who developed Kripke's and Donnellan's picture and turned it into a *causal theory* of the determination of reference. But there are many people who accept the picture without accepting the details of Devitt's approach (as far as I can tell, Kripke and Donnellan among them).
14. In any case, what makes the two approaches difficult to combine is not the fact that they are two incompatible theories of the determination of reference.
15. Evans himself does not characterize his approach as a hybrid theory.
16. And, as we will see, it has in fact been contemplated even by staunch defenders of the chain of communication picture.

17 It is hard to determine though whether this is because nothing fits the associated attributes or rather, as Evans would have it, we conclude that oxygen could not be the origin of such massively erroneous information.

References

Braisby, N., Franks, B. and Hampton, J. (1996), 'Essentialism, word use and concepts'. *Cognition*, 59, 247–274.
Devitt, M. (1974), 'Singular terms'. *The Journal of Philosophy*, 71, 183–205.
Devitt, M. (1981), *Designation*. New York: Columbia University Press.
Devitt, M. and Sterelny, K. (1999), *Language and Reality. An Introduction to the Philosophy of Language*. 2nd edition. Oxford: Blackwell Publishers.
Devitt, M. (2011), 'Experimental semantics'. *Philosophy and Phenomenological Research*, 82, 418–435.
Devitt, M. (forthcoming), 'Should proper names still seem so problematic?' in A. Bianchi (ed.), *On Reference*. Oxford: Oxford University Press.
Donnellan, K. (1970), 'Proper names and identifying descriptions'. *Synthese*, 21, 335–358.
Evans, G. (1982), *The Varieties of Reference*. Oxford: Clarendon Press.
Evans, G. (1985), 'The causal theory of names'. *Collected Papers*. Oxford: Clarendon Press, pp. 1–24. Originally published in 1973. *Aristotelian Society Supplementary Volumes*, 187–208.
Genone, J. and Lombrozo, T. (2012) (GL), 'Concept possession, experimental semantics, and hybrid theories of reference'. *Philosophical Psychology*, 25, 717–742.
Jylkkä, J., Railo, H. and Haukioja, J. (2009), 'Psychological essentialism and semantic externalism'. *Philosophical Psychology*, 22, 37–60.
Kripke, Saul (1980), *Naming and Necessity*. Cambridge, MA: Harvard University Press. Transcription of the lectures originally delivered in 1970.
Kripke, Saul (2013), *Reference and Existence. The John Locke Lectures*. New York: Oxford University Press.
Kroon, F. (1987), 'Causal descriptivism'. *Australasian Journal of Philosophy*, 65, 1–17.
Machery, E., Mallon, R., Nichols, S. and Stich, S. (2004) (MMNS), 'Semantics, cross-cultural style'. *Cognition*, 92, B1–B12.
Machery, E. and Seppälä, S. (2009/2010), 'Against hybrid theories of concepts'. *Anthropology & Philosophy*, 97–113.
Martí, G. (2009), 'Against semantic multiculturalism'. *Analysis*, 69, 42–48.
Martí, G. (2012), 'Empirical data and the theory of reference', in W. P. Kabasenche, M. O'Rourke and M. H. Slater (eds), *Reference and Referring. Topics in Contemporary Philosophy*. Cambridge: MIT Press, pp. 63–82.
Martí, G. (forthcoming), 'Reference without cognition', in A. Bianchi (ed.), *On Reference*. Oxford: Oxford University Press.

Nichols, S., Pinillos, A. and Mallon, R. (forthcoming) (NPM), 'Ambiguous reference'. *Mind*.

Nisbett, R. E., Peng, K., Choi, I. and Norenzayan A. (2001), 'Culture and systems of thought: holistic vs. analytic cognition'. *Psychological Review*, 108, 291–310.

Putnam, H. (1973), 'Meaning and reference'. *The Journal of Philosophy*, 70, 699–711.

Reimer, M. (2010), 'Reference'. *The Stanford Encyclopedia of Philosophy.* Ed. E. N. Zalta, <http://plato.stanford.edu/archives/spr2010/entries/reference/>.

Testing Transparent Ascriptions: A Plea for an Experimental Approach

Mark Phelan

Consider the sentence, "I believe that your keys are in the car". It seems natural to interpret this sentence as saying something about my psychological state, namely, about my beliefs. But now suppose you are desperately searching for your keys, and I tell you, "I believe that your keys are in the car". In this context, this phrase would be typically understood to primarily convey something about the world – about a possible location of the keys. But how can it be that the exact same phrase conveys such different information – about my psychological state, on the one hand, and the external world, on the other?

I will call first-person psychological state sentences that exhibit the context-shiftiness described above *transparent ascriptions*. Transparent ascriptions seem to tell us something about the speaker's psychological state in some contexts, but in other contexts they primarily tell us something about the world. Philosophers and linguists have offered two general strategies for explaining transparent ascriptions. One strategy, which I will call the *Gricean view*, contends that the meaning of transparent ascriptions never changes relative to context. On this view, psychological verbs invariably contribute information about psychological states to the propositions expressed by transparent ascriptions. But, in appropriate contexts, such psychological state propositions imply hedged information about the non-psychological world, and, in such contexts, this implied information is of central importance. The second strategy suggests that the contribution that certain psychological verbs make to the truth conditions expressed by sentences in which they occur varies. Sometimes these verbs only contribute information about psychological states; sometimes they only, or additionally, serve to hedge the clauses with which they jointly comprise sentences. So, according to this *direct expression view*, the meaning of transparent ascriptions changes relative to context.

Here, after briefly explaining how the topic of transparent ascriptions fits into a large debate within linguistics and philosophy, I further explicate the Gricean and direct expression views. Next, I discuss some arguments against each view, and, after showing why each of these arguments fails, suggest that evidence from linguistic processing studies may prove helpful in assessing which view is correct. Finally, I offer three original experiments, which – while far from decisive – provide some initial support for the direct expression view, and, more importantly, suggest that transparent ascriptions present a promising topic for future work in experimental pragmatics.[1]

1. The Gricean picture of communication

The debate over transparent ascriptions can be seen as part of a much larger debate over semantic content and the role of pragmatic processing in linguistic understanding. This debate concerns the accuracy of an influential picture of communication that contemporary linguists and philosophers have inherited from twentieth-century philosophers of language – most notably, Paul Grice (1989). In this section, I discuss Grice's picture of communication in detail, and illustrate an important class of argument – 'context-shifting arguments' – that contemporary theorists have used to challenge aspects of Grice's picture. Transparent ascriptions constitute ideal fodder for context shifting arguments.

According to Grice, what is communicated by an utterance in a particular context can be factored into two elements: what is said and what is implicated. What someone says is 'closely related to the conventional meaning of the words (the sentence) he has uttered' (25). What someone implicates follows from rational inferences from what is said, assumptions about the context of utterance, and knowledge of certain conventional maxims of conversation. In addition to maintaining that what is said is what the spoken sentence means "in virtue of the particular meanings of the elements of [the sentence], their order, and their syntactical character" (87), Grice also maintained that what is said is propositional – or, at least, truth-evaluable – in nature. In fact, the propositional nature of what is said is key to Grice's account of implication. The Gricean framework of conversational implicature is one of rational calculation from conventional maxims of communication, which emphasize properties closely tied to truth-conditions, such as accuracy and informativeness. Thus, on the Gricean picture of communication, what is said is closely related to the conventional meanings of the words that make up the spoken sentence *and* grounds what is implicated in virtue of its propositional nature.[2] But can these two properties of what is said happily coexist? Over the past several decades, linguists and philosophers of language have vigorously debated this aspect of the Gricean picture. Many theorists have argued against sentence meanings that are both closely related to the conventional meanings of words in the way Grice suggested *and* truth-evaluable, and they have employed so-called context-shifting arguments in making their case.

If what is said corresponds to the words that make up the spoken sentence in the way that Grice maintained, then there can be no change in what is said without a change in the particular meanings of the words that comprise the spoken sentence, their order, or their syntactic character. If what is said is propositional in nature, as Grice also maintained, then, in the case of indicative sentences, what is said determines a set of conditions under which the sentence is true. Thus, if what is said is propositional *and* correlated with the spoken sentence in the way Grice maintained, then there can be no change in the truth conditions of what is said without a change in the particular meanings of the words that comprise the sentence, their order, or their syntactic character (setting aside the small class of traditional indexical and demonstrative expressions, which everyone agrees change their truth-conditional contribution relative to context). According to proponents of context-shifting arguments, the truth conditions of what is said sometimes shift across contexts in which there is no change in the words that comprise the sentence, their order or their syntactic character. If they are correct, then either what is said is not propositional (that is, the truth conditions attributed to what is said actually follow from what is said together with something else) or what is said does not correspond to the words that comprise the spoken sentence, their order and their syntactic character. In either case, the Gricean picture must be modified to allow for context-sensitive processes that work at a sub-propositional level. Either we deny the propositional nature of what is said and allow for processes that work to enrich a non-truth-evaluable sentence meaning (perhaps a proposition schema) into distinct propositions in different contexts. Or else we maintain that what is said is propositional and thus deny sentential correlation by admitting sub-sentential pragmatic processes that modify or supplement the spoken words to generate what is said in different contexts. Either way contextually sensitive pragmatic processes initially transform a non-propositional communicative conveyance into a proposition appropriate to figure into the calculation of implicatures. In other words, contra Grice, context sensitive pragmatic processes help generate the propositions sentences *directly express*. (These propositions are directly expressed in the sense that they do not follow from and are not logically posteriori to other propositions expressed through the utterance.)

The key premise in context-shifting arguments, which their proponents accept and their opponents deny, is that the truth conditions of what is said sometimes change across contexts in which there is no change in the words that comprise the relevant sentences, their order, or their syntactic character. Various sentences have been offered as context-shifting examples (see Searle 1978 and Travis 1989 for a number of early examples, and Cappelen and Lepore 2005 for a wider discussion), and various theorists concede context-shifting for certain expressions but not others. In effect, the debate has become one over the extent to which the traditional Gricean picture of communication is accurate. More perspicuously, it is a debate over which of various kinds of linguistic expressions are evidence of context shifting and how best to deal with the shiftiness of these expressions. Although they have not been a focus of debate, transparent ascriptions lend themselves to context-shifting arguments, because the truth-evaluable contents these utterances primarily convey seem to change relative to context and such change is not localized to obviously context-sensitive indexical or demonstrative terms.

2. The Gricean view of transparent ascription

Consider a transparent ascription, the sentence "I think Burger Palace is open until midnight". If Rebecca utters this sentence in a context in which Tina is craving an 11 p.m. snack, there's a natural sense in which Rebecca would only be taken to speak truthfully if Burger Palace is open until midnight. If, however, Rebecca is explaining the practical syllogism to Tina by describing the mental reasoning that led her to turn right on Northland Avenue at 11 p.m. – if, for example, she is saying, "I want a snack; I think Burger Palace is open until midnight; and I believe Burger Palace is on Northland; thus, I turned right on Northland" – she will be taken to speak truthfully only if she actually *thinks* Burger Palace is open until midnight, regardless of whether it actually is or not. Intuitively, then, what Rebecca has primarily expressed by her utterance of this transparent ascription seems to change across contexts, though the sentence she speaks does not.[3] Response patterns to Rebecca's utterance also favor this conclusion. It would be appropriate to object to Rebecca's utterance in the first, snack-seeking context by saying, "No, it's not. It closes at 10 p.m. on weeknights". However, this would not be an appropriate rejoinder to the same statement in a psychological description context. It seems, then, that what is primarily expressed by utterances of, "I think Burger Palace is open until midnight", changes relative to context. And this conclusion generalizes to other transparent ascriptions.

Now, a change in what is *primarily* expressed by utterances of a particular sentence relative to context does not entail a change in what is *directly* expressed by the sentence relative to context. After all, what is primarily expressed by, "Jordan is a bulldog", can change relative to context – whether we are speaking about my new pet or the bouncer at the local bar, for example. But many would deny that what is directly expressed by this spoken sentence changes across these contexts. Context-relativity in what is primarily expressed by utterances of a particular sentence can be dealt with in either of two ways. It can be identified as context-relativity in what is directly expressed, and thus contribute to context shifting arguments. Or, alternatively, it can be explained as an instance in which what is indirectly expressed by an utterance changes across context.[4]

Adherents to the Gricean view would deny that transparent ascriptions are instances of context-relativity in what is directly expressed by a sentence. They would point out that information about the world can be conversationally implicated when speakers make claims about their psychological states, and that such implications – and not what the pronounced sentences actually say – can, in some conversational contexts (but not others), be of primary importance. For example, Griceans would argue that a claim about the world, *that Burger Palace (may) be open until midnight*, is implicated when a sentence that invariably only expresses a claim about one's psychological state, "I think Burger Palace is open until midnight", is uttered in a snack-seeking context. And in such a context, they would maintain, this implication, and not what the spoken sentence actually says, is of primary importance. Since the truth-conditions expressed by transparent ascription sentences do not change on this explanation, this is not an instance of context-shifting.

Kauppinen (2010) offers a succinct statement of this Gricean view.[5] Of the Gricean account of conversational implicature in general, he writes:

> a conversational implicature to the effect that *p* is generated . . . whenever the speaker says (or makes as if to say) that *q* and it is mutually known that the hearer needs to assume that the speaker intended to convey that *p* in order to see the speaker as complying with the Cooperative Principle. (442)

Applying this general account to the present case of transparent ascription, we get the following account of how Tina could work out *that Burger Palace may be open until midnight* from Rebecca's utterance, "I think Burger Palace is open until midnight", in the snack-seeking context (as modified from Kauppinen 2010):

(1) The mutually acknowledged purpose of the conversation is to acquire information about available snack options.
(2) Rebecca's utterance would be irrelevant unless the information she conveys about her psychological state were intended to convey some information about available snack options (from 1 and general considerations of relevance).
(3) By saying what she says, Rebecca only attributes to herself the thought that Burger Palace is open until midnight.
(4) Assume that Rebecca is abiding by the Maxim of Relation.
(5) So, in speaking as she does, Rebecca must intend to convey some information about places that are open where one could acquire a snack, specifically, she must mean to convey that what she thinks is true, that Burger Palace is open until midnight (from 2, 3 and 4).
(6) Given that there is a more direct way for Rebecca to convey information about restaurants that are open, namely a straight assertion like "Burger Palace is open until midnight", she is violating the Maxim of Quantity by being unnecessarily informative in using a psychological verb, unless calling attention to her psychological state plays some role.
(7) The most obvious role that calling attention to her psychological state plays is to make salient the possibility of divergence between how things appear to one and how they actually are.
(8) Assume that Rebecca is abiding by the Maxim of Quantity.
(9) So, in speaking as she does, Rebecca intends to convey that she is not certain that Burger Palace is open until midnight. (from 6, 7 and 8)
(10) So, in speaking as she does, Rebecca intends to convey information about Burger Palace's hours, namely that the restaurant is open until midnight, but also that she is not certain about that information. (from 5 and 9)

As Kauppinen concludes, "the Maxim of Relation explains why an assertion that is literally about the speaker's psychological states can convey information about the world, and the Maxim of Quantity explains why it is hedged" (443). Importantly, in contexts in which the mutually acknowledged purpose of the conversation differed, this assertion would not convey this information.

According to Kauppinen's Gricean view, the truth conditions of what is said do not change across different contexts in which transparent ascription sentences are uttered. On this view, it is something of a misnomer to think of these as transparent ascriptions at all. Instead, what changes across different contexts is what the propositions expressed by these sentences implicate. Transparent ascriptions pose no threat to the traditional Gricean picture of communication on this explanation, since the Gricean picture maintains that what is implicated and the importance of what is implicated compared to what is said can change relative to context of utterance. I turn now to direct expression views, which, in their more plausible form, entail revision of the traditional Gricean picture of communication.

3. The direct expression view of transparent ascription

At the heart of the direct expression view is the claim that the semantic contribution that psychological state verbs make to the propositions directly expressed by sentences changes in the following way: sometimes these verbs contribute to directly expressed claims about one's psychological state, but other times they (at least additionally) facilitate a directly expressed hedged claim about the world.

The classic version of the direct expression view had its origin in mid-century ordinary language philosophy. For example, in *Philosophical Investigations* Wittgenstein (1958) concludes that "believe" is used in the first-person present to express a hesitant assertion, not "an assertion of hesitancy" (192). And, in an influential paper, J. O. Urmson (1952) writes of:

> such philosophical war-horses as *know*, *believe*, and *deduce* . . . that when these verbs are used in the first person of the present tense . . . the assertion proper is contained in the indicative clause with which they are associated, which is implied to be both true and reasonable. (495)

Urmson claims that these 'parenthetical verbs', "function with regard to a statement made rather as 'READ WITH CARE' functions in relation to a subjoined notice, or as the foot stamping and saluting can function in the Army to make clear that one is making an official report" (495–496).

Key to Urmson and Wittgenstein's direct expression view are two ideas, (1) that psychological state verbs makes different semantic contributions in different grammatical constructions, and (2) that in the first-person present tense they do not contribute to the meaning of the sentence, but rather hedge the force of assertion with which the indicative clause is expressed.[6] In fact, there are good reasons to doubt this classic version of the direct expression view. As Kauppinen (2010) points out, a syntactically localized version of the view has as a consequence "that I simply cannot attribute a psychological property to myself by using 'believe', which is wildly implausible" (441). And as Infantidou (1993) shows, the claim that psychological state verbs used in the first-person present tense do not contribute to truth-conditions does not square with a standard test for distinguishing non-truth-conditional from truth-conditional content. The test asks us to consider conditional statements that contain as their antecedents transparent ascriptions. For example, we are asked to compare:

(1) If I believe the keys are in the car, Max will put them in the kitchen drawer.

to:

(2) If the keys are in the car, Max will put them in the kitchen drawer.

The key question is whether the conditions under which the antecedent is satisfied for (1) are the same as for (2). They are not. (1) says Max will put the keys in the kitchen drawer under different conditions than (2). Thus, "I believe the keys are in the car" is not semantically equivalent to "The keys are in the car", as Urmson and Wittgenstein maintained.[7]

These considerations reveal the implausibility of a direct expression view that claims first-person present indicative uses of psychological verbs invariably modulate the force with which the indicative clause is expressed. But they are consistent with other versions of the direct expression view. Direct expression views claim that psychological state verbs sometimes directly hedge the indicative clauses with which they jointly comprise sentences. There are other plausible accounts that would claim this for transparent ascriptions while denying that the hedge is syntactically triggered. For example, the previous considerations leave open direct expression views that claim that first-person present tense psychological state sentences are sometimes used to directly express *only* hedged claims about the world, so long as such uses are triggered by context of utterance, and do not invariably follow in virtue of syntactic features. For such views could maintain that the non-semantic use is triggered only in specific contexts, thus not invariably activated in the first person, as Kauppinen points out is implausible, or in the particular contexts Infantidou's test invokes.

A more plausible version of the direct expression view claims that, in certain contexts of utterance, a first-person, present tense psychological state sentence can directly express, and the psychological state verb it contains can serve to hedge, the claim about the world contained in the sentence's indicative clause. Such a view may or may not also maintain that the utterance simultaneously directly expresses that the utterer is in the psychological state indicated by the main clause. Carston (2002) advocates such a view when she writes of transparent ascriptions that, "the content of the complement clause can, on occasion, be communicated and so qualify as an explicature of the utterance" (211). Relevance theorists, such as Carston, deny a Gricean notion of what is said, that is, they deny a syntactically correlated proposition conveyed by an uttered sentence. Instead, they factor what is communicated by an utterance into explicatures and implicatures, where explicatures are those communicated assumptions that are developments of a logical form encoded by the utterance, and implicatures are communicated assumptions that are not developments of such a logical form. A sentence is seen to convey a logical form, which is insufficient to specify a proposition, but can be systematically fashioned by speakers of a language into a proposition, in virtue of beliefs held common among those speakers, including beliefs about the specific context of communication. Relevance theorists speak of assumptions, not propositions, and this and other terminological differences are not merely terminological, but significant to the theory. Nonetheless, this view maintains that in certain contexts transparent ascriptions can directly express the claim about the world contained in their indicative clauses.

What's more, relevance theory maintains that any extra processing costs must be justified in terms of positive cognitive effects, or worthwhile differences between one's pre and post processing representations of the world. So, since Rebecca might have said simply, "Burger Palace is open until midnight", the extra cognitive costs required to process "I think" must be justified in terms of further, positive cognitive effects. As Infantidou (1993) writes of a similar sentence, "the parenthetical construction *I think* needs to be offset by *extra or different contextual effects*. The different contextual effect in this case is generally a diminished commitment to the proposition expressed" (208). Thus, the inclusion of the psychological verb serves to directly hedge the external world claim contained in the indexical clause on this plausible, relevance theoretic version of the direct expression view.

I do not intend a strong commitment to the relevance theoretic version of the direct expression view. Rather, I take this discussion as an existence proof for a plausible version of the direct expression view. A version of the direct expression view that maintains that the hedging use of first-person psychological statements is triggered only in certain contexts of use has been defended in the transparent ascriptions literature. If that view is correct, then the propositions directly expressed by first-person psychological state sentences change relative to context, and independently of changes in the meaning, order or syntactic character of the words that comprise the spoken sentences. In that case, the traditional Gricean picture provides an inadequate description of communication when it comes to transparent ascriptions.

Which is correct, the direct expression view or the Gricean view of transparent ascriptions? In the next section, I consider some arguments that bear on this question. But, ultimately, I suggest that the best way to answer this question is through empirical investigation.

4. Arguments concerning transparent ascriptions

Our question comes down to this: Do transparent ascriptions sometimes directly hedge the claims about the external world contained in their indicative clauses, or is such hedged information instead implicated in the relevant contexts? In this section, I review some arguments that bear on this question.

Against the idea that transparent ascriptions directly express information about the external world, Kauppinen (2010) writes that:

> Any competent speaker of the language, guided merely by general linguistic knowledge about person and tense transformations, can tell that if 'I believe that p', as uttered by N.N., is true at t, 'N.N. believed that p' will be true at later times. (441)

Here Kauppinen claims that "N.N. believed that p" can be inferred from N.N.'s saying, "I believe that p", in virtue of general linguistic knowledge and nothing else. It is beyond dispute that competent speakers do – and, therefore, can – infer that "N.N. believed that p" from N.N.'s saying, "I believe that p". But it is debatable whether they do so by virtue of general linguistic knowledge and nothing else. Competent speakers are typically competent reasoners. And any competent reasoner can infer that if *N.N. believes p* is true at t, *N.N. believed p* will be true at later times. Therefore, knowledge that "N.N. believed that p" will be true at later times would follow from a hedged assertion by N.N. that p, so long as asserting hedgedly entails some degree of belief in the proposition tentatively endorsed – as it would if, as seems likely, the norm of hedged assertion were tentative belief.

Since Kauppinen does not defend the claim that one can tell that "N.N. believed that *p*" will be true at later times in virtue of linguistic knowledge and nothing else, this argument does not challenge direct expression.

Kauppinen also offers a methodological argument against the direct expression view. He quotes Grice's modified Occam's razor, that "senses should not be multiplied beyond necessity". And writes that, "the fewer primitive semantic axioms we postulate, the better we can explain the systematicity and productivity of language" (441). But these objections are misplaced when it comes to the plausible version of the direct expression view, which claims that there is but one primitive semantic axiom for (for example) "think", but that it is either underspecified and capable of different enrichments in different contexts or else does not contribute to semantic content at all in certain contexts.

The previous arguments do not provide compelling reasons to reject the direct expression view. But arguments against the Gricean view of transparent ascriptions are not very compelling either. One might point out that, as Urmson noted, the verb "know" seems to admit of analogous transparent uses as the verbs "believe" and "think". For example, suppose we have searched for the keys to your office for a very long time, both in the car and in the house. Now, we are really getting anxious about finding them. Earlier in our search I said:

(3) I think the keys are in the car.

But now I say:

(4) I just know the keys are in the car.

In such a context, both utterances would primarily express something about the location of the keys, namely, that they are in the car. According to the Gricean view, both utterances do this by directly expressing something about my psychological state, either that I think or else know that the keys are in the car. But now suppose we subsequently find the keys not in the car but between the couch cushions. Well, then I might say:

(5) I just knew the keys were in the car, but I guess I was wrong.

On the Gricean view, I here mysteriously avow that, indeed, I did know the keys were in the car, while at the same time asserting that I was wrong, presumably about the location of the keys. But if knowledge is factive, how can this be?[8]

Against this argument, a Gricean might contend that sentences like (5) operate through protagonist projection. According to this explanation, when I say, "I just knew the keys were in the car", I am projecting into my own past state when I falsely believed I knew. On this proposal, (5) is like Holton's (1997) sentence, "Sally knew that he would never let her down, but, like all the others, he did". But there is a disanalogy here. Sally would affirm that in the past she really believed that she knew he wouldn't let her down. But one might reasonably deny that he really believed he knew the location of the keys when he uttered (4). Regardless of whether protagonist projection can account for this example, there is independent reason to doubt that I actually attribute knowledge to myself in uttering (4). The utterance sounds more natural when it involves the expression "I just know" rather than "I know". But perhaps "just knowledge" isn't equivalent to true knowledge. Perhaps to say, "I just know", is to say I fall short of knowledge. In that case, expressions involving "just know" do not provide compelling evidence against the Gricean view.

Another potential issue for the Gricean view concerns certain novel utterances that are truth-conditionally equivalent to transparent ascriptions. Remember, according to Griceans, (3) means *that I think the keys are in the car*, and – because that would be irrelevant in a key-searching context – thereby implies *that the keys are in the car*. But were that explanation correct the inferential chain should be preserved in any instance in which (3) is replaced by a semantically equivalent utterance, since conversational implicatures are supposedly non-detachable. But this does not seem to be the case. Consider, for example:

(6)   I occupy a truth-conditional, doxastic attitude that the keys are in the car.

Intuitively, (6) would not serve to primarily express a proposition about the external world in relevant contexts (not even on the assumption that all conversational participants understood the utterance). However, Griceans might object that this utterance fails to primarily express the relevant external world claim because it so obviously runs foul of the maxim of manner. (6) is very verbose and obscure. For that reason, conversational participants may stall on the utterance, trying to make sense of why the speaker so obviously flouts the maxim of manner. Thus, they may all together fail to consider the relevance of the utterance to the topic of conversation, and thereby miss the hedged implication.

None of the previous arguments are very compelling. They seemingly leave us at a stalemate between the direct expression and Gricean views. But note that, while the debate between these two views has bearing on a large debate in linguistics and philosophy, both are views of how a specific class of linguistic expressions is processed in relevant contexts. How these expressions are processed is an empirical question. Therefore, it is only natural to recruit experimental methods to help us settle this debate. In the next section, I will try to get the ball rolling by offering several studies examining people's interpretations of what is said in the case of transparent ascriptions.

5. The experimental pragmatics of transparent ascriptions

Imagine a situation in which Tina is craving a late night snack. She asks Rebecca if any place is still open. Rebecca responds, "*Kate said* Burger Palace is open until midnight". Intuitively, by speaking as she does in this context, Rebecca conveys *that Burger Palace may be open until midnight*. What's more, an inference from what Rebecca says to such a conveyance would be supported by the same mechanisms that the Gricean view of transparent ascriptions invokes; the psychological steps inherent in this inference could be summarized analogously to those enumerated in Section 2 above. The Maxim of Relation could explain how an assertion that is literally about what someone said can be used to make a claim about the world, and the Maxim of Quantity could explain why that claim is hedged.

Since the maxims of communication that the Gricean view appeals to are perfectly general, the same maxims will give rise to the same implication, *that Burger Palace may be open until midnight,* whether Rebecca says, "I think Burger Palace is open until midnight", or, "Kate said Burger Palace is open until midnight". Direct expression views, however, focus on the semantic contribution that psychological state verbs make to the propositions directly expressed by sentences. Since such views are compatible with Gricean implicatures, they allow, "Kate said Burger Palace is open until midnight", to conversationally implicate that *Burger Palace may be open until midnight* in a snack-seeking context. But when, "I think Burger Palace is open until midnight", conveys *Burger Palace may be open until midnight*, it does it in a much different way, according to these views. Thus, a natural way to test these views involves looking at how people treat hedged conversational conveyances in instances involving first-person psychological state implications compared to third-person statement attributions. In three studies, I attempted to draw such comparisons.

5.1 Experiment 1: What is said

5.1.1 Methods

In an initial study, participants (N = 81, male = 57, median age range = 25–34) were assigned to one of two conditions.[9] In a *first-person state* condition, participants read four very short conversation descriptions in which a respondent uttered a transparent ascription – a sentence about her or his own psychological state. In a *third-person claim* condition, a different group of participants read about conversations in which a respondent uttered a sentence about what someone else had said. For example, participants in the *first-person state* condition read the following conversation description (among others):

> *Keys 1st-Person State:* Beth is looking for her office keys. She asks Andrew if he knows where they are. Andrew says, "I think they are in the car."

In the *third-person claim* condition, other participants read this conversation-description:

> *Keys 3rd-Person Claim:* Beth is looking for her office keys. She asks Andrew if he knows where they are. Andrew says, "John told me they are in the car."

Four psychological state verbs (think, suspect, believe, presume) and four utterance verbs (told, uttered, said, remarked) were used in these descriptions.[10] Changes across conditions for this and all subsequent experiments were minimized and related to changes in these verbs.

All conversation descriptions were designed so that a psychological state sentence or a sentence about what someone else had claimed would be naturally taken to convey information about some other state of the world. What were of interest were participants' assessments of what each sentence *meant*. In particular, I was interested in whether first-person state sentences might be more readily understood to mean the same thing as hedged assertions. So, directly after reading each vignette, participants were asked about the meaning of what was said. For example, for the above *keys* vignettes, participants were asked:

> When Andrew says, ["I think they are in the car",/"John told me they are in the car",] does what he says mean, "the keys might be in the car"?

They could respond to this question by choosing yes, no, or not sure. For each participant, I calculated a 'saying score' by awarding 1 point each time the participant judged that the relevant hedged, external world claim was part of what the respondent had said, and 0 points each time the participant judged that it was not or that they were not sure. Given that there were four test vignettes, there was a maximal saying score of 4.

In addition to the four test descriptions, four decoy descriptions were also included, which involved speakers uttering external world sentences, such as, "the art museum is on Meade Street next to the library", and, "we don't sell appliances in this store". I ignored participants' responses to these descriptions. Descriptions were counterbalanced for order. (All descriptions appear in the Appendix.)

5.1.2 Results and discussion

According to the direct expression view, first-person psychological state ascriptions directly express the hedged external world information that analogous, third-person claim ascriptions merely implicate. According to the Gricean view, both statements implicate the relevant hedged external world information, and neither directly expresses it. Given this difference, if the Gricean view were correct, it would be somewhat surprising to find an asymmetry in assessments of what is said between the two conditions. However, if the direct expression view were correct, such an asymmetry would be expected. In experiment 1, there was a significant difference by utterance type in assessments of whether the relevant hedged claims were part of what was said. Contra the Gricean view, hedged claims were more readily identified with first-person transparent ascriptions than with third-person claim sentences (Figure 9.1).[11]

In addition to this significant difference in aggregated saying scores, we can examine participants' responses to individual conversation descriptions. Participants judged that relevant hedged claims about the external world were part of the meaning of what was said much more often for first-person state descriptions than for third-person claim descriptions (Figure 9.2).[12]

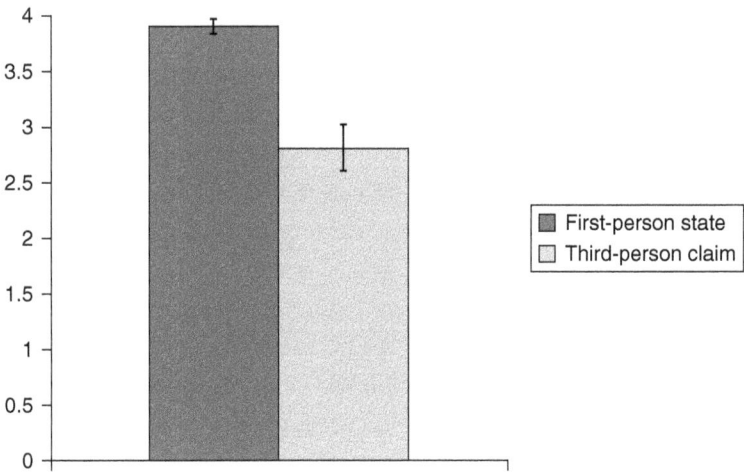

Figure 9.1 Mean saying scores

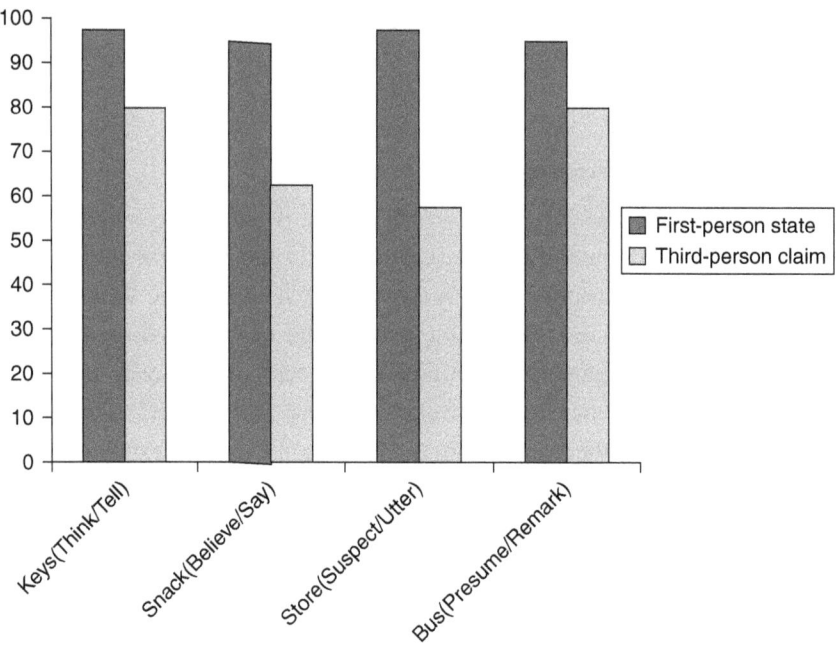

Figure 9.2 Percentage of transparency assessments per vignette

Though far from decisive, these results support the direct expression view of transparent ascriptions over the Gricean view, since they would be less surprising if the direct expression view were correct.[13] Of course, the high level of assessments that what is said includes hedged claims about the external world in the *third-person claim* condition is *prima facie* incongruent with the direct expression view (as well as the Gricean view). But ordinary speakers' assessments that some proposition is part of what is said do not, in and of themselves, constitute good evidence that it *actually is* part of what is said. Support for the direct expression view follows from the inference that a difference in assessments of what is said would be unexpected if the Gricean view were correct, and not from any claim to the expertise of ordinary speakers in assessing what is said as opposed to what is merely meant.

In response to experiment 1, a Gricean might attempt to explain the asymmetry in participant responses not in terms of a difference in the mechanisms that give rise to the relevant hedged information but rather in terms of a difference in what is actually implicated by the two classes of sentences. Perhaps for some reason or other third-person claim sentences actually fail to convey the relevant external world information that first-person state sentences successfully convey in my vignettes. In that case, the asymmetry in participants' responses might be indicative of a desire to indicate an asymmetry in what is conveyed, and not a difference in how it is conveyed.[14] With this potential response in mind, I devised a second experiment that assessed whether both kinds of utterances successfully convey the relevant hedged claims.

5.2 Experiment 2: What is said versus what is conveyed

5.2.1 Methods

As in the previous experiment, participants in experiment 2 (N = 128, male = 65, median age range = 25–34) were assigned to one of two conditions and presented with four very short conversation descriptions containing either first-person state sentences or third-person claim sentences. As before, participants were asked about the meaning of what was said. However, in this experiment they were first asked whether the relevant hedged external world claim was conveyed by what was said.[15] So, for example, in experiment 2 participants read the following keys description:

> Beth is looking for her office keys. She asks Andrew where they are. Andrew says, ["I presume that they are in the car."/"John remarked that they are in the car".]

Directly after reading each description, participants were asked whether hedged information was conveyed by the relevant statement:

> When Andrew says, ["I presume that they are in the car,"/"John remarked that they are in the car",] does he in some sense convey that the keys might be in the car?

They could respond to this question by choosing yes, no or not sure. Participants were then asked about the meaning of the spoken sentence using the same dichotomous measure as in experiment 1:

> When Andrew says, ["I presume that they are in the car,"/"John remarked that they are in the car",] does what he says mean, "the keys might be in the car"?

Participants responded to this question by choosing yes, no or not sure.

As before, I calculated a 'saying score' by awarding 1 point each time the participant judged that the relevant hedged, external world claim was part of what the respondent had said, and 0 points each time the participant judged that it was not or that they were not sure.[16] For each participant, I also calculated a 'conveying score' by awarding 1 point each time the participant judged that the relevant hedged, external world claim was in some sense conveyed by what was said, and 0 points each time the participant said that it was not or that they were not sure. Thus, there were maximal saying and conveying scores of 4.[17]

Aside from the addition of the conveying probe, careful readers will have noticed several other differences between the keys descriptions in experiments 1 and 2. First, note that whereas Andrew talks about what he *thinks* or what John *told* him in experiment 1, in experiment 2 he talks about what he *presumes* or what John *remarks*. Although the same four psychological state verbs and four utterance verbs were used across both experiments, I altered the descriptions so that different verbs were paired with different conversational topics. This was intended to allay a potential worry that something specific about the particular verb-conversation pairs was responsible for the experiment 1 effect. Next, note that whereas in experiment 1 Beth asks if Andrew *knows* where her keys are, in experiment 2 she simply asks where her keys are. Both the keys and store vignettes from experiment 1 included protagonists who, strictly speaking, could be seen as asking about other protagonists' mental states. This potentially biasing phrasing was eliminated from the descriptions included in this and subsequent experiments.[18] Finally, the descriptions were also standardized so that each contained an embedded indicative *that*-clause. So, for example, whereas in experiment 1 Andrew says, "I think they are in the car", in experiment 2 he says, "I presume *that* they are in the car".

The same four decoy vignettes from experiment 1 were also included in experiment 2, and all vignettes were counterbalanced for order.

5.2.2 Results and discussion

The purpose of experiment 2 was to counter the Gricean response to experiment 1: that third-person claim sentences actually fail to convey the relevant external world information that first-person state sentences successfully convey in my conversation descriptions. While lay-participants may lack mastery of semi-technical terms such as "what is said", my assumption in experiment 2 was that all ordinary speakers are (roughly) equally adept at understanding what is conveyed by an utterance in context. In support of this assumption is the manifest fact that all ordinary speakers navigate conversations with roughly equivalent aplomb, a skill that philosophers of language agree rests largely on grasping what is conveyed by utterances in context (not merely what is said).

With this assumption in mind, I compared participants' conveying scores with their saying scores across conditions. My hypothesis was that conveying scores would be high and not significantly different across conditions. I further hypothesized that while saying scores would be – as in study one – high in both conditions, they would significantly differ across conditions, with third-person claim saying scores being lower than first-person state saying scores. These hypotheses were borne out.

I subjected conveying and saying scores to a mixed design 2 (within-subject factor: saying/conveying) × 2 (between-subject factor: first-person state/third-person claim) ANOVA. I found main effects for both the between factor (first-person state/third-person claim)[19] and the within factor (saying/conveying).[20] Importantly, I also found an interaction effect such that people were less likely to judge that relevant hedged claims were part of what was said for *third-person claim* vignettes, than to judge that they were part of what was conveyed for such vignettes, or part of what was said and conveyed in *first-person state* vignettes (Figure 9.3).[21]

Focusing on conveying scores, we can see that participants took both the psychological state sentences and the sentences about what someone else had claimed as they were designed, to convey the relevant hedged information about states of the world. Conveying scores were high and did not significantly differ for *first-person state* and *third-person claim* conditions.[22] Saying scores, however, were significantly different across conditions.[23] These findings tell against the Gricean response to experiment 1. It seems that people do think the relevant

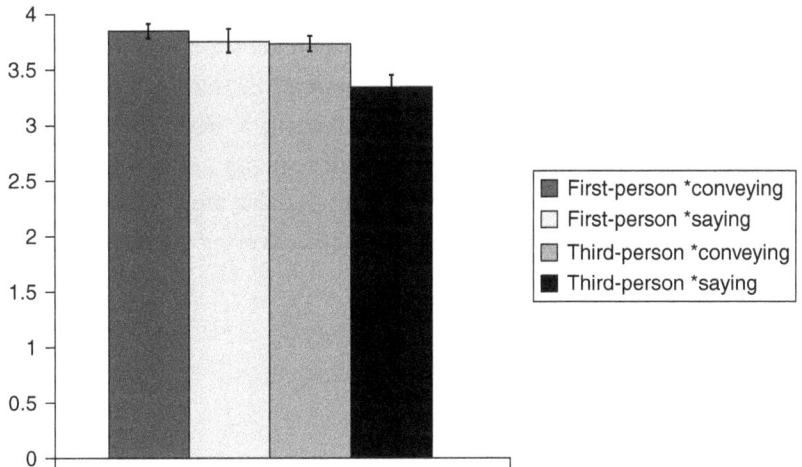

Figure 9.3 Mean saying/conveying scores across first- and third-person vignettes

external world information is conveyed both by first-person psychological statements and third-person claim reports in my vignettes, so a difference at this level of communication cannot explain the difference (found in both experiments 1 and 2) between assessments of what is said.

However, though significant, the effect of condition on saying scores was much smaller in experiment 2 than in experiment 1. Additionally, ignoring the aggregate saying scores and looking at each vignette independently, chi-square tests reveal significant differences in participants' responses to the saying-question for only two of the vignettes (keys and store).[24] What's more, when those participants who did not think or were not sure that the hedged assertion was conveyed by the relevant utterance in the conversational context are excluded from the analyses (as they arguably should be), a significant difference remains only for keys (though store is approaching significance).[25]

Why might the saying-effect observed in experiment 2 be smaller than that observed in experiment 1? Perhaps this difference is explained in part by the pull of consistency. What is conveyed, what is said and what is meant are related notions. Perhaps since participants in experiment 2 had to first assess whether relevant hedged information was conveyed by an utterance, and since they overwhelmingly judged that such information *was* conveyed by both kinds of utterance, they felt some pressure to answer the related question concerning the meaning of what was said consistently – to also answer this question in the affirmative. Such an effect could have led saying-assessments to be higher for third-person claim vignettes than they would have otherwise been, and higher than they were in experiment 1, which did not include the conveying probe.

There are several ways to test this consistency explanation. For example, we could alter the order of the elements of the experiment, asking participants the conveying question after they had already answered the saying question. Or we could alter the measure used in the study, choosing a means of response that would not simply emulate the yes/no/not sure response mechanism appearing in study one. In experiment 3, I devised a new scalar measure for the saying question and altered the order of the saying and conveying questions.

5.3 Experiment 3: Convey after say

5.3.1 Methods

As in the previous experiment, participants in experiment 3 (N = 112, male = 78, median age range = 25–34) were assigned to one of the two conditions, *first-*

person state or *third-person claim*. Within each condition, participants were presented with the relevant four short conversation descriptions (and four decoy conversation descriptions) used in experiment 2. However, in this experiment, after reading each description, participants were immediately asked about the meaning of what was said using a new saying probe, which elicited level of agreement with a meaning equivalence statement:

> How much do you agree with the following statement?
>
> When Andrew says, ["I presume that they are in the car",/"John remarked that they are in the car",] what he says means, "the keys might be in the car".

Participants indicated their level of agreement on a seven-item scale anchored with "Totally disagree" and "Totally agree", and with "Neither agree nor disagree" as the midpoint. Subsequently, after reading each vignette and responding to each saying probe, participants were presented with a new set of instructions informing them that, "Some of the following stories will resemble what you have already read, however, the questions differ", and instructing them to read carefully. Participants then reread the four relevant test descriptions and assessed whether the relevant hedged external world claim was conveyed by what was said. Once again they responded to this question by choosing yes, no or not sure.[26]

For each participant, I again calculated a 'conveying score' by awarding 1 point each time the participant judged that the relevant hedged, external world claim was in some sense conveyed by what was said, and 0 points each time the participant said that it was not or that they were not sure. Furthermore, I generated an 'overall agreement score' for each participant, by calculating their mean level of agreement with the meaning equivalency statements for the four test vignettes.

5.3.2 Results and discussion

As in experiment 2, participants judged that both first-person state and third-person claim sentences conveyed the relevant hedged information about states of the world. Conveying scores were again high and did not significantly differ for *first-person state* and *third-person claim* conditions.[27] However, inline with the previous two experiments, overall scores for the saying probe were significantly different across conditions, with participants agreeing more with the meaning equivalency statements in *first-person state* than in *third-person claim* (Figure 9.4).[28]

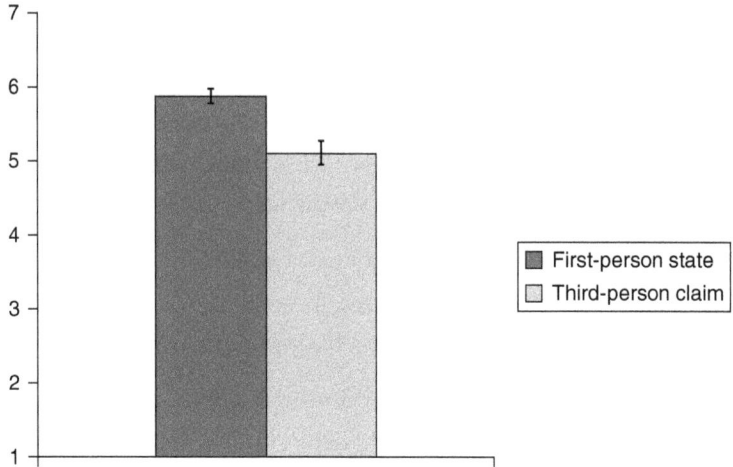

Figure 9.4 Mean overall agreement with meaning equivalence statements

This saying effect size was larger than that observed in experiment 2, and more in line with that observed in experiment 1.

Ignoring overall scores and looking at each vignette independently, we see that participants tended to agree more with the meaning equivalence statements in *first-person state* than in *third-person claim*. T-tests revealed significant differences by condition in participants' responses to the saying-probes for three of these vignettes (keys, store and snack).[29] These significant differences remained when those participants who didn't think or weren't sure that the hedged assertion was conveyed by the relevant utterance were excluded from the analyses (Figure 9.5).[30]

Compared with experiment 2, experiment 3 reveals stronger effects for condition when the saying probe appears before the conveying probe. This suggests that the dampened effect observed in experiment 2 is explained by a desire for consistency on the part of participants.[31] In any case – and as I discuss in the concluding section below – the findings from the three experiments considered in their totality provide prima facie support for the direct expression view of transparent ascriptions over the Gricean view.

6. General discussion and a sketch of future work

The previous experiments reveal a stable difference in participants' understanding of the relationship between, on the one hand, transparent ascriptions (first-person state sentences) and hedged information, and, on the other, third-person

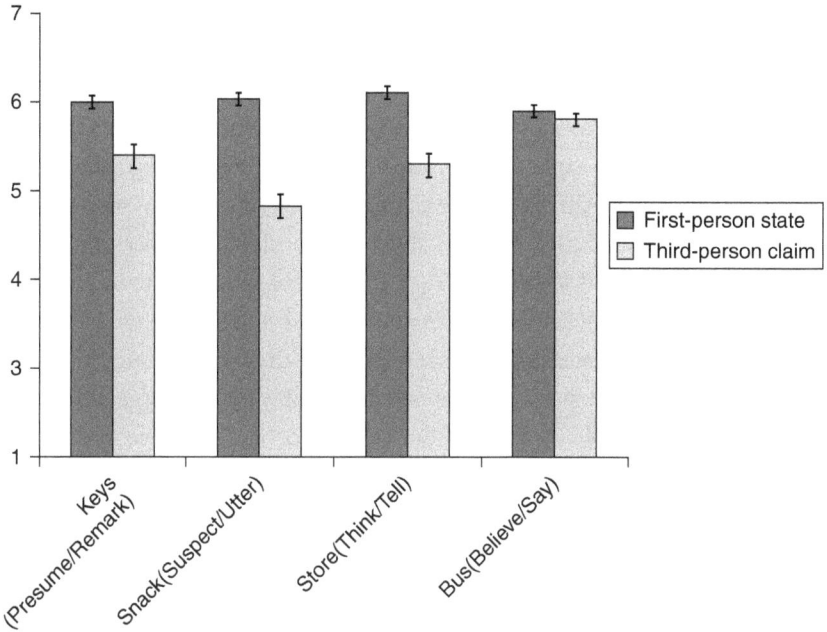

Figure 9.5 Mean agreement with meaning equivalency statements for those who judged the hedged claim was conveyed

claim sentences and hedged information. Across a variety of measures and conversational contexts, participants associated hedged information with the meaning of transparent ascriptions to a greater extent than with the meaning of third-person claim sentences. Despite this stable difference in assessments of what was said, no difference emerged between participants' assessments of what was conveyed. Both *first-person state* and *third-person claim* probes were judged to convey the relevant hedged information at the same high rates. This pattern of responses is entirely unsurprising on the direct expression view, according to which the difference in participants' assessments of what was said is explained by a difference the theory posits in the way in which the two kinds of utterances convey the relevant information. However, the Gricean view posits no such processing difference, so the observed pattern is not explicable from the inner workings of that theory alone. In the absence of convincing deductive arguments, abduction from these experiments favors the direct expression view of transparent ascriptions over the Gricean view, if only weakly. The weakness of this argument to the best explanation is inversely proportional to the plausibility of alternative explanations of the pattern of results. Here, in concluding, I briefly reflect on one possible alternative explanation.

The direct expression view claims that differences in participants' assessments of what is said are reflective of linguistic differences in the way in which two kinds of sentences convey hedged information. It falls to the Gricean to offer a distinct and more plausible account of what the observed asymmetry reflects. One salient possibility attempts to explain the asymmetry in terms not of a linguistic but of an epistemic difference. After all, on the Gricean picture, first-person state sentences report the speaker's belief, whereas third-person claim sentences only report what the speaker heard someone else say. If a speaker is thought to be reliable, his assertion of his own belief that, for example, the keys are in the car will provide reasonably good evidence that the keys might be in the car. However, his assertion that someone else said this is the case, will presumably provide less good evidence regarding the probable location of the keys, since this evidence invokes both the reliability of the speaker and the person he cites. According to the epistemic account of the observed pattern of results, participants' answers to questions about the meaning of what was said reflect (at least in part) their assessments of the quality of information regarding the probable location of the keys. And, since they have lower quality information in the third-person cases, they are less likely to judge that the hedged information is part of what is said in these cases.[32]

This alternative, epistemic account of the pattern of saying responses faces difficulties. For one thing, it seems unlikely that the posited epistemic effect would influence saying but not conveying responses. Nonetheless, consideration of individual vignettes may support the epistemic account. My weakest effects were for the bus vignette, in which the interlocutor is just a random bystander, not, as in the other vignettes, a person with whom the inquisitor seems to have a relationship. Perhaps because the informant is unknown to the inquisitor (and is, in turn, conveying information from someone the informant seems not to know), there is perceived to be little difference in the informational value of what is said across conditions for this vignette.[33]

Now, it is worth noting that bus saying scores are generally *higher* than saying scores for other vignettes in the *third-person claim* condition, which is not indicative of relatively low informational value assessments. But regardless of the ultimate success of the epistemic account, I welcome alternative explanations for the observed pattern of responses, and I think the argument from individual vignettes is on the right track. Effect sizes across my various experiments seem to follow conversation descriptions, not the particular verbs that appear in the target sentences. This suggests an important role for context in explaining the pattern of responses. Such a role is, of course, perfectly consistent with the plausible direct expression view, which favors a contextual trigger for transparent uses. But how this trigger works and what exactly it is triggering remains to be spelled out.

Perhaps real headway on the topic of transparent ascriptions will be made only when the more sophisticated methods of experimental pragmatics are brought to bear on it.[34] Ultimately, I will be satisfied if I have convinced others that transparent ascriptions are a worthy target of investigation. With luck, experimental philosophers and researchers working within experimental pragmatics will answer my plea and help settle this debate. I believe it is a worthy endeavor.[35]

Appendix

Conversation Descriptions for Experiment 1:

Keys: Beth is looking for her office keys. She asks Andrew if he knows where they are. Andrew says, ["I think they are in the car"./"John told me they are in the car".]

Snack: Tina is craving a late night snack. She asks Rebecca if any place is still open. Rebecca says, ["I believe Burger Palace is open until midnight"./ "Kate said Burger Palace is open until midnight".]

Store: Carl noticed that the prices on shoes at his favorite sporting goods store are very low. He asks Dave if he has any idea why. Dave says, ["I suspect that the store is going out of business"./"Fiona uttered that the store is going out of business".]

Bus: Philip has been waiting five minutes for a bus. He asks the man standing next to him how often the buses run. The man says, ["I presume that they run every ten minutes"./ "A passenger remarked that they run every ten minutes".]

Conversation Descriptions for Experiments 2 and 3:

Keys: Beth is looking for her office keys. She asks Andrew where they are. Andrew says, ["I presume that they are in the car"./"John remarked that they are in the car".]

Snack: Tina is craving a late night snack. She asks Rebecca if any place is still open. Rebecca says, ["I suspect that Burger Palace is open until midnight"./"Kate uttered that Burger Palace is open until midnight".]

Store: Carl noticed that the prices on shoes at his favorite sporting goods store are very low. He asks Dave why. Dave says, ["I think that the store is going out of business"./"Fiona told me that the store is going out of business".]

Bus: Philip has been waiting five minutes for a bus. He asks the man standing next to him how often the buses run. The man says, ["I believe that they run every ten minutes"./"A passenger said that they run every ten minutes".]

Decoy Descriptions (Experiments 1, 2, and 3):

Museum: Nate is looking for the art museum. He asks a woman on the street if she knows where it is. She says, "The art museum is on Meade Street next to the library".

Bank: It's Saturday and Martha needs to deposit a check. She asks Evan when the bank closes. Evan says, "The bank closes at noon on Saturday".

Coffee Maker: Heidi is looking for a new coffee maker. She asks a store clerk where the kitchen appliances are. The clerk says, "We don't sell appliances in this store".

Car Lot: Leo is at a used car lot. He asks a man walking by if there's any chance he knows how much the red convertible costs. The man says, "Actually, I'm a salesman here".

Notes

1 While my discussion in this chapter will focus on transparent ascriptions involving doxastic state verbs like "believe" and "think", I take it that much of what I write will have wider application to ascriptions involving the large class of psychological verbs considered by Urmson (1952).
2 This does not entail that it contributes to the actual psychological process of calculating implicatures (see, e.g. Saul 2002). However, many neo-Griceans and contemporary Gricean critics assume that it typically does (and that the significance of the Gricean account hinges on its psychological reality). I will follow most contemporary participants in this debate by making this assumption.
3 A proposition is primarily expressed by an utterance if it is one that hearers would take as a main point of the utterance. I will assume that, if such a proposition were known to be true, hearers would generally judge that the speaker had spoken truly. That a proposition is primarily conveyed by an utterance does not entail that it is directly expressed by the pronounced sentence, since hearers may take an implication of what is directly expressed as a main point of an utterance.
4 Or, alternatively, as an instance in which what is of primary importance – what is said or what is implicated – changes across context.
5 For a different view in the Gricean spirit, see Jayez and Rossari (2004).

6 This classic version of the direct expression view is, in fact, consistent with Gricean tradition.
7 Infantidou (1993, 1994) is primarily interested in what she calls 'true parentheticals', sentences in which the psychological state verbs are relegated to a dependent clause, such as, "The keys are, I believe, in the car". In part on the basis of semantic tests such as those discussed above, she concludes that these sentences are syntactically distinct from main-clause parentheticals, like "I believe the keys are in the car". She then offers a detailed account of true parentheticals, according to which they can be used to simultaneously perform two distinct speech acts. Since my concern is with the semantics of main clause parentheticals, I set aside these reflections on true parentheticals, which I agree are syntactically distinct.
8 Of course, one might simply deny that knowledge is factive, as some recent philosophers have argued.
9 Participants in this and subsequent experiments were recruited and tested using commercially available online platforms (Qualtrics and Amazon Mechanical Turk). All participants were located in the United States. Each was paid $0.40 for their participation.
10 These verbs were selected on the basis of their assessed synonymy with one another in a pre-test.
11 $t(78) = 4.98$, $p < 0.001$ (two-tailed), SE (third-person claim) 0.206, SE (first-person state) 0.064, $r = 0.49$. (One participant was excluded from this analysis due to failure to respond to all vignettes.)
12 Keys: $\chi^2 (1, N = 81) = 6.32$, $p = 0.012$; Snack: $\chi^2 (1, N = 81) = 12.99$, $p < 0.001$; Store: $\chi^2 (1, N = 81) = 18.8$, $p < 0.001$; Bus: $\chi^2 (1, N = 80) = 4.11$, $p = 0.043$. (These data collapse "no" and "not sure" responses. For no vignette other than Store × Third-person claim did more than two participants choose the "not sure" response. For this vignette, nine participants chose "no", and eight chose "not sure".)
13 Two comprehension controls were included at the beginning of this experiment. All significant results stand when participants were excluded for failure to pass one or both controls.
14 Of course, a Gricean who offered this response would face the burden of explaining why the hedged information is implicated by the first-person state sentence, but not the third-person claim sentence.
15 The same four psychological state verbs (think, suspect, believe, presume) and four utterance verbs (told, uttered, said, remarked) used previously were used in these vignettes. However, conversation descriptions were altered so that different verbs were paired with different conversational topics. (This was intended to allay a potential worry that something specific about the particular verb-context pairs was responsible for the previous effect.) The same four decoy vignettes from experiment 1 were also included in this experiment, and all vignettes were counterbalanced for order.

16 "Not sure" responses for the saying question: Keys (4), Store (4), Burger (3), Bus (7).
17 "Not sure" responses for the conveying question: Keys (0), Store (1), Burger (2), Bus (5).
18 Thanks to Wesley Buckwalter for raising this worry in response to an earlier draft of this chapter.
19 First-person/Third-person Effect: $F(1, 126) = 6.725$, $p = 0.011$, $\eta^2_{partial} = 0.051$.
20 Saying/Conveying Effect: $F(1, 126) = 11.208$, $p = .001$, $\eta^2_{partial} = 0.082$
21 $F(1, 126) = 4.076$, $p = 0.046$, $\eta^2_{partial} = 0.031$.
22 Mean conveying scores: first-person state = 3.86; third-person claim = 3.74. $t(126) = 1.29$, $p = 0.2$ (two-tailed), SE (first-person state) 0.055, SE (third-person claim) 0.074, $r = 0.11$.
23 Mean saying scores: first-person state = 3.76; third-person claim = 3.35. $t(126) = 2.727$, $p = 0.007$ (two-tailed), SE (first-person state) 0.067, SE (third-person claim) 0.132, $r = 0.24$.
24 Keys: $\chi^2 (1, N = 128) = 6.79$, $p = 0.009$; Snack: $\chi^2 (1, N = 128) = 2.32$, $p = 0.13$; Store: $\chi^2 (1, N = 128) = 5.18$, $p = 0.023$; Bus: $\chi^2 (1, N = 128) = 0.67$, $p = 0.41$. (As above, this and the next analysis collapse "no" and "not sure" responses. See note 16 for this data.)
25 Keys: $\chi^2 (1, N = 125) = 7.52$, $p = 0.006$; Snack: $\chi^2 (1, N = 122) = 2.14$, $p = 0.14$; Store: $\chi^2 (1, N = 121) = 3.44$, $p = 0.064$; Bus: $\chi^2 (1, N = 118) = 0.16$, $p = 0.689$.
26 I used different saying and conveying measures in this experiment to minimize the possibility of a reverse consistency effect, whereby assessments of the now earlier-occurring saying probe might influence responses to the subsequent conveying probe.
27 Mean conveying scores: first-person state = 3.71; third-person claim = 3.73. $t(108) = 0.128$, $p = 0.899$ (two-tailed), SE (first-person state) 0.085, SE (third-person claim) 0.144, $r = 0.013$. (Two participants were excluded from this analysis for failing to answer the conveying probe for all vignettes.)
28 Mean overall agreement scores: first-person state = 5.89; third-person claim = 5.06. $t(110) = 3.99$, $p < 0.001$ (two-tailed), SE (first-person state) 0.097, SE (third-person claim) 0.188, $r = 0.35$.
29 Keys: $t(110) = 2.69$, $p = 0.008$ (two-tailed), SE (first-person state) 0.129, SE (third-person claim) 0.242, $r = 0.25$; Snack: $t(110) = 4.684$, $p < 0.001$ (two-tailed), SE (first-person state) 0.134, SE (third-person claim) 0.276, $r = 0.4$; Store: $t(110) = 3.271$, $p = 0.001$ (two-tailed), SE (first-person state) 0.153, SE (third-person claim) 0.241, $r = 0.29$; Bus: $t(110) = 1.068$, $p = 0.288$ (two-tailed), SE (first-person state) 0.151, SE (third-person claim) 0.200, $r = 0.1$.
30 Keys: $t(106) = 2.4$, $p = 0.018$ (two-tailed), SE (first-person state) 0.128, SE (third-person claim) 0.229, $r = 0.22$; Snack: $t(100) = 4.216$, $p < 0.001$ (two-tailed), SE (first-person state) 0.129, SE (third-person claim) 0.268, $r = 0.38$; Store: $t(102) = 3.203$,

$p = 0.002$ (two-tailed), *SE* (first-person state) 0.135, *SE* (third-person claim) 0.22, $r = 0.3$; Bus: $t(99) = 0.199$, $p = 0.842$ (two-tailed), *SE* (first-person state) 0.164, *SE* (third-person claim) 0.164, $r = 0.02$.

31 Here it is worth pointing out that two unreported experiments, which had the same conveying-saying probe order as experiment 2, but used meaning equivalence saying probes like those appearing in experiment 3, returned the same general pattern of results reported above. For both of these experiments, however, observed saying effects were smaller, and mean responses were higher overall. This suggests that, while the consistency effect observed in experiment 2 can be dampened by varying the type of probe used, it is best dealt with by changing the order of the probes.

32 I am thankful to Daniel Cohnitz for suggesting this interesting alternative explanation in a referee report on an earlier version of this chapter.

33 I am thankful to Daniel Cohnitz for suggesting this argument.

34 For example, experimental methods such as processing time studies, eye-tracking studies and developmental studies have proven useful in unraveling related questions concerning so-called scalar implicatures. See Phelan (2014) for discussion.

35 I'm grateful to Wesley Buckwalter, Daniel Cohnitz, Jussi Haukioja, Shen-yi Liao and Thomas Ryckman for reading an earlier version of this chapter and offering many important suggestions and searching criticisms. Their comments improved this work immensely.

References

Austin, J. L. (1962), *How to Do Things with Words*, 2nd edition. Ed. J. O. Urmson and M. Sbisá. Cambridge, MA: Harvard University Press.

Bach, K. (2002), 'Seemingly Semantic Intuitions', in J. Keim Campbell, M. O'Rourke and D. Shier (eds), *Meaning and Truth*. New York: Seven Bridges Press, pp. 21–33.

Carston, R. (2002), *Thoughts and Utterances: The Pragmatics of Explicit Communication*. Oxford: Blackwell.

Grice, P. (1989), *Studies in the Way of Words*. Cambridge, MA: Harvard University Press.

Holton, R. (1997), 'Some telling examples: A reply to Tsohatzidis', *Journal of Pragmatics*, 28, 625–628.

Infantidou, E. (1993), 'Parentheticals and relevance', *UCL Working Papers in Linguistics*, 5, 193–210.

Ifantidou, E. (1994), *Evidentials and Relevance*. PhD thesis, University of London.

Jayez, J. and Rossari, C. (2004), 'Parentheticals as conventional implicatures', in F. Corblin and H. de Swart (eds), *Handbook of French Semantics*. Stanford: CSLI, pp. 211–229.

Kauppinen, A. (2010), 'The pragmatics of transparent belief reports', *Analysis,* 70 (3): 438–446.

Phelan, M. (2014), 'experimental pragmatics: An introduction for philosophers', *Philosophy Compass,* 9 (1), 66–79.

Saul, J. (2002), 'What is said and psychological reality: Grice's project and relevance theorists' criticisms', *Linguistics and Philosophy,* 25, 347–372.

Urmson, J. O. (1952), 'Parenthetical verbs', *Mind,* 61, 480–496.

Wittgenstein, L. (1958), *Philosophical Investigations.* Oxford: Blackwell.

Index

ambiguity 142–151, 166–169

Beebe, J. 69
belief ascriptions 49–53, 173–197
"Benjaminus" case 149–151
Braisby, N. 121
Buckwalter, W. 50

Cappelen, H. 28n, 56n, 90
Carston, R. 181
"Catoblepas" case 146–149, 160–161
causal theory of reference 17, 33, 69–73, 88–90, 159–169
Chomsky, N. 36, 79
"Cicero" case 13
Cohnitz, D. 1, 4, 92–94, 97
"Columbus" case 11, 20, 45
communication 91–94, 174–176
context-shifting arguments 176–179
conversational implicature 152–153, 177–179
corpus, the 46–49

Davidson, D. 67–68, 78
DeBlanc, M. 133n, 158
descriptivism 11–14, 33, 69–73, 88–90, 117–120, 140–142, 159–166
Deutsch, M. 3, 90–91, 114
Devitt, K. 50
Devitt, M. 3, 19–20, 24, 27n, 33–46, 78, 90, 93, 97–99, 115–116, 168–169
dispositions, linguistic 92–104
Donnellan, K. 44
Dummett, M. 35

"Einstein" case 11, 20, 45
elicited production 49–51
essentialism, psychological 120–126
Evans, G. 163–166
Expertise Defense *see* intuitions, of experts
extension 66–73, 75–79

externalism 74–75, 91–92, 120–126
eye-tracking 100–104

"Feynman" case 13
Field, H. 68
Franks, B. 121

Genone, J. 47–49, 58n, 125–126, 159–160
Gernsbacher, M. 101
"Gödel/Schmidt" case 7–20, 45, 69–73, 89–91, 95–97, 102–103
Grice, P. 174–179

Häggqvist, S. 4–5
Hampton, J. 121
Haukioja, J. 92–94, 97, 122–125
Hintikka, J. 34
Horwich, P. 68
hybrid theory of reference 33, 123–125, 162–166

"Ibn Kahn" case 165
Ichikawa, J. 18–19, 26n, 133n
implicit scare quotes, problem of 51–53
Infantidou, E. 180–181
internalism 74–75, 91–92, 120–126
interpretation 92–99
intuitions,
    as a priori 35–36
    as evidence in philosophy 8–11, 17–25, 34–39, 92–99
    of experts 40–42, 66–67, 115–116
    fanciful vs. humdrum 19, 44
    linguistic vs metalinguistic 97–99
    memory judgments as 43
    perceptual judgments as 39–42
    in thought experiments 43–45, 95–99
    as the 'voice of competence' 36–37

"Jonah" case 69, 141–142, 144
Jylkkä, J. 122–125

Karabanov, A. 100–101
Katz, J. 34
Kauppinen, A. 177–180, 182–183
Keysar, B. 103
Kripke, S. 4, 7–25, 117–120, 161

LaPorte, J. 126–130
Lewis, D. 78, 140–144
Lewis, G. 128–129
linguistic usage 47–54, 91–95
Livengood, J. 91, 102
Loar, B. 35
Lombrozo, T. 47–49, 58n, 125–126, 159–160
Ludwig, K. 76

Machery, E. 2–3, 17–20, 27n, 31, 45–46, 68–75, 88–90, 109–115, 157–158
McKinsey, M. 35
"Madagascar" case 14, 133n, 165
Mallon, R. 2–3, 17–20, 68–70, 88–90, 109–115, 145–149, 157–158, 160–163
Marslen-Wilson, W. 101
Martí, G. 5, 90, 95–96, 113–116, 158, 167
meta-internalism vs meta-externalism 91–95

natural kind terms 73–75, 117–131, 140–149
Neale, S. 27n
Nichols, S. 2–3, 17–20, 68–70, 88–90, 109–115, 145–149, 157–158, 160–163

Olivola, C. 133n, 158

"Peano"/"Dedekind" case 11
Phelan, M. 5–6

Pinillos, Á. 5, 145–149, 160–163
polysemy 154–155
proper names 7–20, 46–54, 68–75, 95–99, 149–151
psycholinguistics 99–104
Putnam, Hilary 4, 74–75, 118

Railo, H. 122–125
reference 31–32, 66–73, 75–79, 93–94, 111–114
  see also causal theories of reference descriptivism hybrid theories of reference
Reimer, M. 163–164
relevance theory 181
Ryle, G. 65

semantics, descriptive vs foundational 111–114
"Smith/Jones" case 16
speaker's reference 15–16, 67, 71–73, 152
Stanley, J. 132n
Stich, S. 2–3, 17–20, 46, 54, 68–70, 88–90, 109–115, 157–158
Strawson, P. 67
Sytsma, J. 69–70, 91, 102

Thomson, J. 28n
thought experiments 43–45
Tyler, L. 101
"tyleritis" case 47–49

Undercoffer, R. 69
Urmson, J. 179

Wikforss, Å. 4–5
Williamson, T. 133n
Wisniewski, E. 40

Ingram Content Group UK Ltd.
Milton Keynes UK
UKHW022256120723
425048UK00007B/129